THEOLOGY AND THE JUSTIFICATION OF FAITH

Constructing Theories in Systematic Theology

by

Wentzel van Huyssteen

Translated by

H. F. Snijders

WILLIAM B. EERDMANS PUBLISHING COMPANY
GRAND RAPIDS, MICHIGAN

Translation of *Teologie as Kritiese Geloofsverantwoording:*
Teorievorming in die Sistematiese Teologie
published 1986 by the Human Sciences Research Council, Pretoria, South Africa

Library of Congress Cataloging-in-Publication Data

Van Huyssteen, Wentzel.
Theology and the justification of faith.

Translation of: Teologie as kritiese
geloofsverantwoording.
Bibliography: p. 198
1. Knowledge, Theory of (Religion) 2. Theology—
Methodology. 3. Religion and science—1946-
I. Title.
BT50.V3613   1989   230'.01   88-33490
ISBN 0-8028-0366-0

Contents

Preface   viii

Introduction   x

    Systematic Theology and Philosophy of Science   xii
    Some Conceptual Definitions   xv
    Conceptual Models and Theories   xvi
    Outline   xix

Part I: Systematic Theology and Philosophy of Science

1. Logical Positivism   3

    The Vienna Circle   3
    The Unity of Science   5
    The Standard Conception of Science   7

2. Theological Reaction to the Positivist Model of Science:
Karl Barth   11

    Introduction   11
    Theology as a Unique Science   14
    Heinrich Scholz and the Minimum Demands for Science   17
    Theology and Subjectivism   19

3. Critical Rationalism: Karl Popper   24

    Rationality and Objectivity   24
    The Theory-Ladenness of Observation   27
    The Criterion of Falsifiability   29
    The Theory of Verisimilitude   31

4. Critical Rationalism and Theology: William W. Bartley   33

Introduction   33
The Accusation of Loss of Reality   35
Theology and the Question of the Limits of Rationality   36
Pancritical Rationalism   40
Commitment and Theorizing   44

5. The Paradigm Theory and the Question of the Origins of
   Theological Models: Thomas S. Kuhn   47

Introduction   47
The Historicist Turning Point   49
Kuhn in Debate with Popper   55
The Incommensurability of Paradigms   57
Truth, Rationality, and Historicity   60
Kuhn's Relevance to Systematic Theology   61

Part II: The Construction of Theories in Systematic Theology

6. Theology as the Science of God: Wolfhart Pannenberg   71

Introduction   71
The Universal Nature of Theology   74
Theology and Philosophy of Science   77
Theological Statements as Hypotheses   81
The Object of Theology: God as Problem   85
The Scientific Nature of Theological Reflection:
  Critical Evaluation   92

7. Theology as a Critical-Argumentative Science: Gerhard Sauter   101

Systematic Theology as an Argumentative Theology   101
Five Basic Problems in Theology   103
The Origin of Theological Statements   109
The Justification of Theological Statements   114
An Analytic-Theoretical Model of Thought for Theology:
  Critical Evaluation   117

Part III: Systematic Theology: A Critical-Realist Perspective

8. The Nature of Theological Statements   125

Introduction   125
Religious Experience and the Language of Faith:
  The Origin of Theological Statements   126
Religious Language as Metaphoric Language   132

What Is a Metaphor? 133
From Metaphor to Thought Model:
   The Nature of Theological Conceptualizing 137

9. Criteria for a Critical-Realist Model of Rationality in
   Systematic Theology 143

   Introduction 143
   The Reality Depiction of Theological Statements 147
   The Critical and Problem-Solving Ability of
      Theological Statements 172
   The Constructive and Progressive Nature of
      Theological Statements 190

Bibliography 198

Index 204

Preface

Doing theology in the present complex South African situation can be a difficult and demanding venture. Fortunately it is also a challenging and liberating endeavor because theology can never avoid the direct appeal of the problems created by its context.

In South Africa, as in virtually any other complex society, this context creates a specific problem, a problem that in a special way manifests itself in the often opposing and conflicting answers of different theologies trying to be both contextual and confessional for their own time. The problem of conflicting theologies always signals the danger of the ideologizing of theological models and the claim of some theological constructs to demonstrate the only "true" or "biblical" answers for a complicated and confusing situation.

This book does not deal with these issues directly, but it does indeed deal with the theoretical problems presupposed by such issues, that is, the epistemological problems of rationality and of theory construction in theology. Thus the search for valid epistemological criteria for a creditable Christian theology forms the main theme of this project. It is also my contribution to the broader epistemological issues presupposed by the current Theology and Science debate—an issue which has become of increasing importance to me lately.

The publication of this work also offers me an opportunity to express my gratitude to a wide circle of friends and colleagues who have been directly involved with the research and planning that preceded this publication. I am very much indebted to Johann Mouton for the leading role he played in the recent publication of the Afrikaans edition. I am also extremely grateful to Hendrik Hart, in particular, and to members of the Institute for Christian Studies for the hospitality they showed me during my stay in Toronto, Canada, in 1982. The many hours of discussion and the ensuing correspondence played a significant role in the shaping of my thoughts. A special word of thanks also to Gordon

Kaufman of the Harvard Divinity School, who provided, during my stay there, a valuable introduction to the American theological scene.

During both my recent sabbaticals I was privileged to visit Germany again. I do want to thank Gerhard Sauter and his family for the wonderful time I spent with them in 1976 and in 1982. His special interest in my work has always been and still is an inspiration. To Wolfhart Pannenberg I am also deeply grateful. His keen theological and personal interest has always influenced and challenged the evolution of my own theological thought. I remember with appreciation the numerous opportunities for discussion, especially in 1976 and 1982. I am also much indebted to Heinzpeter Hempelmann for the many hours of creative and stimulating discussion we had while I was visiting Bonn; that discussion directly influenced the development of this manuscript.

Since the recent Afrikaans publication of this book I was privileged to revisit the United States of America. To new and wonderful friends, without whose encouragement and sincere interest this publication would never have been possible, I am grateful: Philip Hefner and Carl Braaten (Lutheran School of Theology at Chicago), Bob Russell and Nancey Murphey (Graduate Theological Union, Berkeley), and, of course, Ernan McMullin and David Burrell (University of Notre Dame).

A special word of thanks to Susan Steyn, who in her own perfectionist way prepared the Afrikaans edition for publication. I am also most grateful to Mr. Henry Snijders for the difficult and demanding job of translating this into English. And so too Helena Glanville and Kenneth Carr, students and dear friends, for the many hours spent in preparing the manuscript for publication.

My sincerest appreciation, however, must surely go to my wife, Hester, and to our four children. Without their support and enthusiasm this work would not have been possible.

Wentzel van Huyssteen

Introduction

Theologians of our time find themselves in a situation that not only taxes their intellect to the utmost but might also spur them on to extraordinary heights of creativity. The systematic theologian, in particular, has to learn to balance on the razor's edge separating the demands of an intensely personal and fairly esoteric faith from the sociopolitical diversity of doctrinal, confessional, and ethical claims that faith may imply in a specific Christian community.

In the South African context, especially, both dimensions—the individual and the intersubjective experience of faith—now lie at the core of what must surely be the most pressing theological question of our time: Can theology still speak out contextually in such a manner that the liberating voice of the gospel may be heard loudly and clearly in all facets of our own society?

Behind this question of the relevance and topicality of systematic-theological statements, however, lies hidden the question of an even more profound epistemological contextuality: whether theologians, in their complex network of statement and argument, are in fact saying anything credible about God. For systematic theologians, this question frames the fundamental-theological problem of the validity or credibility of their theological discourse on God. This, the crucial issue confronting modern systematic theology, could also be formulated as follows: What precisely takes place in the theorizing process by which the everyday language of our faith might become transformed into theological theories that would truly appeal to both our insight and our experience?

In itself this difficult question suffices to make us aware of the extraordinary responsibility vested in the theologians of our time. Their task, in fact, is to demonstrate through creative reflection that the Christian faith has its own integrity: an integrity and uniqueness that may integrate the divergent dimensions of our modern experience, to give it the maximum degree of meaning and significance.

In taking up this responsibility theologians profess, at the same time, their willingness to account intelligently and creatively for the essence of their Christian faith and for their hopes for the future (cf. 1 Peter 3:15). That willingness to account implies, above all, that theologians should ultimately be prepared to engage in the creative restructuring of fundamental Christian truths, in order that the Christian message might validly regain its vital relevance to the modern conception of life in its most profound and all-encompassing sense. As a provisional definition I would therefore describe theology—in its broadest sense, but in particular systematic theology—as a process by which we offer a credible and critical theoretic account of our Christian faith.

This willingness to account for one's faith also presupposes, however, that theologians shall have the courage to extend the language of their own faith—and thus also our theological concepts, theories, and conceptual models—to the utmost limits of its meaning. For theologians this task presupposes a conceptual transformation in which they have already confronted, in a positive, critical, and constructive manner, their dual commitment both to the Christian faith and to the demands posed by our awareness of the issues of our time.

For this reason—and despite the fact that it is frequently done in American and European contexts—I prefer not to draw a sharp and deliberate distinction between systematic theology and a so-called fundamental theology, especially not if fundamental theology is to be construed only as an apologetical theology, bent upon using some kind of rational demonstration to convince a modern, secularized world that the claims made by the Christian faith are in fact valid. Such a fundamental theology would not only stand in sharp contrast to the apparent sincerity of a confessional theology grappling with contextual issues; it would ultimately also lack any intratheological relevance to the very issues confronting systematic theology.

To avoid that misconstruction, and because I am convinced that all systematic theologians must sooner or later face the fundamental theoretic question of the nature and structure of their own conceptual model—since any form of fundamental-theological questioning must eventually become fully contextual within the framework of systematic theology—I have chosen to speak consistently of a fundamental-theological questioning of systematic-theological thought as such.

The attempt made in this book to construct a valid conceptual model for systematic theology implies the construction, from a fundamental-theological perspective, of a theory for systematic theology which will ultimately serve not only theology in its apologetical discourse to the outside but also systematic theology itself, by critically analyzing its theorizing as a process ultimately of creative, conceptual construction. This does not imply a less sincere engagement than that of systematic theologians dealing with contextual problems; it implies, rather, a sincerity of a different kind: the sincerity of theologians who—precisely for the sake of the crucial message of Christian faith—would justify theological contextuality by first questioning the validity of their own thinking. In fact, I am convinced that theological contextuality or involvement in reality comes fully into its own only when the question of an even deeper depiction of reality has first been asked: the question of the realist quality, validity, or credibility of our theological statements as such.

Systematic Theology and Philosophy of Science

Accounting critically for their faith presupposes that theologians must be prepared to reflect on their own thought processes, and this places upon them the fundamental task of relating the essence of their faith to the question of the very nature of rationality, as posed in contemporary philosophy of science.

This task holds an exciting challenge for a systematic theology that seeks to assess itself as a form of critical accounting for faith: the question whether the problematic concept of rationality can be validly regained and revitalized for theology. This question, like that of theorizing in theology and of the possibility of creatively constructing a valid rationality model for systematic theology, draws systematic theology into a direct dialogue with philosophy of science. It is, after all, this branch of philosophy which concerns itself with analyzing and critically assessing the premises of science and thus seeks to construct rational theories of science (Koningsveld, 1977:207).

In doing so philosophers of science are performing an invaluable and indispensable task for systematic theologians, for in terms of the former's pursuit of consistent scientific models, and thus of coherent conceptions of the nature and structure of science, they might eventually identify the following for theologians: the epistemological criteria for good science; the complex issues surrounding rationality, objectivity and truth; various interpretations of the structure of scientific theories; and questions on the theoretic and practical aims of science (Mouton and Marais, 1985:17, 25-26).

Inevitably, then, the questions asked in philosophy of science about the nature of systematic theology will direct the focus of this book toward the more theoretic dimensions of theologizing. Of particular relevance will be the epistemological criteria for valid scientific assertions, and thus directly the problems of rationality, objectivity, and truth. My argument will, I hope, demonstrate clearly that this epistemological dimension must form the very foundation of all further methodological and thus also of all hermeneutical questions in theology. The epistemological perspective is vital also because in theology, as in other research in the human sciences, objectivity forms a prerequisite to valid scientific thought. But objectivity—like, in fact, rationality—can no longer be understood in the positivistic sense of impersonal, universal validity. In theology, as in all human sciences, objectivity and the criteria for it are determined contextually and have, as such, a relational character.

The questions asked in philosophy of science about systematic-theological thought are particularly vital in the South African context, because South African theology has no history of scientific precision in its conceptual tradition. In this sense, too, the epistemological questioning of rationality and truth can lead only to greater conceptual lucidity and to a keener critical awareness of the issues surrounding the nature and structure of theological models, in the sense of conceptual frameworks. This process ensures, furthermore, that a theology seeking critically to account to itself for its own nature could never become a-contextual or lapse into theory alienization. It is in fact the theoretic pursuit of criteria for a valid theological model that will ultimately bring us back to the inevitable contextuality of sound theology, whether experiential, confessional, sociopolitical, or historicotheological.

Thus confronted with epistemological questions on the rational framework of their thinking, theologians must address the question of the degree of truth and objectivity of their statements. Even the most basic tenet of Christian faith, that it purports exclusively to be good news for all people of all times, implies a claim to truth and objectivity that can not be religiously relativized (Trigg, 1977:166). This very claim—the so-called absolutist claim of the Christian faith—makes it impossible for theologians, who would pursue their philosophical task both with intellectual credibility and in a personal commitment to faith, to view theology purely as an uncritical cherishing and reaffirmation of tradition. On the contrary, true theology ought to be a constantly creative act: a creative event in which theologians seek to tell the truth as accurately as possible, but at the same time a creative act supported consciously by the traditional sources of theologians, by their explicit dependence upon the Christian events that originally created and gradually helped to shape that tradition, and by their religious conviction that the most profound significance of human life can be revealed only through an understanding of those events.

This puts systematic theologians before their greatest challenge, namely, to attempt to answer the question, What is theology? in a twentieth-century situation, where the Christian religious tradition faces a crisis concerning the cognitive quality of its claims. The question of the cognitive quality of theological pronouncements (cf. A. van Niekerk, 1984:65-66; Peacocke, 1984:43; Tracy, 1978:5; Hesse, 1984:27-28) will play a central role in the last section of this book. The word *cognitivity* is used throughout in the sense of reference or reality depiction in theological statements: in what sense theological statements refer to reality or claim to be true, in the provisional sense of the word. This question of cognitivity deserves serious attention from theology, since it is in its essence concerned with the objective quality, the reality underlying the referential language of theology.

Systematic theologians who seek to convey convincingly the Christian message are now confronted with a series of specifically defined, fundamental-theological problems. The question, What is theology? embraces not only the question, Is theology also a science? but leads to further problematic questions such as the following:

- What precisely do concepts such as *rationality, objectivity,* and *truth* imply?
- Do theologians in fact argue rationally, and can theology claim to have a conceptual model that would stand up to critical evaluation in contemporary philosophy of science?
- What is the nature of theological statements, and how do they differ from prescientific religious statements and official ecclesiastical pronouncements?
- What are the origins of theological statements, conceptual models, and theories?
- What is the structure of these statements and models, and what is the role of theorizing in the formulation of theological statements?
- How does the theologian's own religious commitment relate to theorizing in his theological subject?
- What is the nature of the arguments used by theologians to justify their statements? To what extent, therefore, can theological utterances be made acceptable and accessible to others, or their truth be made susceptible to testing, proof, or justification?
- What is the role of the Bible, as the Word of God, in theological theorizing?
- How do theologians respond to criticism, especially when the Bible is invoked as an authoritative criterion to justify often widely divergent theological stances?

In my view, such questions put upon systematic theology an inescapable obligation to rationality and thus of critically accounting for faith. In more theological terms: in reflecting on God's revelation in history, theologians must be prepared to render a critical account of faith which will eventually make the hermeneutical question the central theological question of our times, also in systematic theology. Epistemologically, however, theologians must remain constantly aware of the eschatological structure of any pronouncement of faith—in other words, that such pronouncements are approximately true, have a provisional quality, and must therefore, as statements about God, be limited and open to correction. This is so because God, the ultimate object of our theological reflection, will always be ahead of our concepts and conceptual models of Him.

The epistemological question of the quality and validity of our theological statements is thus of vital importance, not only because there are no longer any comprehensive, homogeneous epistemological theories without certain defects (Botha, 1977:3), but also because the typically positivistic unitary ideal for science as such is no longer acceptable in terms of truth, objectivity, and rationality.

Some Conceptual Definitions

When theologians inquire from a philosophy of science metalevel about the relevance of God to our everyday experience of reality, they find themselves excitingly involved in the dynamic process of science. And in this process systematic theologians will not only have to take note of the issues and conceptual framework of the problems currently preoccupying philosophy of science but will also have to become critically familiar with those concepts—both for the scientific credibility of their own reasoning and for the sake of that truth on which they wish to make valid, credible statements as lucidly and accurately as possible. That being so, we shall now briefly explain precisely what is meant by certain terms that are used throughout this book and that have a central bearing on the line of reasoning followed here.

It should be clear by now that the central theme of this study is the question of the nature of systematic-theological thought. In terms of philosophy of science, this theme implies an epistemological approach to the question whether the problematic concept of rationality can be reclaimed meaningfully and validly for theology. If theology could validly be described as a rational activity it would, at the same time, have gained scientific credibility, since scientific activity must above all meet the criteria for rationality (Mouton and Marais, 1985:29). What these criteria for rationality imply for theology will have to be examined closely. These criteria will imply, at the least, that systematic theology must aim at the utmost clarity in its thought, conceptual models, and theories.

More particularly, it will be shown that rationality has had various and even conflicting interpretations in contemporary philosophy of science. The new trend toward historicism since Thomas S. Kuhn has to a large extent superseded the positivistic concept of rationality in which rationality was equated with a universally valid, value-free objectivism. Since Kuhn, rationality has become a quality of persons or a particular community, and no longer one of rules, guidelines, or universal laws. The conception of rationality eventually adopted in this book is one that in fact has a historicosociological character but is not exhausted by this contextuality, because certain criteria of rationality are also intercontextually or interparadigmatically valid.

If it is accepted, furthermore, that the term *model* means basically a conceptual framework in terms of which something is explained (Mouton and Marais, 1985:139ff.), then a rationality model is a conceptual framework adopted by a person or a group in order to explain what criteria are needed to make a particular model of thought qualify as rational. This process normally implies a quite specific scientific ideal; in other words, the aims that scientists pursue in their scientific activities. In the sciences the attainment of a specific ideal obviously also determines the formulation of guidelines or criteria, as well as the ultimate evaluation of theories in terms of the specific ideal pursued by a scientist.

As will eventually be shown, since rationality is always determined partly by context, there are good reasons to assume here that rational thought, in turn, is always bound up with certain definitive premises. This intellectual commitment to certain models of thought or theories must at all times be clearly distinguished from an even more profound, ultimate commitment (a term used here mostly in the specifically religious sense). Rationality—particularly in theology—is ultimately always rooted in a quite specific religious commitment and thus also in the conviction that what is believed is in fact real or true (Trigg, 1977:47; Hart, 1983:209ff.).

A further characteristic of all scientific activity is that the sciences embrace a variety of schools of thought. Since Thomas S. Kuhn's work, these higher and often divergent research traditions have been referred to as *scientific paradigms*. The term *paradigm* has acquired divergent and complex meanings, but basically it still stresses the communal character of science and serves primarily as a model for the pursuit of science (Mouton and Marais, 1985:145ff.).

Since theology, too, comprises a variety of schools of thought and traditions, the term *paradigm* is sometimes used in an analogous sense in this book. When paradigm is defined in this sense, as a broad interpretative framework, theology might also, for example, speak of a Reformed, or Roman Catholic, or even a Christian religious paradigm (Barbour, 1976:147ff.). In all cases, however, the reference is to a coherent body of basic convictions, models, and theories functioning as a comprehensive interpretative framework.

Conceptual Models and Theories

It is important that theologians realize that they are authentically involved in their pursuit not only when approaching their field of study critically, observantly, intelligently, rationally, and responsibly, but also when they realize that critical thought does not demand cutting themselves off from their basic convictions and ultimate commitment through a supposed objectivity. Creativity and rationality in a fundamental-theological reflection on systematic theology can never mean abandoning the sources and traditions of theology. They imply, rather, the construction of a model in which the extremes of the content of the Christian faith, on the one hand, and the context of the problems currently engaging philosophy of science, on the other, are transcended in a new and creative conceptual transformation.

In the pursuit of such a model, however, the following will have to receive due consideration:

• To theologians it is of the utmost importance to realize that, despite the diversity of rationality models in the contemporary philosophy of science, the demands of a positivistic philosophy of science still frequently threaten the scientific character of the development of theological thought with absolutist claims to empirical verifiability.

- The questions philosophy of science raises for theology would also lead theologians to appreciate that knowledge—in this case theological knowledge, the knowledge of faith, or the knowledge of revelation—is by no means indisputable or firmly grounded, seen in the light of scientific theory.

The isolation of theologians preoccupied with the problems that philosophy of science raises for theology is exceeded only by the alienation of those who, totally ignorant of the process of theory formation, lay claim to an indisputable scriptural theology or theology of revelation. The attempts of theologians to describe the nature of theology and theological knowledge without taking into account the problems implicit in this thematics in terms of philosophy of science will therefore have to be exposed as illusory.

Thus one of the most significant and incisive shifts in modern systematic-theological thought must surely be the swing away from a type of theology in which seemingly immutable conceptual models cause theological statements to be seen as precise and true dogmatic propositions, toward a new sensitivity to the relational nature of the language of religious experience. The nature of this religious language is profoundly affected by the relationship between the subjective experience of faith and the objectivity of what is deemed to be the content of faith, of which the believer can speak only in the metaphoric language of faith. Consideration of the nature of theological language, however, leads almost naturally to the question of the origins and sources of our theological thought, and thus also to the question of the intellectual credibility of theological language as the specific expression of thought consciously founded on faith.

This question of the nature of theological conceptual models and theorizing is of the utmost importance to me, not only because, in the context of the problematics of the modern philosophy of science, the language of theology often seems to be divorced from reality or even irrelevant; nor just because theological language often shows an ideological streak when a specific conceptual model is absolutized as the only biblical way of thinking and acting; but also because without questioning the peculiar nature of theological thought, one can find no satisfactory answer to the question of the relationship between the personal commitment of believing theologians, their religious experiences, and the specific theorizing that ultimately supports their theological model.

Not only does that theorizing in the origin and development of theological conceptual models play a crucial role in theology; it is also exceptionally problematic because particularly in systematic theology such a theorization of fundamental convictions may readily assume an authoritarian and dogmatic character. This is especially likely to happen when the crucial question of a meaningful and credible premise for systematic-theological reflection is summarily dismissed, for example, with the claim that theology as such is founded on divine revelation and that this revelation has come to us through the exclusive authority of the Bible or the church.

This claim to infallible insight into divine revelation through the unassailable authority of the church or of Scripture poses nearly insurmountable problems to understanding the question of the origins of theological conceptual models and of the question of the truth of theological assertions. Such a theological position always presupposes, as a conceptual model, a certain belief or basic conviction, namely, that God has revealed Himself specifically as posited by the adopted model. However, neither this conviction nor the theorization of its assertions is ever subjected to critical evaluation.

If systematic theologians are to be intellectually honest, therefore, they can no longer simply presume to know what they mean when they use unquestioningly terms such as *God, Bible, confession,* or *revelation.* The very way in which theological models have been theorized prevents theologians from uncritically and unquestioningly assuming to know the meaning of such terms. A much more incisive question would be the historicosociological one of the origin of such concepts: why they were created in the first place, and why they have been developed and adhered to in a particular way.

Not only theological conceptual models, then, but any theological concept—even if it came to us through Scripture and confession—has been shaped by series of traditions and historically determined presuppositions. This is not to deny, of course, that theology, as an act of thought, does find its dominant focus in God's revelation; what must be denied is that this revelation (or rather: our conception of it) can be used unquestioningly as a premise for theological thought. When such a claim is in fact made, systematic theology is confronted with its most acute problem: the dogmatist ideologizing of a particular, exclusively selected conceptual model into the only true or biblical model.

This is the ultimate hazard for a theological model that sees itself as directly committed to a particular broad ideological tradition. If the historical and theological credibility of a particular tradition is replaced by the conception that it is the only possible truth, such a model becomes ahistorical and tends to regard any further development as merely linear and accumulative. This type of development becomes more and more rigoristic, because any insight into the historically defined character of every conceptual model has long been abandoned.

Fortunately the obverse is also true: the more pointed the questioning into the historicosociological origins of theological models, the more intellectually sophisticated such models become; and the more sophisticated the model, the more tolerant and less rigoristic it becomes toward other attempts to interpret God's salvation for this world in terms of concrete, living situations.

Outline

With a view to constructing a valid rationality model for systematic theology and thus attempting to answer the question of the nature of theological language, I shall use the following approach:

In line with the questioning of theology by philosophy of science, Part I will analyze the principal models of rationality from contemporary philosophy of science and in each case evaluate the typical reactions of systematic theology to that model.

Chapters 1 and 2 will concentrate mainly on the almost overwhelming influence exerted on theology by the positivistic conception of science. This discussion will also show why the logical positivist model of rationality, with its ideal of universal laws and thus its objective of basing rational knowledge on final certainties, through the criterion of verifiability, developed into the standard scientific conception of our time. This rationality model, which purported to be so logical, factual, and value-free in its research process that it deliberately sought to eliminate all subjective and metaphysical elements, has raised enormous problems for theology.

Theology's standard reaction to the demands of positivist science was to ignore them totally by setting up its own esoteric ecclesiastical theology. In a subtle sense, however, theology thus came to adopt for itself the rigid structure of the positivist rationality model, both epistemologically and methodologically. We shall examine the typical example of Karl Barth's theological model for the clear-cut profile that standard theological reaction assumed in Barth's confrontation with Heinrich Scholz.

Chapter 3 will deal with Karl Popper's critical rationalism. His rationality model, with its ideal of verisimilitude, in which scientific theories are brought ever closer to truth through the application of the criterion of falsifiability, posed a new challenge to theology. In particular, that objectivity in scientific knowledge no longer depended on nontheoretic, self-evident facts but was redirected toward intersubjective correspondence and thus became a social issue put a more humane face on Popper's rationalism.

What would remain unresolved in this rationality model was the problem of theology's unique object, and especially the fact and effect of the theologian's ultimate commitment. This is clearly evident in William W. Bartley's stringent criticism of theology. The critical-rationalistic charge that theologians constantly take refuge in an irrational ultimate commitment will be dealt with in Chapter 4.

Chapter 5 will concentrate specifically on the incisive change brought about by Thomas S. Kuhn's paradigm theory in respect of the concepts of rationality and objectivity, by which rationality, as the common property of a research community, gained a fully historicosociological character. In my view this broadening of the traditional rationality model has significant and even radical implications for the question of theorizing in systematic theology. Kuhn's conception of the incommensurability of paradigms, however, poses virtually insurmountable problems for the question of truth in theology. We will eventually (in Part III) have to move beyond Kuhn and seek a valid solution to the problem of objectivity and truth in systematic theology inter alia in terms of the contemporary philosophical conception of scientific realism.

Part II will deal specifically with the question of rationality and thus also the question of theorizing in systematic theology. I have opted for an analysis of the conceptual models of Wolfhart Pannenberg and Gerhard Sauter, two modern European theologians who have comprehensively and consciously concentrated on the problematics of theology as posited by philosophy of science.

Chapter 6 will deal with Pannenberg's stand that theology has a commitment to rationality and can never immunize itself ideologically against criticism. It will also be shown how extensively Popper's critical rationalism contributed to Pannenberg's rationality model and, furthermore, how irreconcilable the latter's interpretation of Kuhn is with that conceptual model, when he extends it into a rationality model for systematic theology.

Chapter 7 will evaluate Gerhard Sauter's attempt to establish an argumentative theology, with an analytically theoretic approach, within the context of the close relationship between theology and the church and its confession. We will deal specifically not only with Sauter's positive contribution to the problem of theorizing in theology but also with the problematic extent to which the question of the theologian's ultimate commitment and the danger of an extreme form of ecclesiastical conventionalism remain unresolved in his thought.

Part III develops a rationality model for a systematic theology that purports to be a form of critical accounting for faith. From a philosophy of science point of view, that theology will be described as critical realism.

First, however, Chapter 8 will deal pertinently with the nature of theological statements and will show in detail that theological theories are founded on the metaphoric nature of religious language. This discussion will establish the basis for a referential theory in which referential continuity is found in the consistency with which reality is in fact revealed in the metaphoric nature of religious and theological language. In doing so I also wish to emphasize a certain definitive continuity between prescientific religious language and the language of theoretic theology—a continuity that was possible neither in the rationality models of logical positivism nor in critical rationalism, nor even, in a certain sense, in Kuhn's model.

In conclusion, Chapter 9 formulates three criteria for the structuring of a critical-realist rationality model in systematic theology. Against the background particularly of scientific realism, which undoubtedly heralded a significant change in contemporary philosophy of science, a model is constructed for a form of critical-theological realism in which rationality and progress can be maintained as scientific ideals precisely because theological statements also have the potential for criticism and problem solving, whether cognitively, contextually, or in terms of a definitive problem-solving model.

PART I

SYSTEMATIC THEOLOGY AND PHILOSOPHY OF SCIENCE

1

Logical Positivism

Scientific positivists have their colleagues in theology, for the assumption that it is possible to go directly from observation to theory without the critical use of models has its counterpart in those who assume it is possible to move from the story of Jesus to doctrine without the critical aid of metaphors and models.

> Sallie McFague, *Metaphorical Theology: Models of God in Religious Language* (Philadelphia: Fortress, 1982):89.

The Vienna Circle

Any systematic theologian with a special interest in the intellectual-historical development of theological models will soon come to realize that a metatheological interest in the problematics of philosophy of science is no longer an incidental luxury. On the contrary, the specific (and complex) development of philosophy of science in our time has had a powerful impact on the intellectual course of theological history.

One might fairly say that philosophy of science owes it founding to a group of physicists, mathematicians, and philosophers who, for a number of years from 1922 onward, met weekly in Vienna to discuss scientific and philosophical issues (De Vries, 1984:41ff.). Thus was born the famous Vienna Circle, with which eminent scholars such as Schlick, Carnap, Neurath, and Reichenbach are usually associated. Philosophers such as Nagel, Hempel, and Ayer were to become a kind of second generation of this school of thought, which became known as *logical positivism* and which had a profound effect on the development of metascientific thought.

This group of philosophers was particularly attracted to empiricism, an epistemological approach that sought to base all true knowledge on some form of sensory experience. Science as a phenomenon had, of course, received attention from earlier scholars too, but the activities of the Vienna Circle in the 1920s sparked off truly unprecedented activity in theorizing from a philosophy of science point of view (Pannenberg, 1973b:29ff.).

From the outset, the strong empirical bias of the Vienna Circle made it especially sympathetic to the natural sciences and natural science research. Particularly in its early years, the Circle was also strongly influenced by the philosopher Ludwig Wittgenstein's well-known *Tractatus Logico-philosophicus* (1922), which in fact heralded a revolution in philosophical thought: thenceforth, any type of philosophy that did not meet the stringent demands of lucidity, verifiability, and consistency adhered to in current natural science could be classified as unacceptable, if not meaningless, in terms of a sharply formulated criterion. By this means the Vienna Circle sought to expose any form of speculative thought as a metaphysical fiction, to be superseded by an authentic and universally valid scientific worldview. In terms of that model, only statements that could be proved true or false could have any meaning. And since the meaning of a statement depended on whether it could be verified, this criterion became known as the verifiability criterion of meaning.

This first form of systematized philosophy of science is known as *logical positivism*. As a philosophy, logical positivism strongly resists any possible influences from metaphysics or theological reflection, and logical-positivistic philosophers take their stand on empirical cognition in their efforts to analyze and purify the language and methods of science. This stand was to lead to a logical-positivistic conception of science that many scientists adopted up to the 1960s and are adopting even today, whether consciously or subconsciously.

In this regard it should be borne in mind that any form of positivism assumes some kind of definitive datum as the final basis for all argumentation (Pannenberg, 1973b:31). This could happen even in theology: Dietrich Bonhoeffer, for example, accused Karl Barth of a type of revelatory positivism. As we shall see, Barth assumed uncritically the Word of God or His revelation in Jesus Christ as a premise and base for all argument, without ever questioning the reasons or grounds for this massive assumption. In any form of empirical positivism, however, experience, or rather sensory experience, is posited as the ultimate basis for all forms of knowledge.

World War II and Moritz Schlick's assassination by a student (1936) broke up the Vienna Circle. From then on, the influence of the logical-positivistic philosophy of science was to manifest itself mainly on Anglo-Saxon territory (Koningsveld, 1977:30).

The Unity of Science

One of the most crucial tenets of logical positivism shows up in the expressed conviction that all sciences ultimately have the same epistemological structure (De Vries, 1984:43), which in turn is determined by the structure of the most highly developed science of the times, namely, the natural sciences. Thus was born the typical positivistic belief in the unity of all sciences, and any science that somehow had not adapted to this stringent criterion for science was summarily disqualified.

As a result, the basic tenets of logical positivism have come to focus on a type of unitary science as the ultimate scientific view of the world: a view that would rule out any form of metaphysical and theological dominance, not only in science but also in everyday issues. By this means the empiricist line of the earlier logical positivism was drawn to its logical conclusion. From this viewpoint, the insoluble problems or so-called profound truths of theology, for example, must either be seen as pseudoproblems or be purified to reduce them to truly empirical scientific problems (Koningsveld, 1977:32-33). The ultimate concern of the philosophers of logical positivism, therefore, was to analyze concepts, statements, and theories so as to make explicit their meaning—or lack of meaning. This analysis remains throughout a logical analysis aided by modern logic. Against the background of the empiricism of the Vienna Circle, in which all knowledge of reality was ultimately founded on the irrefutable basis of data obtained from direct observation, logical positivism would define the philosopher's task as follows: With the aid of their logical apparatus philosophers must reduce all empirical knowledge to concepts and statements that refer directly to sensory data. This procedure will enable them to design a system in which all rational knowledge is integrated with the totality of a unitary science.

This approach to philosophy draws a sharp distinction between two kinds of statements: (a) empirical scientific statements (the meaning of which can be elucidated by logical analysis within the system of a unitary science), and (b) metaphysical statements, which have no cognitive content (i.e., they express no knowledge) and can at best express and verbalize certain feelings.

In terms of the fairly rigid natural science worldview of logical positivism, all metaphysical statements must therefore be rejected as cognitively meaningless. This judgment applies in particular to any type of statement that proposes to say something about reality as distinct from personal experience. The only meaningful statements, then, are those that are founded on experience and can be reduced by logical analysis to the basic elements of sensory experience.

Logical positivism recognizes only one other kind of nonempirical statement, namely, analytical statements, or statements of which the truth can be ascertained only by analyzing the meaning of the terms contained in them.[1] It would be contradictory to deny this type of statement, since its truth can in fact be verified independently of any experience. Such analytical statements include those of the formal sciences, logic and mathematics.

Wittgenstein's *Tractatus Logico-philosophicus* may serve as an example of the type of analysis in which the meaning of concepts is elucidated and the language purged of meaningless elements. For Wittgenstein, the philosopher's task culminates in this logical elucidation of language: whatever can be said can now be said lucidly, and what cannot be discussed meaningfully should rather be left unspoken. Through incisive logical analysis, many philosophical problems will simply vanish, since it was the unsound use of language that made them seem problematic.

On the basis of Wittgenstein's thought the Vienna Circle went further and used this logical instrument to excise all metaphysics and to construct the ideal of a comprehensive unitary science. This use of logical means to combat metaphysics and theology gave rise to the name *logical positivism*, which sees philosophical thought as the analysis of the language of science in order to arrive at a reconstruction of science as a unitary science.[2]

To the philosophers of the Vienna Circle, in particular Moritz Schlick and Rudolf Carnap, this approach implied that a given proposition would be meaningful only if it were possible to say what observations (of situations) that proposition could verify. This means that metaphysical propositions must clearly be nonsensical or meaningless, since certain words in such propositions are meaningless because they can have no correspondence with anything empirically identifiable.

The philosophers of the Vienna Circle in fact developed Wittgenstein's ideas on meaningful and meaningless propositions into a systematic theory whereby statements would ultimately be controlled. The leading figures in this development were Moritz Schlick, Rudolf Carnap, and, in England, A. J. Ayer. One important consequence of their work was the conclusion that sensory perception alone could not always provide a logical procedure for testing statements because propositions can be tested only in the context of their relation to other propositions. As a result, more and more attention has been given to the question whether the so-called protocol sentences or basic propositions, which express the content of observations and to which all other propositions can be

---

1. For example, all circles are round; if something is blue, it is not not-blue; all spinsters are unmarried, etc. (cf. Koningsveld, 1977:33).

2. It should be borne in mind that Wittgenstein, in his analysis of the logical structure of language, traces in it the logical form of reality, inasmuch as the coherence of certain words in a proposition (statement) reflects the coherence of certain objects in a situation. In older forms of empiricism and positivism, the individual word or concept was seen as a reflection of reality; in Wittgenstein, the proposition as a whole is that reflection. Therefore only a proposition could be true or false; and its truth or falsehood consists in its correspondence or noncorrespondence with the situation to which it refers.

related in one way or another, can be subjected to a clear and distinct intersubjective formulation. The principle of verifiability has consequently played a crucial role in the further development of logical positivism, but the truly categorical rejection of metaphysical propositions as meaningless was possible only in the earlier stages of this philosophy of science (Pannenberg, 1973b:32).

The Standard Conception of Science

What clearly emerges from the above is that science is seen as a rational activity guided by a certain logic or method in its pursuit of a quite specific ideal of objectivity. Thus originated what we might now call the standard conception of science (Koningsveld, 1977:59-60). This conception links directly with the model of natural sciences in which scientific knowledge is equated with objectivity and rational cognition is invoked in the quest for a true conception of reality. The controlled collecting of experiential data makes it possible to arrive at certain empirical generalizations or laws by way of inductive generalizations. If such hypotheses are successfully tested or verified, a new scientific law has been discovered and can be integrated accumulatively with the growth of scientific knowledge.

The well-known contextual distinction—initially drawn by Hans Reichenbach—now plays a crucial role in the justification of scientific concepts, laws, and theories. Rational reconstruction, and thus also the question of the justification of scientific concepts and theories, is done in the so-called context of justification. How scientists actually arrive at theories is, however, a psychological, sociological, or historical problem and as such lies within the context of discovery. Within this latter context one might ask how scientific discoveries relate to qualities such as intuition, creativity, political and ethical values, cultural-historical and thus also religious factors. Logical positivism maintains that the results of such an inquiry have no bearing on the question of the justification of scientific knowledge: what can justify a theory is not its origin but only correct argument.

In terms of the rationality model of logical positivism the specific influences or considerations that have led a scientist to conclude on a certain theory are, therefore, of no scientific interest. By the same token, the psychological or social reasons for a scientist's acceptance or rejection of a certain conception or theory are of minor significance. Such data may be consigned out of hand to the context of discovery—the province where, for some reason, new ideas arise or are formulated (R. P. Botha, 1977:104).

Philosophers of science are concerned solely and specifically with the context of justification. Their task is to produce a justification for science as such, not for the hidden or implicit reasons researchers might have for constructing or adopting one theory or another. The context of justification is therefore concerned with assessing the merits of scientific theories or ideas. And the highest merit such a theory could have is, of course, its being correct, objective, and value-free: the fact that it corresponds, is correct, and thus expresses the truth in a neutral and controllable manner.

Such a scientific justification of statements proceeds in two phases. First, one must determine whether an assertion or theory in fact belongs to that specific scientific domain, as defined by the logical-positivistic model of rationality. In other words, do the statements of such a theory meet the criterion of verifiability? If so, then the truth or validity of that theory may be further evaluated by asking to what extent it is supported by experience.

The extent to which this contextual distinction has relegated the primary commitments of philosophers, and the effect of any such commitment by scientists on their eventual theorizing, to the context of discovery, thereby declaring them irrelevant to the true progress of rational and scientific thought, was to have a radical impact on the intellectual-historical course of philosophy of science as well as theological thought. This impact will be discussed more specifically later in this book.

For the moment, however, we may agree with Koningsveld (1977:73) that the prime merit of logical positivism lay in the extent to which it facilitated a highly detailed analysis of science as a phenomenon. What cannot be ignored, however, is that the positivistic element of logical positivism invaded the current standard conception of science through its very attempt to explain what science is or ought to be. In consequence, the rationality of science is inseparably linked with its neutral ideal of objectivity, and both rationality and objectivity culminate in the view that each step of scientific theorizing can and ought to be justified only by an appeal to logical argument and/or empirical facts.

In this sense it may be said that logic and factuality are basic to the structure of the positivistic standard conception of science and specifically to the rationality model of the positivistic paradigm. As such, logic and factuality have not only laid down the minimum demands for science but are indeed regulating all theorizing and are making this process a rational activity only in terms of these demands. Scientific development and progress in scientific thought have thus become an autonomous process in the context of justification. Political, social, religious, cultural, and other factors are ultimately seen as not really relevant to scientific growth: they can, at best, affect the growth rate of scientific knowledge, but not the content of hypothesizing or theorizing, since these activities are directly linked to what may be regarded as logical and factual:

- With regard to logic as a minimum requirement for science, it is implied that scientific argument or reasoning must adhere to the rules explicitly formulated by logic. It is demanded, furthermore, that scientific theories shall be free from logical contradiction. Together, these two demands make up the demand of logical consistency: both the process of scientific reasoning and scientific theories must be logically consistent. Therefore any argument containing a contradiction—regardless of its content—is worthless for that reason alone.

- With regard to factuality as a minimum requirement for science: the standard conception of what science is or ought to be demands of scientific theorizing an appeal to objective, value-free facts that have not been distorted by political, cultural, or religious prejudices. In terms of this demand, scientific hypotheses and ultimately theories are constructed on the basis of factual and therefore direct observation. Direct observation implies observation free from theories and ideologies, a factual observation that is open to substantiation by equally objective verification.

The ultimate basis for these minimum demands on science in the positivistic rationality model is the concept of a truly scientific objectivity: through direct observation, facts must speak for themselves, neutrally and freely. Therefore the adoption, rejection, or alteration of a scientific theory is not a matter of belief or disbelief; it can be verified only by an appeal to objective facts: facts that speak the same language to all observers, whether Christian, atheist, or Marxist. It is granted, of course, that this type of objectivity is not always immediately attainable, since observation often suffers interference from ideological or other theoretic influences; nevertheless, any scientific pursuit must remain true to the objective and value-free ideal.

This model of scientific rationality, and therefore also the idea of science as redefined in its modern standard conception, has undoubtedly been made into the norm for our everyday—also scientific—practice. Through the scientification of modern life, by which logical consistency, objectivity, verification, and freedom from values have been elevated to minimum requirements for scientific thought, this standard conception has regained its positivistic character and ultimately reveals itself as an unmistakably ideological line of thought.

Herman Koningsveld (1977:87) may therefore justly maintain that anyone adopting this standard conception has by no means adopted a neutral stance but is in fact a true believer: an adherent to belief in this type of scientific rationality. The standard conception of what science ought to be, defended on the grounds of a positivistic commitment, elevates the ideas of scientific rationality, objectivity, freedom from values, verification, and logical consistency into values: values that society must observe at any price.

The following should now be clear: until the basic tenets of the positivist standard conception are thrown open for discussion, that conception cannot escape the accusation of having an ideological character. More importantly, if a certain standard conception of science has to be defended on the grounds of a belief, there may of course be scientists who think differently and therefore do not share that specific belief in a specific type of scientific rationality. As a result, those tenets that were to serve as a basis for the positivist rationality model might begin to show serious cracks—an event that might, in the long run, lead to both crisis and liberation in our theological reflection.

2

Theological Reaction to the Positivist Model of Science: Karl Barth

Aber die Energie des Glaubens, so hoch sie auch gefasst werden mag, ist natürlich im geringsten noch nicht ein Beweis für seine Legitimität.

Heinrich Scholz, "Wie ist eine Evangelische Theologie als Wissenschaft möglich?" *Zwischen den Zeiten,* 1 (1931):227.

Introduction

The direct effect of logical positivism on the prevailing standard conception of scientific thought was to confront theology with an unenviable dilemma, for obvious reasons: in the theory of science, the question of the nature and status of theological statements would create virtually insoluble problems for theological reflection precisely because of the specifically positivist structured ideal of value-free objectivity and irrefutable verification. In this chapter I shall, therefore, argue that the rationality model of logical positivism might bear down so heavily on theology that the theologian would react almost automatically by devising his own esoteric and peculiar conceptual model for theology. But by its nature and structure such a theological model of thought, even if seen as a theology of revelation or of Scripture, lapses both epistemologically and methodologically into a model of rationality analogous to the standard positivistic concept from which it has sought to escape.

It is now clear that theology has long been wrestling with a crisis of identity (Daecke, 1974:7), one which undoubtedly still prevails because the question, What is theology? has become an unavoidable question of the first order for every critical theologian. What makes the theologians' commitment to the problem of the status and validity of their statements especially compelling is that theology's institutional ties with universities (not only in the European context[1] but in South Africa as well) are, on scientific grounds, still largely unexplored and even uncertain.

The presence of theological faculties and departments of Biblical Studies at our universities derives mainly from a factual situation born of society's pious regard for the convictions of our major ecclesiastical communities—a situation that would pose a serious threat to the survival of such departments and faculties, should there be a change in society's sentiments and convictions. The issue of the nature of theology, and with that the participation of theology in the debate on the philosophy of science, is therefore of vital concern to the theologian simply because theology's position in the cadre of scientific disciplines can by no means be taken for granted. For theology this implies stringent self-criticism, which might, however, lead to its eventual revitalization as a scientific discipline.

Thus the questions that philosophy of science poses for the peculiar nature of theological reflection, as well as the ultimate impulse toward creative reflection on that nature in order to achieve a constructive definition of a creditable theological model of rationality, may lead back directly to the original dilemma into which systematic theology has been plunged by the stringent criteria of the logical-positivistic model of rationality.

This questioning of the nature of theological thought is especially vital to Protestant theologians, with their strong commitment to the Reformation and in particular to Reformed theology, not only because Reformed theological premises such as *revelation* and *Holy Scripture* become central to this questioning of the sources of theological models of thought, but also because the point at issue is the ability of Reformed theology to draw on its own tradition for creditable answers to the questions of our time. It will also have to be demonstrated that systematic theology's grappling with the problems of philosophy of science is no mere ploy to modernize theology, but rather an honest attempt to achieve methodological clarity, especially on the scope and status of its statements.

Owing to the overwhelming impact of the positivistic model of science and the concomitant emphasis on the epistemological unitary structure of all sciences, theology too is now subjected to the so-called question of demarcation: the question as to what types of thought might be demarcated as specifically scientific if they are to be accepted as valid, precise, objective, and thus

---

1. Cf. in detail W. Pannenberg, 1973b:7-8; also S. M. Daecke, 1974b; and G. Sauter, 1975b:283.

as rational reflection. This raises not only the question—as will later become evident—of the confessional determination of theological reflection, but specifically also the question of how, within the broader framework of inter-disciplinary reflection, theologians account for the scientific conception or model of rationality that they consciously adopt (or reject) in their own reflective processes.

In the context of the positivistic view of science, the question of the scientific status of theology would ultimately become a question of its specific procedures or methods. The methodological question, in turn, implies the more profound epistemological question of the true object of theological reflection, and thus also the inexorable question whether theological statements can be justified, verified, or tested. Given due weight by the theologian, the question of the scientific status of theology (within the context of logical positivism) will at the same time be a question of the possibility and justification of a specific theological mode of cognition that meets the minimum demands laid down by the positivist model of rationality.

The problem has been and still is aggravated by the fact that theology usually takes its stand on a highly exclusive claim to truth. God's revelation, as derived from Holy Scripture, is generally defined as the object of theology and is thus seen as diametrically opposed to the demand that no scientific statement can be accepted without testing, and that the accuracy of any such statement must be open to some form of reliable verification. This conflict has gradually led to a sharp distinction between theology and other sciences, usually founded on the premise that whereas nontheological scientists are concerned with reality and can thus make statements only on objectifiable matters, theologians are concerned not with the field of defined objects but with the all-comprehensive Truth (God), which in any event is not susceptible to objectification by accepted scientific methods.

This well-known division of labors between theology and the other sciences has understandably led to mutual suspicion, in which theology has sought to maintain its intellectual integrity by positing that all conceptions—and thus also all scientific statements—are in any event founded on irrationally assumed presuppositions. Unfortunately this kind of strategy would time and again help to pin back theological reflection to a patently irrational and even authoritarian grounding of its claims—a strategy that would, in turn, inevitably become the focus of criticisms of theology.

The reaction of theologians to the stringent rationalistic demands of the positivistic conception of science might well be seen as the standard theological reaction to the standard view of science implied in the positivistic conceptual model.[2] A theology of this type sees itself as a kind of autonomous mental pur-

---

2. Less typical but equally fascinating are the views of theologians who were not only influenced by logical positivism but often attempted to establish direct links with it. In such cases it

suit that can function with no regard for the minimum demands of the standard positivistic conception of science.

By this means theology, grounded on the unique authority of its unique object (i.e., God and His revelation), might develop into a fully autonomous science, thus producing a theology based exclusively on an ultimate commitment which, defying any deeper questioning, leads the obedient to the development of a dogma of divine revelation that directs, authoritatively and infallibly, all theological reflection.

This type of theological reaction to the standard positivist conception of science occurred particularly among the so-called dialectical theologians of Germany in the 1930s and 1940s, and also in some schools of thought within the Reformed theological paradigm. A much more fruitful response to the dilemma that logical positivism has posed for theology might be a critical exploration of logical positivism's empirical criteria for meaning (namely, the verification of propositions by reference to sensory perception or to basic propositions embracing such perceptions), rather than reaction to or an accommodation of logical positivism. Such an analysis, which would revive the question of the structure of scientific conceptual models and of the nature of rationality, occurs especially in the works of theologians who had closely followed the debate on philosophy of science and were thus strongly influenced in their approach to problems by the thought of philosophers of science such as Karl Popper and Thomas S. Kuhn.

Theology as a Unique Science

Before discussing this response in more detail, however, I should like to deal with a typical standard theological reaction to the positivistic conceptual model—the theology of Karl Barth. It is a theology which is not only vast in content but also, in its questioning of the nature of theological reflection, typical and exemplary of the conscious (and especially also the unconscious) grappling of theologians with the critical demands of the positivistic model of rationality. In Barth's case this is highlighted by the direct challenging of his

---

is clearly stated that religious and theological propositions are not intended to make any statements or assertions about a reality beyond ours—a reality as indicated by the Word of God. It is also maintained that religious propositions are not assertions about a particular reality but merely expressive statements of certain religious needs or sentiments. As such, religious and theological statements have no cognitive quality. R. M. Hare sees religious statements as expressions of a vision, a special way of looking at empirical reality (Hare, 1957:176-193). Following Hare, Paul van Buren denies that religious language has any cognitive meaning. Here, too, religious commitment, and therefore religious language, is seen as an expression of a very specific worldview (Paul van Buren, 1963). For a further discussion of this issue, see Roger Trigg, 1977:86ff., 131ff.

theology, on the basis of the positivistic rationality model, in the critical and polemical works of Heinrich Scholz (1971a, 1971b).

Karl Barth's theological thought—from the publication of his well-known *Römerbrief* in 1918 to his masterly *Kirchliche Dogmatik*—may be seen, methodologically, as largely a reaction to the collapse of attempts by nineteenth-century liberal theology to ground Christian faith on some form of knowledge of the historical Christ. Barth's compelling insistence on the priority of God's revelation in Jesus Christ eventually became perhaps the prime leitmotiv of his theology.

These revelatory events were held to be the only avenue to a belief in God, since history as such could provide no basis for faith. By this means Barth also sought to stress the infinite qualitative distinction between God and mankind. The fact that a human being can never—even with the most exact historical methods—succeed in testing or even justifying God's truth became the most basic premise of his reaction to any form of so-called natural theology. Ordinary history, he maintains, can in no way contain God's revelation so as to enable sinful humanity to approach or assess it rationally; on the contrary, revelation is an incidental experience in which humanity is confronted *senkrecht von oben* (vertically from above) with God's overwhelming presence.

By this means Barth strove to transcend the crucial problems of nineteenth-century theology, namely, historical relativism and psychological subjectivism (Klooster, 1977:36), by finding a new and rediscovered focal point in the absolute priority of God's revelation in Jesus Christ. The price he was prepared to pay for this attempt was the total severing of the kerygma on the fate of Christ (as *Geschichte*) from ordinary history (as *Historie*).

Thus, too, the gospel/kerygma on Jesus Christ would become inaccessible to any form of positivistically structured attempts at historical reconstruction. A further implication was that man, as a finite being, could never independently—bypassing God's revelation—and rationally conclude to the transcendence of God.

Barth's emphasis on the fact that man on his own can gain no access to God in His transcendence is therefore an attempt to avoid any form of psychological subjectivism. The implication was, however, that there had been no direct and lasting revelation of God in history—neither a scriptural nor a general revelation (as this stand was later commonly typified in the Reformed conceptual model).

Barthian theology is vast and complex, but this cursory outline of his essential perspective will have to suffice here. Of far greater relevance is the question of the kind of rationality model that emerges from this mode of theologizing. For Karl Barth, theological reflection is authentic only if and to the extent that it is a theology of revelation that finds its object in God, who, in His omnipotent revelation, is in fact the Subject of theology.[3]

---

3. Cf. Karl Barth (1928:269): God is the "in sich selbst begründeten Grund, der nun wirklich in keinem Sinn 'Objekt', sondern unaufhebbares Subjekt ist."

This turning to a conception of theology as a science *(Wissenschaft)* of God and His revelation is so radical with Barth that God and His Word become the only possible fount of theological thought. In opting for a theology derived directly from revelation, Barth not only rejects any form of natural theology but also makes a methodological choice of immense magnitude: *true theology is possible only "from above," from God's revelation down to mankind,* who receives that revelation in concrete obedience.[4] Of further interest is that Barth did not see this direct origin of theology in God's revelation as a product, or *Setzung,* of the human mind, since that revelation impacts on our reality with such authority that it establishes itself as the great *Gegenüber,* or counterforce, to our minds (Barth, 1928:270). It should by now be clear that Barth's stand on this point would ultimately lead to the total isolation of theology. Heyns points out that through such isolation theological thought must ultimately be transformed from a science into a doctrine of faith (Heyns, 1974:155ff.).

In a recent thesis, Erasmus van Niekerk (1984:1-34) also voices the justified reservation that, so far, no generally recognized methodological course had been identified in Barthian thought. Even more important, the problems surrounding the methodological aspects of Barth's conceptual model should not, from a contemporary stance on methodological problems, be modernized unhistorically in a way which is inadmissible from both a hermeneutical and a sociology of knowledge point of view, thereby not doing justice to the aims and contents of Barthian thought as a whole.

The critical question that must, however, be asked about the rationality model of Barthian thought is not only the exposure—from a Reformed paradigm—of a reduced conception of revelation (thus Heyns, 1974:157), but also the question whether Barth did succeed in finding the basis of a true theology in God and His revelation, or whether he found it in a subjective conception of God and His revelation.

The ultimate question, then, is whether the rationality model used by Barth did enable him to achieve his ideal of transcending historical relativism and psychological subjectivism. In the end it will become apparent that Barth, in his severe reaction to the demands of a positivistic conception of science, actually remained caught, in a subtly theological sense, within the framework of precisely that kind of conceptual model.

Karl Barth sought to found his theology of revelation on an impressive choice for revelation rather than experience, theology rather than nontheological sciences, kerygmatic authority rather than rational argument (van Huyssteen, 1978a:338). As a result he could unequivocally state that the question of the scientific status of theology was never a vital question for theology (Barth,

---

4. "Ausser dem Weg von oben nach unten gibt es hier überhaupt kein Weg" (Barth, 1928:276). Barth is also explicit on theology as "Akt des Gehorsams" (1932:2).

1932:5), since theology is a function of the church which, in obedient faith, serves the gospel through critical guidance.

And yet Barth speaks of the scientific nature of theology, since theology too must be relevant and to the point (Barth, 1932:6-7). That relevance is determined by the question whether theology interprets the Word of God in obedient faith. To Barth, that relevance—a commitment to God's revelation—is the prime criterion for scientific validity in theology, not the methodological and cognitive issues. The uniqueness of theology needs no scientific, theoretic basis, since the object of study (God and His revelation), and no presupposed concept of method and scientific validity, guarantees responsible and correct progress in theology.

If Karl Barth's forceful statements are considered from the current perspective on the problems of philosophy of science, it is still understandable that those statements were strongly criticized in terms of the contemporary positivistic model of rationality.

Heinrich Scholz and the Minimum Demands for Science

It was Heinrich Scholz who, as long ago as 1931, sharply rejected Barth's basic premise that, in theology, methodological questions were subservient to its relevance. Although the debate has become dated, and although Scholz was arguing from a positivistic model of rationality that would now not be left unquestioned in philosophy of science, he was in my view correct in pointing out that Karl Barth could ultimately offer no reliable criteria by which to test the relevance of his theology.

In this confrontation, Scholz (1931:221-264) lays down certain specific minimum criteria for the claim to true scientific thought. His aim was to probe the conditions on which any theological conceptual model might claim to qualify as a science. His minimum demands for scientific thought were formulated as follows (Scholz, 1931:231):

1. *The demand of assertiveness (implying, also, the demand of irrefutability):* In any science, only certain special kinds of statements or claims—apart from questions and definitions—are permissible: statements that can claim to be objectively true. This demand is met when a statement has a cognitive quality, as we would now call it; that is, when in that statement something is claimed to be real and true. And in claiming that such a statement is true, the scientist not only endeavors somehow to strike a correspondence with what is being claimed, but obviously also claims irrefutability and therefore the logical exclusion of any untruth in that statement. To put it simply: a statement is either objectively true or not true, which logically implies that it can never be both true and untrue at the same time.

2. *The demand of coherence:* In terms of this minimum demand, every science should focus on a certain definitive and coherent field of objects. It is also important that this field should be specifically identifiable, and as such should be distinct from any statement about it. This point follows logically from the provisional or hypothetical nature of a scientific statement—one in which a scientist, as subject, rationally makes a statement about an objective fact, object, or datum. Different statements may, of course, be made on the same matter from various perspectives, provided these statements do not contradict each other logically. From this it is self-evident that the so-called coherence postulate is ultimately the basis of Scholz's first minimum demand, namely, the demand of irrefutability, which makes it possible to lay claim to objective truth.

3. *The demand of testability:* For Scholz, this demand follows logically from the previous two minimum demands. According to him, one can demand not only that a science should consist of statements and claims that purport to be true, but also that the nature of these statements should be such as to permit some form of testing or verification of their claim to truth.

To Scholz it is self-evident that theology—as, in fact, any human science—cannot evade this stringent demand if it would avoid the stigma of being branded a mere creation of fantasy. Therefore theology's claim to truth should also be accessible to some form of convincing control, testing, and thus verification.

Karl Barth's reaction to Scholz's clearly formulated demands was remarkable: in the very first pages of the first volume of *Kirchliche Dogmatik* he firmly rejected them, without ever again dealing with them (Barth, 1932:7). Barth's reaction finally confirmed Scholz's surmisal (1931:259) that Barthian theology was not concerned with science and scientific reflection, but was much rather a personal religious credo expanded into a comprehensive doctrine and thereby placed beyond any form of control or testing. Ultimately, Barth, in the interests of his type of revelationary theology, consciously rejected any attempt to integrate that theology with the broader spectrum of nontheological sciences. It is ironic, then, that Barth consistently attempted to defend the esoteric quality of his theology of revelation by crossing swords with nontheological thought in general—a type of thought his own reflection could not dispense with, precisely because it sought to be typified as revelationary (cf. E. Van Niekerk, 1984:6-7).

In my view the reasons for Barth's reduction of theology to a type of monological doctrine lie not in a reduced conception of revelation (thus Heyns, 1974:157), but rather in a unique conception of revelation constructed with great and impressive authority on a basis of personal belief, to serve as the only meaningful—in fact, the only correct and true—foundation for theology.

It is not hard, therefore, to find in Barth—despite his rejection of Heinrich Scholz's positivistically structured model of rationality—that very same structural positivistic element at work in his overriding emphasis on a Barthian structured concept of revelation as the foundation and focal point of a true evangelical theology. Methodologically, then, Barth ultimately fell prey to precisely that psychological subjectivism from which he had sought to escape.

If it were in any way possible to construct a theological model of thought within which one could find, without methodological problems and directly, a foundation for theological reflection in God and His revelation, that model could perhaps provide the ideal or only correct method of theological reflection. God and His revelation, however, can now no longer be seen positivistically as a type of objective fact. On the contrary, God and His revelation, as brought to us by the Bible, are now accessible to us solely through an interpretative act. And in the construction of a valid theological model of thought for our time, the full hermeneutical implications of this fact would have to be faced.

Barth's revelationary theology, as a so-called theology *from above,* is methodologically in essence a specifically Barthian theology *from below,* since the assumed authoritative premise of that theology as a conceptual construct, founded on a profound personal conviction, has ultimately been elevated into an authoritarian premise for a comprehensive program of thought.

Theology and Subjectivism

As a Reformed theologian, Karl Barth not only developed his program of thought within the broader paradigmatic context of the influential Reformed theological tradition, but ultimately also exerted a strong influence, both directly and indirectly, through his comprehensive and impressive theology.

In this context it is especially interesting and illuminating to note J. A. Heyns's methodological criticism of Barth's conceptual model. Heyns's comment is noteworthy because his contribution in *Op weg met die teologie* (1974) earns him the recognition of being the first South African systematic theologian to have focused specifically on the philosophy of science question of the nature and status of theology as a science. His critical assessment of Barth's stand and his own construction of a theological model of thought lead inevitably to the question whether such a structured Reformed theology can succeed at all in avoiding the vicious circle of the positivist model of rationality.

In developing his stand, Heyns (1974:215) makes it clear that theology, as a mental activity, is to him indisputably a science, concerned with obedient reflection on God's revelation. He also maintains that the object of theology must always be the revelation of God but that in addition it forms part of mankind's broader cultural task. He continues: "This implies, however, that theology's mode of thought and labor cannot be deduced solely from the structure and demands of the revelatory truth, but that it is essentially also directed by the structure and demands of a larger entity of culture. . . namely, science, and specifically a general theory of science" (1974:14).

This leads to two important provisional conclusions: (1) that the structure and scope of theological statements are determined by the objective as well as the historical, and therefore provisional, character of theology; (2) that theology cannot exist in isolation, as a mere doctrine of faith apart from other sciences, but that it shares, as a science, the problems of scientific theory. Whether the implications of these conclusions are in fact pursued consistently will have to become apparent from a closer evaluation of Heyns's stand.

In seeking clarity on the implications of Heyns's assertions—not only for his own stand, but also for the question of the formulation of methods and theories in theological reflection—it may be profitable to begin with the second conclusion from the excerpt quoted above: that theology cannot exist in isolation, as a mere doctrine of faith apart from other sciences, but that it shares, as a science, the problems of scientific theory.

Heyns (1974:60, 155ff.) repeatedly takes issue—in my view correctly—against the notion of isolating theology as a science and reducing it to a mere monological doctrine. In this regard his assessment of Karl Barth's stand is especially noteworthy. Heyns (1974:155) discusses Barth's conception of theology and maintains that Barth's Christomonistic conception of revelation must ultimately lead to the total isolation of theology from other sciences. To Barth, theology is a function of the church; although it consists of human statements about God, it does not come within the scope of a general scientific critique but must nevertheless maintain its sui generis character as a relevant science. Heyns maintains that Barth's stand on this point leads to the total isolation of theology—a consequence founded, as we have seen, on Barth's reduced conception of revelation.[5]

Heyns (1974:60) rejects such a monological theology in favor of theology as a relational science that links dialogically with the other sciences of our world. In the context of a scientific theory in which scientific language is held to be factual and descriptive, and science itself is seen as the progressive knowledge of reality gained systematically, verifiably (1974:21, 28), by the correct methods (1974:24), and thus logically, Heyns sees theology as indisputably a science, simply because theology meets the requirements set for sciences (1974:126). This conclusion, as well as Heyns's critical rejection of Barth's conception of theology, is firmly in line with his stand as quoted above, namely, that the thought and functioning of theology are not derived solely from the structure and demands of revelation, but also from reflection on a general theory of science.

Both Heyns's rejection of the Barthian stand and his own theoretic basis

---

5. "'n Gereduseerde openbaringsbegrip—van die algemene tot die besondere, en laasgenoemde gekonsentreerd in Jesus Christus—lei tot die isolasie van die teologie en die *sekularisme van die wetenskappe*" (Heyns and Jonker, 1974:157).

for theology become problematic, however, when he considers the nature of theology in greater detail (1974:126). Although he regards theology as a science, specific nuances have to be added to this conception of science: theology is a science sui generis, with its own character and its own rationality. These nuances are evoked by the structure of revelation and of the act of faith founded on it; thus theology is once again distinguished from other sciences. God's revelation, as the object of theology, as well as the faith evoked by that revelation, gives theology a correspondingly unique character, so that the earlier formulated need of founding theology in the context of a general theory of science dwindles before an existential founding in the theologian's personal vocation.[6]

The unmistakably Barthian aura of these statements is further exemplified in highly problematic statements, for example, that the dynamics of theology is the risk of faith, and in the outspoken preference for paradoxical thought in theology—a pattern of thought that Heyns (1974:146-147) also calls dialectic and qualifies as analogical rather than logical. The vast problems that this raises for the nature of theological statements—especially if contrasted with the implications of the earlier claim that such statements are also arrived at by systematic and logical methods—will be analyzed later. For the moment it may be concluded that this approach offers no escape from Barth's drastic isolation of theology. On the basis of a certain conception of revelation so many nuances are added to the scientific status of theology that any true theoretic grounding of theology becomes impossible, and it eventually lapses—at least structurally—into the same isolation as Barthian theology.

As a technique of immunization, Barth's flight from the (albeit positivistic) minimum demands for scientific status was doomed to failure. In fact, his rejection of those demands would ironically avenge itself in the inevitable positivistic structure of the Barthian conceptual model.

I therefore see dangers in Heyns's conscious opting for paradoxical and dialectical thought in theology even after he had initially posited correctly that theological thought could not be deduced solely from the structure of revelation but must be essentially determined also by the debates of contemporary philosophy of science, and had therefore rejected any conception of theology as a type of monological doctrine. In my view that option is in conflict with his earlier demand of systematic and logical method and leads inevitably to his typifying theology as a risk of faith (1974:136). That stand, too, must lead to a drastic isolation of theology, simply because there can be no way of assessing the truth or falsehood of a risk.

At this point I should make it quite clear that I am not concerned with questioning the nature of faith as an act of submission beyond all rational veri-

---

6. Theological reflection "kom voort uit die roeping waarmee God die hart van die mens aanspreek . . ."; and "Teologie is die antwoordende spreke op die spreke van God in die Skrif" (Heyns and Jonker, 1974:132).

fication. What I do question is the founding on personal faith of a conception of revelation that purports to function unproblematically and uncritically as the basis of a theological program and that must ultimately transform theological method to such an extent that theology will once again lapse into total isolation, inspiring conviction only in initiates.

Whether faith, as certain knowledge and trust, does imply some kind of risk is wide open to discussion. But when the basis of theology—God and His revelation—becomes a risk accessible only to paradoxical and analogical thought, one can never be sure whether what one is saying really relates to God (and also to the Bible), or whether it perhaps emanates from a subjective conception of God (and of the Bible)—a conception that can be justified only existentially.

Barth is justified in rejecting the reduction of the object of theology to mankind's religious consciousness (Pannenberg, 1973b:274). Heyns, in turn, is justified in objecting to Barth's isolation of theology. But the assumed axiomatic datum of God and His revelation offers no escape from this dispute, because the positive quality thus given to revelation can offer no alternative to subjectivism in theology. A positivistic theology of revelation that adopts a highly esoteric method makes it extremely difficult to convince others that the basic tenets of theology—God, revelation, Holy Scripture, inspiration, etc.— are not the constructs of subjective whim, whether personal or directed by an influential tradition.

Therefore, when Heyns maintains (1974:128) that knowledge of the Bible thus also means knowledge of God, and that such knowledge is the course of theology, I find myself in wholehearted agreement—from a certain perspective. But if that knowledge is obtained paradoxically and analogically and the dynamics of theology is seen as a risk of faith, severe problems arise simply because it becomes virtually impossible to formulate criteria for valid and creditable statements about God and His revelation: statements which, in any event, are always human and provisional, and which moreover must try to avoid at any price the abyss of subjectivism that opens up before any positivistic attempt (albeit subconsciously, more often than not) to formulate an absolute, immutable, and objective truth.[7]

Heyns's conscious rejection of Barth's stand and his deliberate construction of a theoretic basis for theology show quite clearly that he had no intention of subjectivizing and isolating theology; yet it has become equally clear that a theology seeking to conceive of itself as an autonomous mental act on the basis

---

7. I found theological subjectivism in its most extreme form in Eberhard Jüngel (1967). Cf. statements such as: "Die Freiheit der Theologie ist die Ausübung des Rechtes der Theologie, ausschliesslich Theologie zu sein" (1967:26). "Die Freiheit der Theologie is die in der Freiheit der christlichen Existenz begründete Freiheit theologischer Existenz" (1967:27). And: "Indem die Theologie sich die Freiheit nimmt, das Glauben zu wagen und im Glauben das Behaupten zu wagen und das Glauben sowohl wie das Behaupten denkend zu wagen, wagt sie zu hoffen" (1967:20).

of its unique Object, and thus seeking to found a unique—and ultimately esoteric—science on the basis of an unquestionable commitment of faith, must eventually lapse into a model of rationality analogous to that of logical positivism: a scientific model which, by phasing out meaningful nonempirical (metaphysical) statements, ultimately created a nearly insoluble dilemma for systematic theology.

The question of truth, and thus also the question of the scientific status of theological reflection, is in my view by no means subservient to some or other (positivistically structured) verification process. It is bound up first and foremost with the question of the origins of theological statements. Interestingly enough, new nuances have been added to the question of the truth of theological statements, not by developments within systematic theology itself, but rather by fascinating shifts in philosophy of science away from the positivistic model of rationality.

3

Critical Rationalism: Karl Popper

My point of view is, briefly, that our ordinary language is full of theories; that observation is always observation in the light of theories. Theories are nets cast to catch what we call "the world": to rationalize, to explain, and to master it. We endeavour to make the mesh ever finer and finer.

Karl Popper, *The Logic of Scientific Discovery* (London: Hutchinson, 1968):59.

Rationality and Objectivity

At this point it ought to be clear that the term *rational*—especially because of the negative connotations of the contrasting *irrational*—has come to be associated increasingly, thanks to logical positivism, with scientific status, and has even been annexed as a synonym for scientific discourse on our reality (Van Niekerk, 1982:150-151). Fascinating shifts within contemporary philosophy of science have led away from this ideologically structured positivistic conceptual model. In particular, the extent to which that rigid definition of rationality and the minimum demands for rational (and therefore scientific) thought have been transcended by Karl Popper and Thomas S. Kuhn makes it imperative for systematic theologians not to accept that one model of rationality uncritically, thinking that it offers a full and adequate description of their own rational reflection.

This standard theological reaction is clearly evident when theology re-

24

sorts, in self-defense, to its own positivistic final or indisputable basis, such as God, His revelation, or the inspired Bible as God's Word—as if concepts such as God, revelation, inspiration, and Bible did not also originate in mankind's provisional conceptualizing and theorizing as theoretic concepts or constructs within a historically developing conceptual process.

Any theologian who, in the interests of credibility and of the status of his own mode of argument or reasoning, emerges from the sanctuary of his field of study to grapple with these metatheological questions, which have become so inescapable in our time, soon realizes that the postpositivistic philosophy of science presents an exciting and challenging field, but one which might strike the uninitiated as confusing and complex. In my view, the essence of contemporary philosophy of science, up to and including the so-called scientific realism of our time, derives partly from the works of Popper and Kuhn. For this reason alone, but also for the liberating and broadening perspectives opened up by reflection on a valid theological model of rationality, this book will devote a chapter each to the works of Popper and Kuhn.

The works of these two philosophers of science have led to incisive questioning of and finally the transcendence of the standard model of rationality. In particular, Karl Popper gained renown initially for his remarkably creative engagement with the fundamental assumptions of logical positivism. The ideas that lie at the core of Karl Popper's reaction to the rationality model of logical positivism—whether directed specifically at the Vienna Circle or more generally at his positivistic contemporaries—appear in his very first work, *Logik der Forschung* (1934). The English translation of this book in 1959—*The Logic of Scientific Discovery*[1]—played an especially important role in gaining wide renown for Popper's so-called critical rationalism, and in expanding its influence.

The central themes of Popper's thought, which were to become seminal to modern debates on philosophy of science and specifically to shifts in crucial concepts such as rationality and objectivity, can be summed up as follows (cf. De Vries, 1984:49):

1. A clear-cut distinction is needed between dogmatic and critical thinking.
2. As a rule, people learn from their mistakes. To put it more formally: our knowledge never grows simply through the addition or accumulation of new fragments of proven knowledge; on the contrary, it grows through out attempts to enhance it by eliminating errors.
3. The objectivity of knowledge is determined neither by the way it has been acquired nor by its susceptibility to inductive proof or grounding. Objective knowledge is, rather, knowledge that will stand up to the test of criticism, and therefore to critical questioning.
4. The origins of our knowledge can be traced back to various sources.

1. The 1968 edition will be cited from now on.

Critical questions about those origins and about the truth of our assertions must be defined much more sharply than has been customary in
philosophy of science.

5. There is no ultimate or final basis for true knowledge. All our hypotheses and theories have and always will have the status of conjectures.
Therefore, although the scientist should always pursue truth, he should,
in doing so, take care not to fall into the error of pursuing some final certainty.

Careful analysis of these crucial ideas soon shows that Popper brought
a radically new perspective to the problems engaging philosophers of science.
The central task of the philosopher (and ultimately of every scientist) is no
longer to find proof or justification for true scientific knowledge; it is, rather, to
attempt to show—in the context of interdisciplinary debate—how a specific
critical method can be used to enhance knowledge in science.

In close conjunction with the above, Popper also developed his primary
objection to logical positivism, namely, to its criterion of verifiability, which he
rejected as totally untenable in the development of scientific knowledge. Popper (1963:39-40, 50-51) linked fundamentally his rejection of the principle of
verification and his criticism of the principle of induction. Regarding the latter,
he saw clearly that no number of identical observations—no matter how numerous—would necessarily lead to the conclusion of a general law, valid for all
similar cases.[2] There must therefore always be a discrepancy between any
limited number of observations and the general validity of any law that might
be deduced from them. Consequently, the confirmation of an assumption by
numerous observations can offer no final verification of that assumption even
if only one observation that could disprove the assumption might still be outstanding.

This method of induction, and with it the typical empiricist view of
knowledge as proved knowledge, verified knowledge—even when watered
down to probable knowledge—Popper regarded as typical of the logical-positivistic ideal of basing knowledge on final certainties: a method that purported to
guarantee scientific rationality, objectivity, and freedom from values. By rejecting the notion of inductive confirmation and the basis of objective facts obtained
through objective observation, Popper thus rejected some of the most fundamental features of the positivistically structured standard conception of science.

In this regard Popper draws a sharp distinction between a dogmatic and
a critical approach: the dogmatic approach focuses on confirmation or verification; as a pseudoscientific approach it is more primitive than the critical approach, in which, owing to its true rationality, free discussion of theories oc-

---

2. For example: the fact that someone has seen a thousand black crows cannot lead to the
general objective law that all crows are black; after all, it is theoretically possible that someone
might encounter a white crow somewhere (cf. Koningsveld, 1977:96-97).

curs—discussion with one primary object, namely, to locate the weak spots of such theories in order to improve them. Popper (1963:51) could therefore say: "The demand for rational proofs in science indicates a failure to keep distinct the broad realm of rationality and the narrow realm of rational certainty: it is an untenable, an unreasonable demand."

The Theory-Ladenness of Observation

To gain an even better understanding of Popper's concept of the critical approach, one should appreciate that he totally rejects any possibility of naked, neutral, or objective observation. In fact, all possible forms of observation presuppose a point of view, a perspective, an expectation, a theory from which such an observation becomes possible.[3]

According to Popper, statements about observations are therefore always interpretations of facts in the light of either clearly formulated or subconsciously entertained theories. He thus sought to make the point that scientific knowledge does not proceed from observation to theory; on the contrary, the scientist's point of view or angle of observation is determined by his theoretic interests, by the particular problem engaging him, by his conjectures and anticipations, by his total spectrum of expectations.

To the notion of any naked observation of objective facts, Popper opposes unambiguously the theory-ladenness of all observation. The theory or theories that facilitate a particular observation illuminate reality like a searchlight; what becomes visible, what ultimately passes for our facts, is therefore dependent on our searchlight theories. Therefore: "My point of view is, briefly, that our ordinary language is full of theories; that observation is always observation in the light of theories." In other words, "Theories are nets cast to catch what we call 'the world': to rationalize, to explain, and to master it. We endeavour to make the mesh ever finer and finer" (Popper, 1968:59).

Therefore, although Popper, too, acknowledges that gaining scientific knowledge requires an empirical basis, he clearly rejects any independent or objective empirical basis: the observer himself has to make and establish that basis, so that the basis must necessarily be determined by history and is thus directly the product of culture (cf. Koningsveld, 1977:103). Unlike his predecessors in philosophy of science, Popper does not use the term *experience*—as a basis for all forms of true knowledge—as a relatively unproblematic term. To Popper, experience, in the earlier logical-positivistic sense of the word, is no

---

3. "Observation is always selective. It needs a chosen object, a definite task, an interest, a point of view, a problem" (Popper, 1963:46).

longer the basis of all true science. He strips this word of its common connotations and eventually makes it a more technical term (cf. De Vries, 1984:56).

Experience is thus no longer the criterion by which a theory is tested but rather a concept indicating the method of testing theoretic systems. And such a theory, as a system of statements, can be tested in various ways. First, the logical consistency of a theory may be examined by checking whether contradictory consequences may be deduced from that theory. Second, the logical form of a theory may be examined in order to ascertain whether it meets the relevant minimum conditions in this respect or is perhaps nonfalsifiable. Third, a theory may be compared with its predecessors—earlier theories—to determine whether it represents any advance on one of them. Fourth, a theory may be tested by empirically applying the conclusions derived from that theory. This type of testing ascertains to what extent a theory might be confirmed in experimental situations. If it failed the test, one would be forced to conclude that the theory itself must be unsound. The last method of testing makes it clear that a given theory can no longer be tested directly against experience. The scientific investigator stands between experience and its testing, and so does his decision to accept or reject any conclusion that might emanate from an experiment.

Popper's term for the kind of conclusions by which a theory might be tested is *basic statements* (cf. De Vries, 1984:57). Such testing is no longer, however, an attempt at verification; it is an attempt at falsification: a theory becomes falsifiable if at least one basic statement can be formulated that contradicts the theory in question. Popper's basic statements should not be confused with the protocol sentences of logical positivism: the latter were theory-free statements, founded on pure experience, which had to be irrefutably and obviously true. To Popper, however, these protocol sentences were mere philosophical fictions, precisely because observation always occurs in the light of some theory or other and as such must always contain theoretic elements. At this point one can state that no observation or experience, and hence also no statement about an observation or experience, can ever be pretheoretic. In theology this insight could, I suggest, lead to momentous shifts in questions about the formulation of theories on the relationship between religious experience and theological conceptualization. We shall, however, return to this at a later stage.

As Popper did speak of an experiential or empirical basis for science, that basis—and hence all basic statements—had no absolute or immutable qualities. All science is man-made, and even the most basic scientific statements are hypothetical and therefore provisional in structure. It is by now clear how profoundly Popper's concept of theorized observation involves the researcher in the process of evaluation, in contrast to the ideal of neutral, objective observation in the standard model of rationality.

For Popper the process of scientific cognition begins with problems: not only does our immediate sensory perception occur via interpretation, but our knowledge as such begins with speculation, models, anticipations, hypotheses, conjectures; and it can advance only through a testing process of trial and error. Thus Popper could say (1980:86): "From the point of view of this methodology, we start our investigation with problems. We always find ourselves in a certain problem situation; and we choose a problem which we hope we may be able to solve. The solution, always tentative, consists in a theory, a hypothesis, a conjecture. The various competing theories are compared and critically discussed, in order to detect their shortcomings; and the always changing, always inconclusive results of the critical discussion constitute what may be called the science of the day."

From the above it should now also be clear that Popper turns the objectivity of knowledge into intersubjective correspondence: here objectivity becomes the characteristic of the thought of a specific group, realized through mutual criticism. For Popper, then, objectivity in scientific knowledge is a conventional or social matter and can no longer be founded on atheoretic, self-evident facts. Koningsveld (1977:104) is therefore justified in saying that the rationality in Popper's model is once again founded on logic and facts, but since these facts have no theoretically independent status, rationality ultimately bears a more human face.

The Criterion of Falsifiability

In this context it has also become apparent that scientific theories are not mere logical and inductive conclusions—as in the positivistically structured standard conception of science—but are, rather, free mental constructs, emanating from particular problematic situations. And as free mental constructs, theories may be motivated by nonscientific forms of thought—myths or speculations, for example. Popper therefore rejects the logical positivistic claim that metaphysical assertions are meaningless; if a theory cannot be tested in the strictly scientific sense, it does not necessarily follow that it is trivial, meaningless, or even false. "What we should do, I suggest, is to give up the idea of ultimate sources of knowledge, and admit that all knowledge is human: that it is mixed with our errors, our prejudices, our dreams, our hopes; that all we can do is to grope for truth even if it be beyond our reach."[4]

Although metaphysical statements are not necessarily meaningless or even false, Popper rightly demands a principle of demarcation that would distinguish between statements that might be recognized as scientific and ones that could not be scientific. He found this principle of demarcation in the criterion of falsification. We have seen that Popper unambiguously rejected the principle

---

4. Popper, 1963:30. Cf. also Popper, 1980:80: "Metaphysical ideas are often the forerunners of scientific ones."

of verification: assertions made in scientific statements are not truly verifiable, since it would never be possible to test all instances to which they might apply. Scientific assertions are, however, falsifiable, since the confirmation of any general assertion would fail the moment even a single contradictory instance occurred. If, however, an assertion resisted attempts to falsify it, that might be seen as provisional confirmation.

In Popper's view, then, scientific knowledge grows not through accumulation but through anticipations, conjectures, and tentative solutions to problems. Such conjectures are then controlled by criticism; in other words, by attempts to refute or falsify them. Theories might survive or resist refutation, but they can never be confirmed positively and finally.[5]

In this context the phrase *degree of confirmation* or *corroboration* is often used of scientific theories. The degree of confirmation of a theory tells us how and to what extent that theory has stood up to a test (or tests) up to a given moment. The theory with the highest degree of confirmation is one which has up to a certain point best withstood all the critical tests applied to it (cf. De Vries, 1984:61).

Theories that offer a high degree of resistance to criticism and prove to be the best approach to a particular problem at a given point may therefore be described as the science of a certain time. But since no theory can be positively and finally verified, it is the critical and progressive nature of theories that constitutes the true rationality of science. It is clear, then, that the rational character of science is to be found not in the accumulation of confirmed certitudes, but in the discovery and elimination of errors—in other words, in stringent criticism.

Human knowledge remains the product of our intellectual activities. According to Popper, science creates a theory in response to a problem, and that theory, as a conjecture, is a creative construct and thus a product of human reason—hence the term *rationalism* for Popper's model of scientific philosophy. Such mental constructs are, however, continually subjected to critical testing, which might refute them, and thus Popper's rationalism becomes a critical rationalism—a critical process of free and constructive rationality in which the strongest theories survive and the weaker ones are eliminated.

This definition of Popper's critical rationalism also directly implies his criterion of demarcation. At this point it is essential to realize that Popper (1968:311-312) consistently saw falsification as a criterion for demarcation (of science from nonscience) and definitely not as a criterion for meaning. Thus is constructed, at the same time, a model of rationality that enables us to stress the progressive and critical nature of the growth of knowledge. With his criterion of falsification, Popper draws the line between science and nonscience in yet a further sense, and at the same time shows a much more positive appreciation of nonscientific statements or assertions than was shown in logical positivism.

---

5. "The very refutation of a theory—that is, of any serious tentative solution to our problem—is always a step forward that takes us nearer to the truth" (Popper, 1963:vii).

It may justly be said (Koningsveld, 1977:94) that logical positivism could never do justice to the historical dynamics of the development of human thought. In fact, Popper could point out that myths and metaphysics played an important role in mankind's pursuit of truth. In terms of logical positivism, non-scientific statements such as *God is a personal reality* are totally meaningless; to Popper, however, such statements may be meaningful. In fact, they may even be true, even if they cannot be tested in the strict scientific sense.

Popper assigns a clear and positive function to metaphysical statements. Not only do metaphysical ideas help to form a certain conception of the world, especially in areas where, as yet, no scientifically verifiable theories are available; such ideas are also—as we have seen—implicit in all forms of scientific inquiry. Our scientific hypotheses are often accompanied by the nonscientific, the metaphysical. By this means Popper sought to accommodate the numerous instances where metaphysical and even religious assumptions have played a major role in the history of modern scientific thought.

The Theory of Verisimilitude

A question that must, of course, be asked, is whether these so-called metaphysical ideas are merely the external, historical circumstances for the sources of scientific knowledge, or whether the structure and validity of scientific statements have metaphysical implications (as Pannenberg claimed, 1973b:41) or ontological references. The latter would have to be the case, given Popper's view of truth and his conception of scientific theories as free mental constructs, as anticipations, or as conjectures.

According to Popper, successive theories might in fact enable us to gain a better grasp of the truth. This concept has come to be known as the theory of verisimilitude (cf. De Vries, 1984:78ff.): theories with an ever-increasing degree of confirmation gradually move closer to the truth. In terms of the theory of verisimilitude we can never be really sure whether a statement is true or untrue. We can, however, accept that the theories and concepts we have adopted for sound critical reasons are closer to the truth than competing theories. Accepted basic statements correspond with what we have provisionally accepted as a fact or reality.

It has been seen that Popper totally rejected the notion of a criterion for the confirmation of a final truth. Yet he accepted the idea of truth as a regulatory principle (Popper, 1963:226). To him, the crucial issue is, therefore, not the question of the justification or confirmation of truth, but how untruth may best be exposed and eliminated. In the scientific process of trial and error, the strongest theory survives and is provisionally adopted as the best approach to truth. This anticipation of truth by theories undoubtedly implies that metaphysical ideas cannot be seen merely as part of the incidental historical conditions for the growth of scientific knowledge, but must, in their ontological reference, help to constitute the meaning and validity of scientific theories.

In the light of the earlier logical-positivistic distinction between the contexts of discovery and justification we must finally point out that to Popper, too, it was imperative to distinguish between knowledge as a product and the actual process of gaining knowledge, in which the basic convictions of the scientific thinker may play a subjective role. Questions about the origin and development of our modes of thought and utterance are proper to the context of discovery and should be clearly distinguished from questions relating to the creative product of our (albeit provisional) bodies of knowledge. The latter belong to the context of justification, and in this field theories may achieve a certain degree of verisimilitude and also a high degree of objectivity. This, then, is the context that should form the focal point of scientific reflection.

This important distinction would be taken up by Wolfhart Pannenberg when, as a systematic theologian, he made the problematic concept of God the theme of his attempt to escape from all forms of religious subjectivism through a broader model of rationality, and it is in the light of this distinction that William W. Bartley was to accuse Protestant theology of loss of reality and an irrational withdrawal into an ultimate religious commitment.

4

Critical Rationalism and Theology:
William W. Bartley

Both philosophers and theologians, unable to answer the questions of the scep-
tics, stop defending their positions and begin to describe and expound them—
to preach them.

William W. Bartley, *The Retreat to Commitment* (New York:
Alfred Knopf, 1962):129.

Introduction

One can hardly overestimate the profound influence of critical rationalism, as
one of the leading schools of thought in modern philosophy of science, on our
intellectual climate. At the center of this influence lies the break away from the
stringent logical-positivistic model of rationality. I am convinced that intellectual sensitivity to the range of implications of this break will enable any theologian to tackle the problems surrounding the fundamental questions of systematic theology with renewed enthusiasm and excitement.

For the systematic theologian, the fundamental problem remains the
question: Precisely what kind of activity is theological thought?—a question
inextricably linked with another: How do theologians arrive at the statements
and concepts on which their theories are founded? And even more important:
Is there any methodical way in which the theologian can test the quality and

verisimilitude of his theories, or are theological statements ultimately always founded on irrational religious commitments? If that were the case, theology would run into the same structural difficulties with critical rationalism as with logical positivism. Although theological statements cannot simply be dismissed as nonsensical, it remains difficult, if not impossible, to credit theological reflection with any kind of scientific validity. In this chapter we shall have to concentrate specifically on that problem.

The question of the objectivity or realism of theological statements remains an unavoidable and vexatious problem. In different terms, it is the problem of the cognitive quality or reference of our assertions about God and His revelation. This problem confronts us once again—now most specifically and pertinently—with the question of a creditable model of rationality for theology; the question, that is, whether the structure of our theological reflection qualifies inherently as a valid and rational mode of thought. Such a model would not only have to be creditable in terms of contemporary philosophy of science, but would also have to integrate, meaningfully and validly, the basic conviction and commitment of the theologian as a believer in Jesus of Nazareth.

For systematic theologians who see their mental activity as a highly specialized form of critical accounting for their faith, these basic questions culminate in one crucial question: How can we critically expose the presuppositions of our theological models in order to gain clarity on the origins of theological concepts and theories?

Within the context of critical rationalism, the ideological character of the positivistic model of rationality and its one-sided empirical criterion for meaning have finally been exposed for what they are. And yet, despite the fact that Popper ascribes a much more positive role to metaphysical statements, these statements remain meaningless in scientific terms, because they are in principle unfalsifiable (cf. Hempelmann, 1980:261, 266-267).

In giving such a central position to the falsifiability of theories in his model of philosophy of science, Popper clearly intended, first and foremost, to find a criterion for distinguishing science from nonscience (metaphysics). But he gave a much wider and more basic significance to the concept of falsification; in fact, he consistently stressed the point that this principle led to a unitary scientific method—a method that must ultimately be applicable to all theoretical sciences, whether physical or social. Social sciences, too, are thus expected to formulate hypotheses and theories—concepts that would be open to criticism and thus to the test of falsifiability.

Popper's stand has, of course, direct implications for systematic theology. If theology were to follow critical rationalism in its rejection of the positivistic demands of verification and thus of inductive confirmability, would it then be able to maintain its position in the face of the demands of critical rationalism? More crucially, even: it might then become possible to examine the ways in which critical rationalists themselves justify their basic premises—especially when these concern a unitary method for all sciences—as well as the so-called objective context of justification.

The Accusation of Loss of Reality

Although critical rationalism was to liberate theology by offering it a broader model of rationality, theology would soon come under sharp attack from leading critical-rationalistic philosophers of science such as Hans Albert in Germany (cf. Albert, 1968; 1982) and William W. Bartley (Bartley, 1962) in the English-speaking world. Ultimately, then, the meaning and status of metaphysical statements remain highly problematic for critical rationalism too. Hans Albert, in particular, launched a vehement attack on both the dogmatic apologetic claims of theology and its unashamedly authoritarian conception of revelation. The essence of his criticism hinges on two further points:

First, Albert (1968:113) makes it quite clear that in his view theology can never be a truly critical pursuit, but has a merely hermeneutical, interpretative function. He thus distinguishes between hermeneutical and critical mental attitudes. To this should be added that theology, in its hermeneutical approach to traditions, has adopted the kind of immunization tactics that Popper labeled a *revelatory model:* a conceptual model that could never stand up to the principle of critical examination.

Second, Albert maintains that theology seeks to salvage the concept of God through a further immunization tactic. He points out that the concept of God formerly did have an explicatory function in cosmology, until that function was made redundant by modern physical sciences. Instead of maintaining its intellectual integrity and abandoning those outdated and untenable theories, theology has attempted to change the concept of God by placing it beyond the influence of changes in our views of reality. To Albert this was especially true of the thesis of God's unobjectifiability, since questions about the truth or falsehood of theological statements about God would thus be excluded virtually in principle.

In essence, Albert's critical-rationalistic charge against theology might be summed up as the reproach that it has lost its commitment to reality and that its statements thus lack any form of objective reference. Few theologians have responded directly to Albert's criticism. Apart from the well-known but fruitless Albert-Ebeling debate, only theologians such as Gerhard Sauter, Wolfhart Pannenberg, and recently the young German theologian Heinzpeter Hempelmann have positively taken up the challenge of critical rationalism. This point will be dealt with specifically in later chapters.

Theology and the Question of the Limits of Rationality

The first direct confrontation between critical rationalism and the systematic-theological thought of our time arose when William W. Bartley, a student of Karl Popper's, published his well-known work *The Retreat to Commitment* in 1962.[1] In this book Bartley is concerned specifically with the relationship of systematic theology to the tradition of critical thought. He offers an acute analysis of theologians' reaction to criticism of the presuppositions and premises of their theological thought models, and also of their claims to validity and objectivity in their statements on God and His revelation.

The central focus of Bartley's analysis (1962:1-12) is the problem that arises from the critically reflective intellectual's concern with a so-called ultimate commitment: are all religious, moral, and philosophical premises perhaps ultimately founded on a final, irrational, extreme, and unquestionable commitment? Bartley appreciates, correctly, that the question of the role and function of that ultimate commitment is, at the same time, the problem of the limits of our rationality. The crucial question in this regard might also be put as follows: Is it possible to make any kind of rational choice between diverse and even competing religious, theological, moral, or philosophical premises, or is that choice ultimately a random one?

As a critical rationalist, Bartley takes issue with the notion that choices of this kind, between competing basic convictions, have to be made on irrational grounds. He maintains firmly that any attempt to fall back on a kind of irrational subjectivism in dealing with questions about the origins of any premise should be exposed as an immunization tactic against criticism. It is this evasion of the imperative to advance rational grounds for choices that Bartley terms a *retreat to commitment*.

Furthermore, any scientist or philosopher who opts deliberately for such a conceptual model is not merely retreating behind the barricades of irrational subjectivism, but ultimately suffers an inescapable loss of reality, thus sacrificing the objective status of the subject of his assertions. Such a choice finally sacrifices the credibility of a rational-critical framework of justification, since the assertions made in such subjective statements can no longer be subjected to the critical test of falsification.

This confronts the theologian with a crucial question: Is it in any sense necessary or even essential for theology to construct—in the Popperian sense—a domain of objective knowledge, a context of justification in which the subjective religious commitment can play no ideologizing and thus no dogmatistic role? This question implies a further one: whether the theologian, given his religious commitment and his identification with a specific theological tradition,

---

1. Bartley's sharp criticism of Protestant theology is also discussed in van Huyssteen, 1981:291-302.

is still capable of making statements based on that commitment in such a manner that theology can maintain its intellectual integrity. It is in this regard that Bartley was set on exposing the vulnerability and weakness of the theologian's religious claims to credibility.

A recurrent theme in Bartley's book is that twentieth-century Protestant theology, in particular, consciously takes its stand on the philosophical premise that rationality is in itself limited and that every individual must ultimately fall back on some irrational religious choice or commitment. This view he formulated (Bartley, 1962:215) in terms that leave no room for misconstruction: "The leading protestant theologians of the twentieth century have embraced as fact the philosophical contention that rationality is logically limited, that every man makes some ultimately irrational commitment; and they have used this contention to excuse rationally their own irrational commitment to Christ."

Bartley's central contention, reflected in the title of his book, is that virtually any form of twentieth-century Protestant theology suffers primarily from a retreat to commitment. This retreat to an ultimately irrational commitment is at the same time an evasion of any form of critical debate—an evasion Bartley sees as a reaction to the failure of the Old Quest of the nineteenth century—the attempt to base Christian faith on some historical knowledge of Jesus of Nazareth. The failure of this one-sided historical quest has led theologians to react with a retreat to an ultimate, irrational commitment, founded solely on a subjective religious choice. Bartley found a prime example of this retreat in the theology of Karl Barth.

According to Bartley, the central theme of Barth's theological thought is in fact his unconditional involvement with and commitment to the Word of God, as revealed above all in Jesus Christ. An irrational commitment to God's revelation in Jesus Christ implies, however, that this revelation is in itself placed beyond any question or criticism (Bartley, 1962:128), and that implies that any form of apologetic theology must be rejected as both futile and impious: futile, for if the Word of God has been accepted in faith, it becomes unnecessary to advance grounds for it; and impious, since the revelation of God's Word in Jesus Christ must correlate with piety and especially with absolute obedience.

To Bartley (1962:61), a theological stance such as Barth's is conceivably the most rational form of irrationalism. His most fundamental, and in fact most serious, objection to Barth is the total and absolute irrational religious commitment—and thus also concept of faith—on which Barth founded all his further theological theories, perhaps most fundamental of all his irrational assumption that the revelation of God's Word in Christ happened precisely as formulated by Barthian theology.

Karl Barth's systematic-theological construct is, in Bartley's view, a typical example of how Protestant theology relativizes all theological discussion by subjugating it to a prior act of religious commitment. Eventually it seems as if such an irrational commitment has become an essential prerequisite to any theological statement. In this regard, however, Bartley (1962:103) makes the incisive point that the right or privilege of being able to choose irrationally is gained only at the expense of the right or privilege of being able to criticize. For systematic theology the crucial question thus remains whether it can expose itself to any critical discussion; whether its structure allows any elimination of unsound ideas; whether, therefore, it can justly claim to have rational integrity.

In the light of the above, Bartley states unambiguously that many of the arguments employed by theologians to justify their theological premises actually make no difference to their maintaining or abandoning those premises. Even when their arguments are proved false, some theologians adhere to their premises, but then on the grounds of an irrational commitment rather than rational argument. Bartley (1962:89) is rather cynical about such arguments— they are, he suggests, "the neon lights, not the foundations, of the theological edifice."

Bartley justly contends that the only truly serious argument still offered by modern theologians in support of a pretheoretic commitment to a specific religious stand (and thus a conception of faith) is the *tu quoque* argument. In their retreat to an irrational commitment, theologians have typically always been able to invoke this one notable argument in defense of their intellectual integrity: the contention that any stand, statement, or scientific procedure is also and always founded on presuppositions which are not only adopted as a premise for further argument but figure equally irrationally as an ultimate commitment. In this *tu quoque* argument it is strongly emphasized that any scientific statement refers to a set of basic axioms or premises, which serve as the accepted basis for all further argument.

If this *tu quoque* argument were valid, there would be no difference between the ways basic, unproven axioms functioned in the arguments of, for example, theologians, mathematicians, or physicists. In rational defense of an irrational commitment, the *tu quoque* argument is constructed as follows (Bartley, 1962:90ff.):

1. Insight into the limits of our rationality leads to the insight that rationality is so limited that everyone is compelled to accept some or other dogmatic, irrational commitment.
2. For precisely that reason the Christian, and therefore also the theologian, is entitled to his own choice of commitment.
3. And since everyone is compelled to make such ultimate, irrational choices, no one has the right to criticize Christians or theologians for their specific choice.

For Bartley, this *tu quoque* argument is clearly still the basis of modern theology's apologetic defense. The notion that rationality ultimately has definite limits enables theologians not only to commit themselves openly—according to Bartley—and irrationally to a basic choice of faith, but also to make this choice without sacrificing their intellectual integrity.[2] Against this background, Bartley (1962:129) is led to the disturbing conclusion: "Both philosophers and theologians, unable to answer the questions of the sceptics, stop defending their positions and begin to describe and expound them—to preach them."

In his critical approach to the problem of an axiomatic or ultimate commitment, Bartley arrives at a fundamental insight: the right to withdraw irrationally to some axiomatic commitment is gained only at the expense of the privilege of criticizing. Those advancing the *tu quoque* argument are not merely isolating themselves in a dogmatistic and therefore a positivistic position, but are also forfeiting the privilege of critical debate with proponents of divergent positions.

The burning question that now arises can be formulated as follows: Is there any escape from the relativism to which the *tu quoque* argument must ultimately lead, or are all theologians ultimately committed, subjectivistically and irrationally, to their own pretheoretic axioms?

Bartley seeks to demonstrate that it should in fact be possible to choose nonarbitrarily between different and even diverse or competing modes of thought or paradigms, and that this can be done with Popper's method of critical examination through trial and error. This method, however, will not only confront systematic theologians with their most stringent test; in Bartley's view, the question whether it is possible to make a rational choice between various paradigms is an even more fundamental problem than demarcation (that is, the question of the division between science and nonscience).

In an attempt to evade both the relativism of the *tu quoque* problem and irrationalism, one might opt for some accepted form of valid authority. Thus Karl Barth could opt for the authority of God's Word, as revealed in Christ, as opposed to the authority of any natural, rational theology; thus, in Roman Catholicism, one might opt for the authority of the Church, and therefore of the Pope; and thus, in the Reformed world, it might be correct and rational to opt for the authority of Holy Scripture and the confessional writings. Within the context of these alternatives it might be rational to accept correct authorities. But when the question arises, What is a correct authority, and by what criterion is its correctness or truth determined? it becomes apparent that the choice of a

---

2. Of special interest is Bartley's view that the two mainstreams of modern philosophical rationalism, namely, empiricism and idealism, show exactly the same structure: here, as in any form of theological positivism, all knowledge is derived from ultimate certainties, which as such need no justification—either sensory observation or indisputable intellectual certainties (Bartley, 1962:109ff.). According to Bartley, both empiricism and idealism are founded on premises just as irrational as those of modern Protestant theology: both adopt a revelatory model for knowledge, since both assume a source of knowledge which is in itself indubitable. The only difference is that the authoritative source is not the revelation of God or the Bible but the authority of sensory perception or intellectual certainties.

correct authority is ultimately a commitment, an irrational choice of one construct or another.

Precisely because theological fideism so often presents itself in the form of an authoritarian ideology, it might be meaningful to join Bartley (1962:132) in asking whether a more rational stance might be achieved by consciously abandoning any commitment to some axiomatic premise or authority. One might then opt critically for a commitment to the outcome of arguments, regardless of where they might lead. Even such an approach would be stronger than the *tu quoque* argument, since the commitment to accepting the outcome of rational argument is not the same as the irrational religious commitment of some Protestant theologians.

This approach implies that an argument in favor of any stand, mode of thought, or paradigm already presupposes a rational attitude, if it would claim any kind of relevance. Therefore a commitment to rationality already has a rational advantage over any other stand or argument. An argument in favor of Christianity (or even Communism), for example, would presuppose a rational approach by other parties in the debate. But an argument in favor of rational argument does not by any means presuppose a Christian (or Communistic) stand on their part. In this sense, Bartley maintains, critical rationalists have a certain argumentative advantage over their fellow-disputants. This advantage might be explained in part by the fact that the rational stand, characterized by a commitment to the results of rational argument, is logically more basic and fundamental than other stands or ideological premises, even if it is in itself ultimately not justifiable.

Bartley must also concede yet another point to irrationalism: here, too, the residue of a subjectivistic commitment shows itself, since rationalists ultimately commit themselves irrationally to the results of rational argument. Bartley (1962:133) is honest enough to face up to this: "The idea that a rationalist is committed to rational argument appears, on the face of it, as convincing and inescapable (whatever the differences) as the idea that a Christian is committed to Christ." Thus even a rational commitment to the results of argument conceals a concession to irrationalism—a concession that leaves the dilemma of an ultimate commitment unresolved.

Pancritical Rationalism

Bartley eventually found an escape from this dilemma in what he called a comprehensive or pancritical rationalism: a philosophical program in which the central question is no longer the traditional one of justification, or How do you know?, but the critical construction of hypotheses that presuppose no ultimate certainties. The central question now becomes a critical one: How can we approach our mental world in such a manner that all our convictions, views, sources of ideas, traditions, and hypotheses may be exposed to the maximum criticism and intellectual errors be eliminated as far as possible?

From the authoritarian question of justification (How do you know?—which still uses the criterion of a norm that presupposes an ultimate commitment to that norm), Bartley (1962:140ff.) shifts the problem to a question of criticism and critical thought from which all implications of an ultimate justification have been excluded specifically and in advance. By this means Bartley sought to establish that the dilemma of a final and ultimate commitment can never be resolved within the framework of an authoritarian and fundamentalistic epistemology. In contrast with any form of authoritarian epistemology, he posited a nonauthoritarian, nonjustificational approach to the formation of knowledge, which is in fact possible through pancritical rationalism.

Bartley's essential concern is an alternative and new model of rationality, through which he tried to avoid the dilemma of an ultimate commitment and the confines of the *tu quoque* argument. His pancritical conceptual model enables rationalists to keep all their convictions, their most basic religious grounds and premises, open for criticism. The pancritical rationalist will therefore never stop an argument by retreating into faith or an irrational commitment in order to evade stringent criticism. By this means Bartley sought to move beyond both positivistic rationalism—characterized by a comprehensive and ultimate rational justification—and any irrational justification through a retreat into a personal religious commitment.

If, then, rationalism is to be sought in open, critical thought, anything can be subjected to criticism and constant testing, including rationality itself. Through this pancritical rationalism, in which rationalism knows no bounds, Bartley is able to avoid the dilemma of an ultimate commitment and of the *tu quoque* argument. Since the question of a final testing or justification (whether rational or irrational) has been abandoned, rationality is no longer confined by an inevitable commitment to faith. For pancritical rationalists, their commitment to rationalism forms part of their rationalism. They are not trying to protect some hidden belief against criticism; therefore criticism of commitments no longer boomerangs (Bartley, 1962:151).

Bartley does not, however, maintain that pancritical rationalists can have no strong beliefs—beliefs that might even prompt them to act with firm conviction. Truly critical thinkers may be convinced of the truth of something without being irrationally committed to the specific truth; they should have the courage of their convictions, but also the courage to keep criticizing them.

For Bartley (1962:152) this pancritical rationalism is, moreover, in keeping with a certain healthy skepticism: "It is only a way of saying that we learn through trial and error—by making conjectures and trying to criticize them—and that we are still learning." This critical attitude enables one to test hypotheses and thus eventually eliminate error. Bartley (1962:158) has four criteria for such rational control:

1. The control of logic: the question whether a given theory is logically consistent.
2. The control of sensory perception: the question whether a theory is empirically falsifiable through sensory perception.
3. The control of the theory of science: the question whether a given theory is in line or in conflict with other scientific hypotheses and with the formulation of problems in philosophy of science as such.
4. The control of the problem: the question of which problem a given theory is supposed to solve, and of whether a given theory is successful in its solution of that problem.

In Bartley's view, these criteria should also hold good for theological theories. Since theological theories, too, can be judged only in terms of a definite problem, one must always ask: Does a certain theory really solve a problem, or does it merely shift the problem? Does it solve the problem more effectively than competing theories, or does it merely raise new and worse problems?

In the light of Bartley's criteria, it becomes impossible to retreat into the safe haven of the *tu quoque* argument, since it is no longer an adequate counter-argument to maintain that the rationalist, too, is arguing from irrationally adopted axioms. His criteria also imply, however, that theology can no longer claim intellectual integrity by falling back irrationally on a fideist stand as ultimate basis and premise for all argument.

Ultimately, systematic theologians will find themselves confronting Bartley's provocative conclusion, which they will have to evaluate and judge critically: People can be engaged without being committed.[3] This conclusion underlines the direct influence of critical rationalism on the structure of Bartley's conceptual model. Like Popper, Bartley reacts sharply to the effects of logical positivism, giving a decidedly new content to concepts that are central also to the systematic theologian engaged in an examination of basic postulates—concepts such as rationality and objectivity. It thus becomes clear that Bartley has opted for an open, critical line of thought, one no longer bound by confirmation and verification, but rather to free discussion of theories and theoretic presuppositions, specifically aimed at exposing and eliminating the weaknesses in such theories. And for Bartley, as for Popper, metaphysical statements fall in the context of discovery, not in the objective, rational context of justification.

Bartley's stand is of special significance to theological questions since

---

3. Bartley, 1962:217. Cf. also p. 151: "We can assume or be convinced of the truth of something without being committed to its truth. As conceived here, a rationalist can retain both the courage of his convictions and the courage to go on attacking his convictions."

his rejection of a positivist model of rationality (and with that any objective, value-free observation) is, as with Popper, a candid admission of scientists' subjective involvement in their own thought and in the growth of scientific knowledge. This sharp insight enables Bartley to pinpoint the problem with which scientists' subjectivity confronts them: the question of the role and function of scientists' subjective involvement in the development of their own thought is also the question of the role and function of scientists' pretheoretic commitment—of the theorizing implied in the methodological basis of their thought.

For systematic theologians, the problem of their ultimate commitment is of the utmost significance. Bartley confronts us with the question whether it is possible to be committed, to opt for faith, without thereby retreating into a pretheoretic, irrational haven of personal commitment as the basis of our theoretic reflection.

In concrete terms, this problem might be formulated as follows: Does the ultimate commitment of systematic theologians inevitably function as an immunization strategy whenever they face the thorny problem of the role played by possible preconceptions in the formulation of theological axioms? Surely the personal faith of theologians, their devotion to God and His revelation and to Holy Scripture, can offer no guarantee of methodological lucidity and creditable theorizing. To put it simply: a devoted theologian (in the sense of one experienced in sincere personal faith) is not a good theologian (in the critical scientific sense) merely by virtue of that devotion. This is so because that devotion, which functions on a pretheoretic level, presupposes theorizing. Ultimately, faith is accessible to us only through our statements of faith, and statements of faith refer directly to conceptions of faith, which in turn are rooted in premises and convictions.

If the theorizing implicit in these conceptions of faith and the content of faith are not consciously recognized, systematic theologians lapse readily into theological fideism, an authoritarian theological stand in which their subjective notions of God and the further content of their faith are uncritically vested with the authority of revelation, to be presented finally as true, correct, or revelatory theology.

When Bartley cautions us against such an uncritical adoption of any ultimate commitment as an immunization strategy, his very commitment to noncommitment exposes him, in my view, to the same charge of a retreat to commitment with which he taxed the standard Protestant theology. As a critical rationalist, Bartley not only adopted empirical criteria for all observation, but also shared Popper's inheritance of a unitary ideal for science in general: a unitary ideal demanding of all sciences, including the social sciences, the formulation of hypotheses and theories that would be open to criticism and thus to falsification. Like his rigid distinction between rational and irrational, this unitary ideal appears to be a relic of positivism.

When Bartley, therefore, joins Popper in maintaining that there can be no naked, natural, value-free observation, but that any observation presupposes a point of view, an expectation, a theory (and as such is already problem-oriented), the theory-ladenness of all observation implies in my view more than Bartley is prepared to admit: not only our observation is contextually or para-digmatically determined, but our criteria for scientific status, too, are ultimately codetermined by our conception of science and the world. In terms of the so-called contextual distinction, the subjective involvemert or commitment of the scientist plays a role not only in the context of discovery, but also in the context of justification. Even Bartley's pancritical rationalism could not lead him to this insight; it virtually compelled him to adopt a view of rationality in which any form of commitment had to be seen as irrational.

We are led to two clear-cut and significant conclusions:

1. Bartley is ultimately also bound by his commitment to noncommitment; that is, by his personal commitment to the so-called pancritical mode of thought.

2. From Bartley's point of view, the theologian's ultimate commitment must obviously be seen as an immunization strategy, a retreat to com-mitment. Nor, given his particular critical-rationalistic view of reality, can the systematic theologian's commitment to a religious Reality be anything but an irrational retreat—a commitment deemed to be ir-rational, however, only because Bartley is still employing a traditional model of rationality, which leaves no room for an ultimate commitment.

Commitment and Theorizing

Bartley's positive contribution should not be ignored. There are indeed system-atic theologians who fail to recognize the theorizing implicit in their theolo-gizing premises, and who only too often invest these axiomatic premises with great authority, despite their subjective origins. It is understandable, then, that Bartley's critical-rationalistic stand led him to confront the systematic theolo-gian with the claim that people can be engaged without being committed. In my view, however, the question should not be how the theologian can succeed in eliminating any commitment from his reflection, but how the methodological violation and abuse of that commitment can be exposed and eliminated.

The crucial truth in the *tu quoque* argument is that all scientists found their thought on some kind of commitment. On the one hand Bartley was right in point-ing out that an ultimate commitment cannot serve as an irrational retreat into some final, unquestionable certainty, but on the other hand we ought not to cherish the illusion that the pancritical approach eliminates any ultimate commitment.

On the level of philosophy of science, theologians confront the problem of formulating a model of rationality in such a manner that the theorizing implied by their own subjective involvement can be accounted for from the outset. Only if they could do so would it also be possible to expose critically the dogmatistic prejudices uncritically presupposed in that basic theorizing, and to eliminate them as weaknesses in systematic-theological theorizing. Only if theologians were capable of doing that could it be true that an ultimate commitment need not necessarily lead to an inevitable limitation of rationality that would force them into an authoritarian retreat behind some kind of dogmatisim precisely because of their irrational commitment.

In the light of the problems critical rationalism has highlighted for systematic theology, I would once again formulate the following crucial question: Is it really possible for theologians to identify with their own theological tradition while nonetheless preserving their rational integrity? Furthermore, can systematic theologians formulate grounds for their choice of any theological model or framework, or are they truly doomed to an ultimate, irrational, relativistic choice, beyond all questioning?

Bartley was correct in pointing out that Barth had totally denied and ignored all the theorizing hidden in the adoption of any authoritative revelatory principle in theology. But the solution to such a problematic, dogmatistic retreat into commitment, and thus into a specific conception of faith, does not lie in the suspension of any pretheoretic commitment; it lies in the exposure of the theorizing implied in the choice of a specific commitment. Bartley is fully justified in demanding that systematic theologians leave their most basic premises open for criticism. Strictly speaking, however, it is not the so-called irrational commitment of theologians that should be exposed; it is their statements about, and thus their concept of, that commitment that ought to be exposed to full criticism.

As a provisional counter to Bartley's commitment to noncommitment I would therefore suggest that systematic theologians can be committed without being methodologically compromised. Only theologians who have tied themselves to an authoritarian axiomatic theology find themselves in a highly hazardous position, since they consistently ignore the theorizing hidden behind their supposedly authoritative stand.

I would suggest that meaningful debate between critical rationalists and believing theologians becomes possible only if each is prepared to yield some ground: theologians would have to be prepared to make provisional (and corrigible) statements that must be open to criticism, precisely because they seek the highest possible degree of certainty about the Truth of which they speak. In fact, the intangibility and inaccessibility of God's revelation makes it impossible to grasp fully or dogmatize that revelatory truth in order to immunize it against all forms of criticism (cf. Hempelmann, 1980:263).

Critical rationalists, on their part, would have to be critically prepared— at least in principle—to face the possibility that the provisional nature of their own critical statements might anticipate a truth of such essential objectivity that it could never be typified as a purely human rational projection. I believe Popper's theory of verisimilitude allows, in principle, for this dynamic growth of scientific statements in terms of a regulatory concept of truth.

We have seen, finally, to what extent Bartley followed Popper in making critical rationalism applicable to systematic theology. The question is, however, whether systematic theology should in fact ultimately be judged by the criteria of critical rationalism.

Immanent criticism has shown that Bartley himself failed to meet the demands he laid down for systematic theology, and in philosophy of science the basic principles of critical rationalism have been challenged incisively (and even more fruitfully) by Thomas S. Kuhn. Kuhn's thought would not only spark off a revolution in philosophy of science but would also have profound implications for the question of the fundamental grounds of systematic theology.

5

The Paradigm Theory and the Question of the Origins of Theological Models: Thomas S. Kuhn

Frameworks must be lived with and explored before they can be broken.

Thomas S. Kuhn, "Reflections on My Critics," in *Criticism and the Growth of Knowledge* (Cambridge: Cambridge University Press, 1970):238.

To translate a theory or worldview into one's own language is not to make it one's own. For that one must go native, discover that one is thinking and working in, not simply translating out of, a language that was previously foreign.

Thomas S. Kuhn, *The Structure of Scientific Revolutions,* 2nd ed. (Chicago: University of Chicago Press, 1970):204.

Introduction

The discussion of Karl Popper's and William W. Bartley's contributions to the debates of philosophy of science has clearly shown that the significance of the break between critical rationalism and the inquiries of the earlier logical positivism can hardly be overestimated. Apart from exciting new possibilities in the redefinition of concepts such as rationality and objectivity, however, critical rationalism has also created radically new problems and challenges for systematic theology.

The following questions now become all the more pertinent and call for specific answers:

- What model of rationality functions in specifically identifiable theological traditions, or in the intellectual frameworks of strongly individualistically thinking theologians?
- What is the nature of theological language as such, and how do theologians arrive at the theoretic mesh of concepts on which their doctrines or theories are founded?
- What precisely becomes of the question of the rationality and objectivity of theological statements as we become increasingly aware that theologians can never—in the process of theorizing—escape their (preconceptualized) beliefs and commitments?

Our discussion of critical rationalism has shown how Bartley further developed Popper's positive assessment of metaphysical ideas in his acute analysis of the role of an ultimate commitment in scientific thought. By this means Bartley not only emphasized the question of the limits of rationality in particular, but also succeeded admirably in demonstrating the futility of ideologizing any theological stand in an attempt to immunize it against criticism. This confronts systematic theologians with a particularly thorny question: Can they, despite their pretheoretic commitment to what they regard as God's revelation, maintain their intellectual integrity by advancing valid reasons for claiming a certain objective or cognitive quality for their statements, and for claiming that a certain theory (or network of theories) can better express the problems of their pursuit than competing theories or concepts?

From the above the following also becomes apparent: After Bartley, theologians will have to prove that they are not attempting to evade the demands of critical discussion. Those who fall back desperately and irrationally on their (pretheorized) ultimate commitment are not only isolating themselves in a dogmatistic and authoritarian position, but also forfeit irrevocably the privilege of critical debate with proponents of divergent views. In answer to Bartley, however, we have also seen that the critical theologians' problem is not so much the elimination of their commitment as the exposure of their statements on that ultimate commitment to the maximum criticism.

In breaking away from positivism's ahistorical model of science, Karl Popper succeeded in placing not only the question of scientific method but also the growth of scientific knowledge irrevocably within a historical perspective. We have seen that Popper regarded science as a dynamic, continuous process of critical testing and progressive questioning. The historical perspective he thus opened up on the development of scientific thought soon came to dominate the viewpoint of various philosophers of science.

The Historicist Turning Point

From the younger generation of philosophers of science, Thomas S. Kuhn has emerged as the most prominent and notable theorist of his time. His well-known and widely discussed work *The Structure of Scientific Revolutions* (1962, 2nd ed. 1970) must rate as one of the most original and influential alternatives yet to the positivist scientific tradition. At the same time, however, he was to become the foremost critic of Popper's work. Kuhn aligns himself especially with one important perspective initiated by Popper: the historical development of scientific theories—a dimension in the development of scientific thought that had always been woefully neglected or obscured by the standard positivist model of science.

Our examination of William Bartley's analysis of the implications of critical rationalism for theological thought has left us with an acute impression of the role of ultimate commitments in the choice of scientific theories. On this very point, Thomas Kuhn maintained that not only the choice of our scientific theories but also the very nature of the scientific pursuit should be explained in sociohistorical terms. This implied that Kuhn would eventually, in contrast to Popper, reject the idea of a growth of knowledge toward truth. Even more significantly, he would thus also reject the rigid distinction between problems relating to the origins of our knowledge (the so-called context of discovery) and those relating to the ultimate evaluation and justification of knowledge (the context of justification).

In his earlier phase, especially, Kuhn saw scientific thought as a socially and historically determined activity dominated by the role played in it by *paradigms*. In that activity, scientific knowledge is no longer growing accumulatively through the gradual addition of new elements to the existing corpus; on the contrary, scientific thought develops through shocks—through radical shifts in which one vision gives way to another. To understand what Kuhn means by these radical shifts or scientific revolutions, and to appreciate his enormous influence on the development of thought in both the physical and the human sciences of our time, one needs to know fairly precisely what he meant by the term *paradigm*.

In Kuhn's work (1970a:182-183), *paradigm* means primarily an exemplar or problem-solving model by which scientists approach the aspect of reality that interests them. Such a paradigm may also be seen as a frame of reference or a tradition of research founded on clear-cut and implicitly predefined premises. In *The Structure of Scientific Revolutions* the term undoubtedly gained a broader and more versatile meaning; it began to include the totality of a researcher's basic commitments and metaphysical premises. To avoid confusion, Kuhn later also used the term *disciplinary matrix* for the theoretic framework with which scientists approach reality in their pursuit of solutions. We shall later return to the important concept of the paradigm.

At this stage, however, we need to note precisely what Kuhn meant when he said that scientific thought did not develop accumulatively, or did not necessarily grow toward the truth, but that it developed in shocks as one paradigm gave way to another through radical shifts. According to Kuhn, the development of scientific thought always takes on the following typical pattern:

1. First, the history of science shows clearly that any research tradition begins with a preparadigmatic phase.
2. At a given point, this phase changes into a period of normal science— a phase in which scientific inquiry takes place entirely within the accepted framework of a very specific paradigm. This phase is usually characterized by great stability and agreement (Koningsveld, 1977:155), especially on which problems are worth investigating and on the standards to be met by solutions (cf. De Vries, 1984:92).
3. Such a period of normal inquiry, directed by a specific paradigm, may experience a crisis leading to a radical shift or revolution in the paradigm or parts of it. Such a shift can be resolved only by the development of an alternative paradigm heralding a new period of normal science.

From this summary it is clear that, for Kuhn, scientific thought develops not through accumulation but through a revolutionary process in which radical shifts play a crucial role. To assess the philosophical implications of Kuhn's revolutionary model—eventually also for systematic theology—we shall have to make a closer study of these three phases in the development of scientific thought.

The Preparadigmatic Period

Although Kuhn states clearly in the preface to the second edition of his book (1970a:ix) that he does not wish to distinguish too schematically between the various phases in the development of science, he nevertheless isolates an initial preparadigmatic period (1970a:13ff.) in the development of every science. This is a period of conflicting ideas, because various schools have no common foundation or paradigm within which scientific explanations can be provided; each school has its own facts, hypotheses, and theories—a typical phase of scientists lacking a science.

According to Kuhn, the transition from this diverse and complex situation to *normal* science cannot be effected only by the traditional means of logic and factuality, since each scientist or group has its own favorite body of data, facts, concepts, and logic. The history of science shows that a particular paradigm becomes dominant at a given point only when scientists refrain from endless philosophical debate and concentrate on detailed problems that may lead to practical solutions for concrete problems. Thus the eventual choice of a paradigm is no merely rational activity, but in fact a complex event determined jointly by historical, social, and psychological factors.

Normal Science

In Kuhn's view, normal science—as we have seen—is the pursuit of science within the confines of a commonly accepted paradigm. He is thus led from a sociology of knowledge analysis of scientific groups or communities to the discovery of the dominant and definitive role played by paradigms in scientific research.

Initially, Kuhn (1970a:viii) defined paradigms as follows: "These I take to be universally recognized scientific achievements that for a time provide model problems and solutions to a community of practitioners." Kuhn later added further nuances to this definition, stating that he used the term *paradigm* mainly in two senses: first, sociologically, as the total body of convictions, values, and techniques common to members of a particular community; second, however, the term paradigm may also denote a particular element in that totality, namely, the concrete puzzle-solutions which, as models or examples, create a (paradigmatic) basis for the solution of the remaining puzzles of normal science (1970a:175).

This type of paradigm or disciplinary matrix provides the theoretic, conceptual, and methodological apparatus with which the scientist formulates theories to explain reality. Thus this kind of paradigm constitutes a scientific view of the world sanctioned by the community of scholars within a certain discipline—in periodicals, at congresses, in textbooks, and in typical formulations and solutions of problems.

In the first case, a paradigm may therefore be defined as the total body of theories, philosophical premises, and values enshrining the area and procedures of a certain scientific group in normal research. In the second case a paradigm may be seen more specifically as the source of a certain methodology recognized by a group, as that which defines the area of problems for scientific activity and provides the criteria by which solutions may be found.

In both cases, however, the term *paradigm* denotes a recognized scientific vision—a vision, for example, inculcated in students in the course of their studies and often reinforced later in their professional practice. It is also clear that Kuhn sees a paradigm as that which the members of a particular scientific community have in common and which forms a characteristic bond between them. He therefore put it as follows (1970c:238): "Whatever scientific progress may be, we must account for it by examining the nature of the scientific group, discovering what it values, what it tolerates, and what it disdains." This gives a clear indication of Kuhn's sociological founding of the growth of scientific thought: scientific thought, too, is determined by group values. And in scientific thought, choice imperatives are at work which are directly referable to (often dogmatistic) commitments.

Asked whether a scientific discovery should be seen as normal or revolutionary, Kuhn would therefore respond: Normal or revolutionary for whom? The answer would always have to be: For a particular group or groups. Thus Kuhn (1970c:253) could maintain that such groups should be seen as units producing scientific knowledge, and this again reveals the sociohistorical basis of his model: scientific activity is always the activity of a certain group or of an individual belonging to that group. And what is seen as scientifically true is therefore always true for a certain group within a given paradigm or research tradition.

Normal science, then, is a group-based activity. Its analysis demands prior examination of the changing structure of a community in a given period, since "a paradigm governs in the first instance, not a subject matter but rather a group of practitioners" (Kuhn, 1970a:180). It is clear that, for Kuhn, a paradigm directly determines the scientist's view of his or her reality: and this view not only includes a broader outlook or metaphysical conception of reality but ultimately also implies that a scientist's basic convictions will inevitably play a role in the actual process of theorizing in scientific thought.

Furthermore, normal science is directed not so much at anything new, but at the precisioning, articulation, or explication of a certain dominant paradigm. In normal science the scientist is confronted not so much with objective problems that have to be explored, but rather with puzzles that have to be solved in terms of the paradigm. In this sense it may be said that, in normal science, not only certain theories but also the experimenters themselves are tested. Even in the most rigorous science this would ultimately mean that the negative outcome of an experiment is by no means proof of the falsehood of a given theory.

Kuhn's view of normal science, therefore, leaves no room for Popper's stringent falsification test. The scientific status of a theory is characterized not by its falsifiability but by its ability to solve puzzles. In this wider Kuhnian model of rationality, this type of intraparadigmatic solution to problems may serve as a scientific ideal. Kuhn (1970a:192) also points out that even in the physical sciences the testing of hypotheses does not normally take the course of direct attempts to falsify them, but rather constitutes a comparison of the capacities of various theories for handling certain data and solving puzzles. Thus the capacity of such a hypothesis for integrating and making sense of available data (cf. Pannenberg, 1973b:66-67) becomes the primary principle in the testing of hypotheses. This raises a question of radical significance not only to the physical scientist but ultimately also to the theologian: How is the scientist enabled to choose between competing theories if testing as such (whether verification or falsification) no longer plays a determinant role in the development of scientific reflection? We shall later have to deal specifically with this question.

Meanwhile, Kuhn regards it as highly significant that a given paradigm not only shapes certain theories but also becomes constitutive of scientific research through those very theories. It is by now also clear that the paradigm of a certain group or community forms part of its totality of thought. When, however, a certain paradigm or conceptual model becomes dubious and begins to falter, that model is invariably reduced to clearly formulated rules and laws; and at the same time strong claims are made, with firm conviction, for the reliable authority of the recognized paradigm.

Revolutionary Science

If more and more puzzles become insoluble within the confines of a given paradigm, and the list of unresolved problems keeps growing, confidence in the recognized paradigm begins to falter. In a stabilized normal science this might precipitate a crisis in which both the paradigm itself and the method of solving the puzzles or problems emanating from it become highly problematic. From this crisis situation, a creative leap might lead scientists to a totally new view of reality and their problems. Thus an often unforeseen conceptual transformation might lead scientists to a new paradigm.

This paradigmatic transformation is what Thomas Kuhn (1970a:92ff.) termed a scientific revolution. It becomes even clearer, then, that he sees scientific development not as a linear, rational accumulation of knowledge, but rather as a series of shocks in which the scientist shifts to a new paradigm through a *gestalt switch* or *conversion.* Such a scientific revolution, as a conceptual transformation, brings drastic change to the historical perspective of the person or group concerned. Thus a revolutionary phase in the history of science is characterized by the jettisoning of trusted theories, the recognition and examination of new problems, the acceptance of other criteria in the testing process, and the total reinterpretation of existing or previously collected data.[1] Eventually, once the group concerned has accepted the new paradigm as a framework for scientific research, a lengthy period of consolidation usually begins, characterized by normal inquiry and research. In this sense the development of scientific thought shows a pattern vacillating between normal and revolutionary science.

It should also be noted that scientific revolutions include not only exceptional events such as those associated with, for example, Copernicus, Newton, Darwin, or Einstein; on the contrary, Kuhn sees scientific revolution as "a special sort of change involving a certain sort of reconstruction of group com-

---

1. For a detailed discussion of Kuhn's concept of scientific revolutions, see A. de Ruijter, 1979:217ff.

mitments" (1970a:181). That change need not be major or conspicuous, nor need it appear to be highly revolutionary. For Kuhn, any creative breakthrough that enables scientists to observe and understand what had previously defied them may be seen as a conceptual transformation and thus as a paradigmatic revolution.

Scientific revolutions, then, are those peculiar moments when a shift of professional commitment is made—moments leading to the transformation of concepts, ideas, methods, and theories because the traditional procedures and their effectiveness are broken irrevocably. Thus a newly discovered scientific insight, as a gestalt switch, is never significant merely as a fact; on the contrary, such a switch, bearing all the marks of a total conversion, brings a qualitative transformation to the world of the scientist, enriching it with new facts and new theories.

Kuhn (1970a:23) made the following point about the effective success of such a new paradigm: "The success of a paradigm is at the start largely a promise of success discoverable in selected and still incomplete examples." This implies that the creative choice of a certain new paradigm is by no means founded on its success in the past, but rather on its promising nature. And in this conceptual transformation the scientist's belief or conviction that the new paradigm will prove more adequate than the old plays a constant role (Kuhn, 1970a:155-156).

The creative discovery of new theories can be achieved, however, only if a number of earlier standard premises and procedures are replaced by a totally new approach, through a conceptual and methodological transformation. Thus a certain scientific group might come to reject an obsolete, inadequate paradigm in favor of a new, more adequate, and more promising one. At the same time there is also a shift in what are seen as truly relevant problems.

Such a revolution is always preceded by a period of unrest, by the discovery of anomalies in the way the accepted paradigm copes with certain problems. Growing vagueness and waning usefulness of a theory or theories is therefore always the prelude to paradigmatic crisis. As Kuhn (1970a:84) put it: "All crises begin with the blurring of a paradigm and the consequent loosening of the rules for normal research." And finally: "A crisis may end with the emergence of a new candidate for paradigm and with the ensuing battle over its acceptance." For Kuhn, then, scientific revolutions are those noncumulative moments of development when an older paradigm is replaced by a newer one. His sociohistorical founding of this development of scientific knowledge is clearly apparent in his statement (1970a:94): "As in political revolutions, so in paradigm choice—there is no standard higher than the assent of the relevant community."

And it is this specific scientific group, led by a newly accepted paradigm, that brings new means to bear on puzzles and sees solutions where none had previously existed. Changes in paradigms thus bring changes to the way scientists see their field of research. In this sense one might even say: after a revolution, scientists react to a different world. Therefore a new paradigm can never arise out of normal science through purely rational argument. On the contrary, a new paradigm is born through what Kuhn (1970a:123) calls "flashes of intuition"—a form of conversion that cannot be enforced by any logical means (1970a:151).

Kuhn in Debate with Popper

From our discussion of milestones in the history of philosophy of science it should now be clear that Thomas Kuhn's theory is in itself a new paradigm in the course of that history. His model broke through Popper's critical rationalism in three important respects (cf. Koningsveld, 1977:174; De Vries, 1984:95):

1. In what Kuhn calls *normal science,* a process of ideologizing might ultimately make it possible for an accepted paradigm to harbor a segment of dogmatism—a dogmatism hard to reconcile with the current conception of science. Since a given paradigm in itself provides the criteria by which to judge what constitute relevant problems (while the paradigm as such is taken for granted), such a paradigm may also result in a certain group or community eventually immunizing itself against truly relevant problems.
2. What Kuhn calls a *scientific revolution* contains a form of conversion—a creative leap normally associated only with religion.
3. In both of the above, Kuhn makes it clear that the development of scientific thought is vitally affected by external historical, social, cultural, psychological, and economic factors. What Wolfhart Pannenberg (1973b:44) said of the implications of Popper's positive assessment of metaphysical factors and ideas is explored to its full consequences in Kuhn: metaphysical ideas can never be seen as merely part of the external and incidental conditions for the growth of scientific knowledge; such ideas are in fact intraparadigmatically constituent of both the meaning and the validity of scientific theories themselves.

This insight once again raises the question of the relationship between Kuhn's conceptual model and Popper's critical rationalism. It is interesting that Kuhn himself (1970a:iv) makes it clear that he and Popper have in a sense an almost identical view of science: both are more concerned with the dynamic process in which science originates than with, for instance, the logical structure of the results of scientific research; both also reject the view that science develops through accumulation, emphasizing, rather, the revolutionary process in which an older theory is ousted by a new one.

Kuhn also emphasizes that he and Popper are united in their opposition to one of the most central and classical tenets of logical positivism: both stress the inseparable blending of observation and theory, and both are therefore skeptical of any attempt to create a neutral perceptual language in which theories are founded directly on experience. Both also emphasize that tradition is the main source of scientific knowledge (Kuhn, 1970a:2; Popper, 1963:27).

In fact, Kuhn sees his differences with Popper not so much as actual disagreement, but rather as a gestalt switch, a different way of looking at the same data, which must ultimately lead to different conclusions. Thus, for example, Kuhn describes the scientist as a puzzle-solver, whereas Popper calls him a problem-solver. Although these terms sound similar they differ in important ways. On the one hand, in Popper's view science begins with problems: problems arise when we are disappointed in our expectations, when our theories ultimately land us in all kinds of trouble and contradictions. On the other hand, Kuhn uses the term *puzzle* to emphasize that the problems confronting scientists challenge their creative originality in the same way as chess problems or crossword puzzles. Scientists themselves, their creative ability, are the problem being tested, rather than the problematic theory.

Therefore, when Kuhn finally breaks away into a historicist direction, not only from the logical-positivistic standard conception of science but also from the criteria of critical rationalism, it is to posit a truly different view of science, despite notable parallels. His view differs from Popper's not only in respect of the problem of demarcation but also in that it is founded on a new insight into the nature of scientific thought. This eliminates not only the positivistic quest for universal laws but also Popper's theory of verisimilitude.

In scientific terms, puzzle solving as such is of more vital concern to Kuhn than any rigorous process of testing. Thus astrology, for example, is to him nonscientific not because its data cannot be tested and falsified but rather because it has no tradition of puzzle solving. In fact, Kuhn (1970a:10) could state emphatically: "To rely on testing as the mark of science is to miss what scientists mostly do and, with it, the most characteristic feature of their enterprise." For Kuhn, scientific thought is therefore primarily concerned not with testing—whether as verification or as falsification—but with the capacity of a theory or various theories for adequately explaining certain data and thus providing solutions to puzzles (Kuhn, 1970a:145).

In the light of the above Kuhn strongly criticizes Popper's principle of falsification as a criterion for demarcation. No theory is capable of solving all or any puzzles confronting it at any particular time. Furthermore, solutions that have already been found are seldom perfect; in fact, inadequacy may be seen as characteristic of the problems and theories that govern normal science. Therefore: "If any and every failure to fit were ground for theory rejection, all theories ought to be rejected at all times" (Kuhn, 1970a:146).

According to Kuhn, many of the misunderstandings about the differences between his and Popper's theories could have been avoided if it had been appreciated that they were concerned with two separate processes: what Popper sees as anomalous and therefore as problematic experiences are important to science because they highlight competing elements in regard to an existing paradigm. Falsification, however—although certainly possible—does not simply occur with or as a result of the occurrence of an anomaly or falsifying instance. On the contrary, falsification is a successive and separate process, which might just as well be called verification since it constitutes the triumph of one paradigm over another (Kuhn, 1970a:147). Thus Kuhn could justly maintain that it would make little sense to the historian, for example, if it could be claimed that verification had established a correspondence between fact and theory. Any historically significant theory corresponds with facts, but then only to a greater or lesser extent. No precise answer exists to the question of how well or to what extent any individual theory corresponds with the facts. This question can, however, be asked when theories are considered collectively, or even when pairs are compared. Therefore, "It makes a great deal of sense to ask which of two actual and competing theories fits the facts better" (Kuhn, 1970a:147).

The question of how the scientist must ultimately choose between competing theories, and therefore how science progresses as a mental activity, may then be answered as follows: In contrast to Popper, in whose view the problem of choosing a theory must ultimately be solved by logical criteria, Kuhn maintains that both the choice of theories and growth in scientific knowledge are ultimately explained by sociological and psychological factors. This means that a certain value system always plays a role in the scientist's choice of theories. If, therefore, we know what scientists value we might also understand what kind of problems would engage them and what choices they would make in given situations. These choices, however, are in the last instance never rationally explicable, and therefore Kuhn maintains that there can be no strict distinction between the contexts of discovery and of justification—especially not on the level of revolutionary science.

This may well be the prime difference between Kuhn and Popper: all scientific language and scientific theories are in themselves already an expression of a comprehensive paradigm or vision. For Kuhn, therefore, there can be no context of justification in which the scientist's ultimate commitment plays no determinant role in the development of his or her thought.

The Incommensurability of Paradigms

The problem of accounting for choices of theories is, of course, closely linked with that of divergent and conflicting views in science. Not only do scientists disagree about the standards to be met by science and scientific thought; proponents of certain stands, and especially of competing paradigms, ultimately pursue their sciences in different worlds. And two groups of scientists, operating in divergent paradigmatic and thus conceptual worlds, will see different data while facing in the same direction and from the same position. For these reasons the insights of proponents of an older paradigm are incompatible with the insights and vision of proponents of a new one. Therefore a new scientific tradition emanating from a scientific revolution must be incompatible and often also incommensurable with its predecessor (Kuhn, 1970a:103).

It is impossible, then, simply to integrate the insights of two divergent paradigms: here, too, the transition from one paradigm to another in a paradigm switch becomes possible only as a kind of conversion process. And this paradigm switch can never be made purely rationally, argumentatively, or gradually. Such a gestalt switch has, of course, a rational core, and argument does play a certain role; but ultimately faith in the force and capacities of a new paradigm is more decisive. Paradigm choices are therefore founded more on the promise a paradigm holds for the future than on the results already achieved through it.

For Kuhn the incommensurability of paradigms goes hand in hand with a certain form of relativism (De Ruijter, 1979:218). Since our scientific thought is paradigm-bound and no supraparadigmatic criteria exist, it is not possible to establish objectively whether one paradigm necessarily provides a more rational, true, or reliable perspective on matters than an earlier one. Therefore Kuhn also rejects the notion that competing paradigms can be tested for superiority in terms of rational criteria.

Paradigms are basically incommensurable because paradigm switches imply a conceptual transformation, both sociologically and epistemologically. Consequently, competing paradigms no longer speak the same scientific language, no longer observe the same data, do not ask the same questions, do not solve the same problems, and do not construct valid methods of proof in the same manner (cf. Doppelt, 1978:35). *Incommensurability*—a term Kuhn borrowed from geometry (cf. De Vries, 1984:97)—therefore denotes a specific problem of communication.

In Kuhn's view, modern scientific theories are not a logical continuation of earlier, older ones. This discontinuity implies, for example, a dissonance of communication between a person who has and one who has not been influenced by a conceptual revolution. And since competing paradigms have no rational criteria in common, it also becomes impossible to advance purely rational grounds for a shift of loyalty from one paradigm to another.

It is important, however, to note that for Kuhn this irreconcilability of paradigms does not imply an absolute and extreme discontinuity between paradigms, as if each paradigm is entirely trapped within its own conceptual world. Dissonance between paradigms does not mean there can be no rational core, nor that the switch from one paradigm to another must be reduced purely to a conversion, a leap of faith in which the scientist is mystically converted to a new language game. Kuhn by no means suggests that paradigm switches must be ascribed to purely irrational factors. His vision does not, therefore, imply an absolute epistemological break between competing paradigms (cf. Doppelt, 1978:39), nor should we interpret him as being indifferent to development in scientific thought (cf. Kuhn, 1970c:260ff.).

What he justly emphasizes is that logical criteria alone are never sufficient for paradigm choices, precisely because the scientist's ultimate commitment plays such a definitive role in the so-called context of justification, and therefore no supraparadigmatic criteria are adequate reasons for preferring one paradigm to another. This again implies not that each paradigm is and remains trapped in its own conceptual world in an absolutely relativistic sense, but rather that competing paradigms do not identify in similar manner the problems confronting them. For Kuhn there can therefore be no question of striving to attain truth.

Although competing paradigms sometimes have problems in common, they do not always assign the same priority, significance, or magnitude to those problems. Therefore intraparadigmatic discussions are often at cross-purposes, not so much for lack of a common language but because there is no common cognitive approach or sensibility to problems, criteria, and possible solutions. And for precisely that reason rational consensus between divergent paradigms is so unattainable, since each paradigm implicitly defines its own criteria for scientific status, which inevitably favor its own research program, solutions, and achievements.

The crux of Kuhn's position on the incommensurability of paradigms is that competing paradigms differ fundamentally on what should be seen as problematic or as data. This highlights his concept of the underdetermination of theories by data. In other words, his stand implies a radical broadening of the standard model of rationality, since data alone are no longer enough to adjudicate between theories, and since human decisions—the value judgments of scientists—are now seen as influencing scientific evaluation.

The question of which paradigm offers us the best solution in respect of given data can therefore never be answered purely rationally. It betrays, in fact, a more deeply rooted normative problem in which sociological, historical, and psychological factors play a crucial role in the gestalt switch from one paradigm to another.

Given the central role Kuhn assigns to such a conversion in the development of scientific thought, one might justly ask in what sense he would still see the progress of scientific thought as a rational one, and whether he is not in fact explicitly adopting an irrational stand. Kuhn (1970c:261-262) clearly states that there may be sound reasons for switching from one paradigm to another but that such reasons can never be compelling. This relativizing of rationality should not, however, be construed as sanctioning irrationalism. Even sound reasons in favor of one paradigm or another are never final and compelling; the switch requires a conceptual transformation, and for Kuhn this event is an essential element of a rational process that naturally includes rational argument (cf. Doppelt, 1978:53).

Kuhn's use of concepts such as conversion and gestalt switch does not necessarily signify a preference for irrationality. The arguments advanced to justify a theory, however, depend ultimately on which paradigm's internal criteria have been adopted, and this choice is closely linked with rational argument and sound reasons, although not totally governed by them.

Kuhn's strong emphasis on sociological, psychological, historical, and other factors in scientific revolution is therefore by no means a lapse into irrationalism; it means, rather, opting for a much wider concept of rationality. By this means he offers us an exciting attempt to explain the social process by which a scientist might reasonably adopt a new paradigm. In Kuhn's view science is first and foremost a paradigmatically governed social activity in which—often unexpectedly—revolutionary steps may be taken. Within such a concept of science and the development of scientific thought it is the task of the philosopher of science to attempt to explain the rational structure of scientists' activities and beliefs, and to enable others to follow them. This underlines even more clearly the difference between Kuhn's and Popper's conceptions of science. Whereas Popper sees the growth of knowledge toward truth in the creatively rational construction of theories that must ultimately be subjected to critical testing, Kuhn sees no role for an ultimate testing by definitive methodological criteria in the development of science.

For Kuhn it is of paramount importance that testing does not play the dominant role in the development of science that is normally claimed for it. In fact, agreement on the results of observation and on the course and results of experiments is possible only in periods of normal science. In a phase of revolutionary science, however, there are fundamental disagreements on how to interpret and formulate the results of experiments. The possibility of arriving at valid testing is ruled out, since coexistent and competing theories are in any event incommensurable for lack of commonly accepted testing criteria. This clearly emphasizes once again that, in Kuhn's model of rationality, the choices made by scientists in periods of revolutionary science can never be reconstructed purely rationally. And it is this accounting for the determinant role of pretheoretic commitments in responsible choices that gives Kuhn's view of science a much broader grasp of rationality.

Truth, Rationality, and Historicity

In Kuhn's view, the concept of truth can be used only intraparadigmatically; therefore truth has a certain local (cf. De Vries, 1984:98) and definitely provisional character. *Rational* means that on which a certain scientific community has decided jointly, and any ahistorical concept of rationality must then be shown up as illusory. If accused of falling into a kind of relativism, Kuhn answers that the theoretic language of science does not necessarily develop toward truth, but that there is definite growth in theories as instruments—instruments that gradually becomes better, more refined, and more functional. This does not, however, imply more or better knowledge of the truth about our realities, as Kuhn clearly states (1970a:206): "Later scientific theories are better than earlier ones for solving puzzles in the often quite different environments to which they are applied. That is not a relativist's position, and it displays the sense in which I am a convinced believer in scientific progress."

Kuhn's *The Structure of Scientific Revolutions* soon became one of the most sensational and contentious publications in contemporary philosophy of science. Questions about his concept of truth, about precisely what he meant with the ambiguous term *paradigm*, about how radical the so-called incommensurability of paradigms really is, and about the distinction between normal and revolutionary science, soon became an essential part of discussions in philosophy of science.

Less remarked upon, however, was the new challenge he had created for theology. Kuhn's conception of science would relativize the standard image of logical positivism even more than Karl Popper's had done. The essence of that challenge lies in the new bearing given to crucial concepts such as rationality and objectivity, precisely because of a conscious methodological recognition of the indissoluble bond between the scientist's basic commitments and the theorizing that eventually occurs in scientific reflection.

Kuhn's Relevance to Systematic Theology

In my view, that transformation of concepts has created a basis for a new, alternative conceptual model in theology, which may finally break and transcend the rigid boundaries of the standard theological reaction to the positivistic model of rationality. However, Kuhn's broadening of the concept of rationality will ultimately have to account for the problems his concept of truth must pose for theology, most notably the question to what extent his model of progress in the history of science holds good for other fields—in this case for systematic theology.

Kuhn (1970a:208; 1970c:244) admits that his conclusions are applicable to a wide area, especially since he portrays scientific development as a succession of tradition-bound periods punctuated by (often unexpected) noncumulative breaks. In fact, periodization in terms of revolutionary shifts in style, taste, and structure has always formed part of the history of human thought, especially the history of art, literature, and music, as well as in philosophy and politics. He sees his originality mainly in having applied this structure to the sciences—fields that have generally (under the influence of the standard conception of science) been thought to develop in a different way (Kuhn, 1970a:208).

Although Kuhn deals tentatively with the question of the applicability of his model to the development of the human sciences, and fairly traditionally typifies most of the human sciences as preparadigmatic sciences (cf. De Vries, 1984:210), his vision does open up vital perspectives on the question of the origins of our traditional theological models. Therefore, apart from the thorny problem of demarcation in respect of theology, Kuhn offers us even at this stage the possibility of evaluating the development of systematic-theological models in sociohistorical terms. He justly emphasized not only that the choice between conceptual models must be explained in sociohistorical terms, but also that the question of the nature of scientific thought must be answered in this way.

The Kuhnian model opens our eyes to the fact that the so-called pure sciences have much more in common with other conceptual models than could ever be recognized in a positivistic standard conception of science. In fact, what we have here is a definite relativization of the rigidity with which the positivistic demarcation question is usually formulated. Since Popper—but especially with Kuhn—it is no longer possible to draw a simplistic equation between nonscience and non-sense. This also implies that the dogged but futile efforts of systematic theology to cross the boundary into the field of true, formal science can be provisionally abandoned in favor of a new, freer, and open question about the nature of rational thought as such. For systematic theology this is a question of the utmost importance, and especially so for a systematic-theological model that would develop into a form of critical accounting for faith.

We have seen that Kuhn regards science as a sociohistorically determined activity characterized and dominated by the impact of paradigms. As an intellectual activity, systematic theology is also a sociohistorically determined conceptual model and therefore always governed by paradigms. This is where the theologian's commitment to a certain integral basic commitment plays such a vital role. Not only do the systematic theologian's basic convictions commit him to certain paradigms or research traditions backed up, historically and otherwise, by definitive group values, but even our specific religious experiences are determined by our language and tradition, since no religious experience can ever be truly prelinguistic or pretheoretic (cf. Kaufman, 1979:7). Thus a given systematic-theological paradigm or conceptual model may also—for instance, through its confessional implementation by a church—come to determine how religious commitments are theorized, and thus it may determine even the nature of our religious experiences.

Theological reflection, too, is therefore always and everywhere a group-based activity. If we are to explore changes and even radical breaks in this intellectual activity, and to understand why one (possibly outdated) model may be replaced at a given stage by a new, promising one, we shall have to explore the nature and needs of, as well as changes within, a particular group structure. For in theology too a particular paradigm determines primarily not only the data studied but also the person or group of persons studying those data in terms of it. Within the context of systematic theology, therefore, the intellectual activity of a certain group will be governed decisively by a common basic conviction or convictions. Individual conceptual models are ultimately influenced and even decisively determined by factors such as personality, education, and the course of a previous research pattern.

For systematic theology, Kuhn's major contribution may well be the insight that scientific knowledge does not accumulate through the gradual addition of new elements to an existing body of knowledge; on the contrary, scientific knowledge shows no such logical growth but develops by shocks, through radical breaks or revolutions in which one vision has to make way for another.

The discussion of Kuhn's paradigm theory has shown repeatedly that a particular group's paradigm embraces the total structure of that group's thought. When problems begin to surface within the context of such a paradigm, so that the paradigm becomes insecure and may even begin to falter under the accumulation of insoluble problems, such a model is often quickly reduced to sharply defined and precisely formulated rules and laws, with the authority of the paradigm itself invoked rigorously and with the utmost conviction.

These may also be typical symptoms of developments within systematic theology, especially an authoritarian axiomatic theology in which the authority of its conceptual model is derived directly and unquestioningly from God's revelation, for instance, as given to us in Holy Scripture. Within systematic theology a stable and dominant research tradition, as the accepted and trusted paradigm, may fall into a crisis in which both the tradition and its solution of problems may become highly problematic. Perhaps the most outstanding example of such a crisis is the Reformation of the sixteenth century. As Kuhn has clearly demonstrated, such a situation may, owing to various sociohistorical factors, lead theologians to the creative transformation of their mental world and thus to a totally new view of reality and problems. In fact, such a paradigmatic revolution may also lead theologians to identify problems they had previously resisted on ideological grounds, because they could not identify them.

As in the development of strict scientific thought, any new conceptual model or approach begins—precisely as a new theory or discovery—in the thought of single or a few individuals. Such a person or persons would be first to see the reality of systematic-theological problems in a different light. This reminds one, of course, of the two factors to which Kuhn ascribed the process of substituting one paradigm for another. Referring to the role individual thought plays in scientific revolutions, he wrote (1970a:143): "Invariably their attention has been intensely concentrated upon the crisis-provoking problems; usually, in addition, they are men so young or so new to the crisis-ridden field that practice has committed them less deeply than most of their contemporaries to the world view and rules determined by the old paradigm."

In any disciplinary tradition a paradigm switch is therefore also heralded by a period of disquiet and the discovery of anomalies in the way a given paradigm copes with certain problems. This, in turn, leads to the type of crisis mentioned above, and ultimately, it is hoped, to the reformulation of old theories and the discovery of new ones. In systematic theology, too, a paradigmatic shift, as a conceptual transformation, can occur only if it spreads integrally over the entire front of a theologian's vision. If the theologian is to be spared superficial eclecticism and the uncritical conflation of elements from often divergent systematic-theological traditions, there must be a fundamental and creditable transformation of certain formerly standard axioms and procedures—a transformation that may have not only conceptual but also sweeping methodological implications.

The rejection of an obsolete and inadequate conceptual model may, in systematic theology too, lead to a radical shift concerning the relevance of problems. In theology such a shift becomes particularly difficult, however, because a subjective commitment to trusted basic convictions may only too easily put a cloak of authority on conceptual models. In systematic theology a true conceptual transformation may be characterized by the jettisoning of trusted but obsolete theories, the identification and examination of new problems, the adoption of other criteria in assessing certain data, and often also the total reinterpretation of extant and previously collected or processed data.

For theologians who have experienced a radical paradigm shift, such a conceptual transformation usually implies, in addition, a reconstruction of their total field of study from a new or reformulated basic commitment—a reconstruction that might lead to drastic changes in the most basic thematic structuring of a discipline. Eventually the theologian might still be dealing with the same data, but then from a new perspective, within a totally new conceptual framework or paradigm.

Kuhn has rightly pointed out that some form of crisis in thought is always a prerequisite to the birth of new theories. And in systematic theology, as in the natural sciences, a new revolutionary phase need not always be associated with prominent figures such as St. Augustine, Calvin, Luther, Barth, Moltmann, or Pannenberg. On the contrary, a breakthrough or conceptual transformation phase in systematic theology can be any special change or departure that may lead to the restructuring of a person's or group's basic commitments.

In systematic theology, conceptual transformations are those rare moments in which a shift of basic commitments occurs, moments in which the theoretic configuration of a certain basic commitment is broken and transformed. Such moments may occur in the theologian's own conceptual development, but they may also show themselves in the periodization of the history of systematic theology in all its many forms. All such revolutionary moments imply a transformation of ideas, concepts, theories, and methods—a transformation by which the traditional procedures, as well as their efficacy, are breached once and for all.

In theology, too, new ideas or theories (for example, on the story of creation, the historicity of persons such as Adam and Eve, Jonah and Esther, or of Israel's migration from Egypt and settlement in Palestine) are never important merely as facts or data. A new theory may, as such, carry implications with all the characteristics of a total conversion, which might qualitatively transform and enhance the theologian's own conceptual model. Here, too, a theologian's creative choice of a new paradigm or conceptual model is based not on what was achieved through it in the past, but rather on its potential—on the conviction that the new paradigm will prove more adequate and creditable than an earlier, obsolete one.

Resistance to a new (creditable) model—one that has shown convincingly that it holds promise in the context of current problems—may come from a theologian or group of theologians who have not shared the conceptual transformation. As our discussion of Kuhn's stand has shown, a dominant theology, trusted by a group, may through ideologizing inject an element of uncritical dogmatism into a paradigm or conceptual model.

Since any authoritarian theological model in itself provides the criteria by which the precise relevance of problems and the authenticity of biblical solutions are evaluated, such a conceptual model may eventually cause a certain group to immunize itself against truly relevant problems. What makes this possibility so hazardous to theology is what both Popper and Kuhn have rightly pointed out: that the primary source of our conceptual models must naturally be a tradition—one which, especially in theology, may be vested, surreptitiously and subtly, with a cloak of seemingly infallible revelatory authority.

Closely related to the problem of paradigmatic commitment and its offshoot, the question of the nature of paradigm shifts, is the problem of divergent and even conflicting stands in systematic theology. Not only do systematic theologians disagree patently on what they regard as theology; protagonists of certain theological traditions—especially of divergent and competing ones—actually conduct their theology in different worlds. What Kuhn called the incompatibility, and even the incommensurability, of paradigms is therefore particularly noticeable in systematic theology. Theologizing within different paradigms or conceptual models, two theologians or groups of theologians might identify different problems and initiate different solutions while apparently working from the same basic commitment or premise (such as the "authority of Scripture" as the "revealed" Word of God) in the same direction (a biblical solution to the problem).

For this reason alone the insights and adherents of an earlier or older theological conceptual model can never reconcile themselves entirely to the vision and insight of adherents of a new or alternative model. Theologically, it would therefore be both irresponsible and superficial to attempt a simplistic reconciliation of two divergent theological models.[2] Here, too, the transition from one conceptual model to another becomes creditable only after a radical and comprehensive new insight has been gained—a conceptual transformation that can never occur through mere logic or argument.

With his sociocultural evaluation of the development of thought Kuhn also demonstrated convincingly that purely logical grounds cannot account for a shift in the systematic theologian's loyalty from one paradigm or conceptual model to another. This is why the communicational conflict between theologians and frameworks of theological interpretation is so often radical and irresolvable. When theologians talk at cross-purposes from divergent philosophical traditions, the cause is not so much a lack of a common language but rather the lack of a common frame of thought, a common perception of problems, criteria, and possible solutions.

On the rational scientific level, however, kindred spirits are people who have experienced (or missed!) a common conceptual transformation. Therefore, before theologians too can communicate meaningfully, some paradigmatic shift has to occur. Such a transformation is never made gradually; it is a conversion, a sudden gestalt switch that cannot be forced rationally or otherwise.

When a theologian is finally confronted with a choice between divergent models or theories, that choice is never made entirely on rational or irrational grounds. The arguments finally accepted, however (for example, in favor of a better theory or theories), depend directly on the theological paradigm or conceptual model whose internal criteria have been adopted. By its nature such a choice—in theology too—is closely linked to but not totally governed by rational argument.

In terms of Kuhn's model the demarcation question in respect of systematic theology—whether systematic theology could qualify as a scientific activity—remains difficult and complex. In his well-known essay "Reflections on My Critics," Kuhn (1970c:243) states clearly that everything he has said, although specifically directed at formal science and scientists, is more generally applicable to a wide variety of other fields. For Kuhn, therefore, it is essential that no progression distinguishes the strict, established sciences from philosophy, theology, or the other human sciences (which he also called protosciences). Even if these mental activities failed to meet Popper's demarcation criterion for a strict science, they might nevertheless progress and develop in a manner similar to that of the sciences.[3]

What is true of strict science—or what Kuhn also calls *mature*

---

2. Such a superficial eclecticism could conceivably occur if isolated elements of the thought of Bonhoeffer (for instance, the secularization motif), Barth (such as his concept of revelation), Moltmann (the hope category), and Pannenberg (for example, the historicity of the resurrection) were introduced a-contextually and arbitrarily in a strictly Reformed paradigm.

3. Kuhn, 1970c:244: "In antiquity and during the Renaissance, the arts rather than the sciences provided the accepted paradigms of progress."

science—is true of rational activity in a broader sense. What Kuhn said in respect of philosophy and other proto-sciences is also true of theology: here, too, creative breakthroughs (revolutions) cannot encompass and govern the total essence of this activity. Such revolutionary shifts must alternate with stabilized phases. In fact, Popper (1970:51) emphasized that scientists inevitably and necessarily develop their ideas within a particular framework—a view that led directly to his incisive and influential conclusion: "we approach everything in the light of a preconceived theory" (1970:52).

In theology, then, radical breakthroughs presuppose definitive paradigms, precisely because such breakthroughs always imply the rejection and replacement of a framework or essential parts of it. For systematic theologians a particular, definitively structured paradigm and specific conceptual models are therefore inevitable. Without them their critical accounting for their faith could never break free from obsolete concepts to a model with new promises and new possibilities. Kuhn (1970c:242) put this succinctly: "Frameworks must be lived with and explored before they can be broken."

Thus a particular theological tradition may indeed be our only access to the truth of God's revelation, but this in itself can never be the reason why that tradition is the only true one. It seems to me that this cautions us against theologians who claim authoritatively that their theological tradition is the only true (or biblical) one. Any form of dogmatic exclusivism is not only theoretically unrealistic and irresponsible, but also emanates from a conscious (and often even deliberate) blindness to the presence and action of God in ways for which traditional theological frameworks more often than not leave us totally unprepared.

In any strictly defined theological paradigm (for instance, the Reformed tradition) we must therefore be prepared to recognize that the situation in which we are theologizing has changed to such an extent that it is impossible to fall back unthinkingly and easily on trusted and infallible positions within that tradition. Here, too, new situations and new experiences demand new insights, a conceptual transformation in a new manner of Christian thought and understanding. This broader concept of rationality is to be found in Kuhn's paradigm theory, which may offer a surprising and meaningful insight into the sociohistorical process by which the theologian is led to a rational acceptance of a new conceptual model.

Finally, it becomes possible to identify a clearly defined—albeit provisional—model of rationality for systematic theology: one with minimum demands and criteria that might also be recognized as valid and creditable in the broader postpositivistic philosophy of science, while nonetheless doing justice to the peculiar nature of the Object of our theological reflection. Before we can tackle this difficult and responsible task, however, we must first consider the work of two systematic theologians who did in fact accept the challenge of debate in contemporary philosophy of science.

PART II
THE CONSTRUCTION OF THEORIES
IN SYSTEMATIC THEOLOGY

6

Theology as the Science of God:
Wolfhart Pannenberg

Für Menschen, deren Leben einen Inhalt gefunden hat, so dass sie wissen, wofür sie leben, gewinnt auch das Vielerlei des Alltags ein Profil. Wo ein Ziel alles im Leben umgreift, da wird unser Leben ein Ganzes. Das Leben gewinnt Stil.

Wolfhart Pannenberg, "Ein Leben mit Stil," in *Gegenwart Gottes: Predigten* (Munich: Claudius, 1973):55.

Introduction

From the preceding chapters it should be clear that any responsible reflection on the factors ultimately governing theological theorizing must reckon with the inevitable implications that those central questions asked in philosophy of science have for current systematic-theological discussion. A new, exciting grasp of the origins of theological models has been gained, to manifest itself also in the language of specific theological statements.

The perspectives gained through contemporary philosophy of science have opened up a broad range of issues for systematic theology, some of which have been dealt with explicitly, others implicitly. Within this complex whole we might now turn more pointedly—albeit provisionally—to the following problematic themes:

First, the dominant and all-encompassing question remains the critical issue of the type of (intellectual) activity theological thought represents in its most profound sense. Inextricably linked with that must always be the question of the rationality models employed by particular theologians, and how they have chosen those specific models. Ultimately it must become clear that the key to both metaquestions lies in the answer to another one: how theories are formed specifically in systematic theology.

Second, theologians have to consider the question of the origins of their systematic-theological statements; and this general question leads to other, quite concrete questions, such as: What is the source of our theological statements? Can we trace the sources of our theological models and, in doing so, attempt to identify the factors that determine the actual character of our theological statements (and models)? The answer to this question would, however, lead systematic theology to the crucial and central question of the decisive role the theologian's personal, and therefore subjective, religious convictions play in the eventual choice of a particular theological model and in its further structuring. No critical theologian can evade the question of the role personal commitments play in the shaping of particular theories within a conceptual model.

The issue of the origins of our theological statements is ultimately also the question of how our personal religious experiences are shaped by traditional historical factors, and thus of the influence—including the sanctioned influence—such conceptual models or paradigms may have on current theorizing in systematic theology. The question of the origins of theological models is, furthermore, the question of the social structure within which theology functions, and thus the question of the meshing of theological theories with the social structure in which they occur.

Third, the inclusive question of the factors bearing on the formulation of methods and theories in theology leads inevitably to the problematic question of what, precisely, the direct (or indirect) object of theological statements is. This difficult question also opens up the further one of the precise nature and determinant influence of the theologian's own relationship with that object, including its influence on his or her formulation of theological theories. Ultimately, we are faced with the decisive question of the effect that the nature and availability of systematic theology's object have on the nature, structure, and scope of theological theories.

Fourth, systematic theologians will have to face the crucial question of the nature and structure of their theological statements, not only in consequence of their response to the question about the rationality model of their theology, but also because God is the directly or indirectly implied object of all their statements. This immediately raises the further question of our theological statements' objective quality, cognitive nature, or reality depiction. We are thus confronted yet again with the question of the provisional or hypothetical character of theological statements, and whether that provisionality can be validly integrated, in terms of philosophy of science issues, with the fundamental question of the nature of all rationality. This question of the nature and structure of our theological statements obviously also implies the question of the similarity and differences between everyday statements of faith, official ecclesiastical and/or confessional statements, and theological statements as such.

Fifth, both the unique character of the object of systematic theology and the problematic nature of theological language lead inevitably to the question: To what extent can others follow the assertions made in our theological statements, and thus in our theological theories too? In other words, can theological statements really be made accessible to others, and thus be exposed to some form of evaluation and checking? More pointedly: is it in fact possible to examine the truth or validity of theological statements in order to justify them in one way or another, or to rid them of error? The problem this question raises is whether the claims to truth in theological statements can be checked in any way. This question is important also because it might lead us to clarity on the kind of arguments theologians use to justify, validate, and maintain their positions.

Quite clearly, then, no theologian can evade the question of the status and validity of theological statements in terms of contemporary philosophy of science. And yet, although there have always been theologians who questioned the nature of theological thought, only a few modern ones have specifically and purposefully taken up the challenge of justifying theology in the wider context of philosophy of science. Among these theologians, the most notable must be the Germans Wolfhart Pannenberg and Gerhard Sauter. Apart from them, the young German theologian Heinzpeter Hempelmann and American theologians such as Gordon Kaufman, David Tracy, and Sallie McFague have focused intensively on these issues, although by no means always specifically within the problem-context of contemporary philosophy of science.

Anyone who wishes to keep abreast of current trends in theological theorizing and model-construction will have to take note of the theological models handled by these theologians. However diverse their conceptual models and those of others concerning themselves directly with these problems may be, each in his or her own way proceeds from the basic premise that the believing Christian theologian is in fact capable of an intellectual achievement that could be rated rationally valid and responsible—an intellectual approach capable of regulating language according to definitive criteria, of responsible and accountable theorizing and model-formulation, and ultimately of a form of valid control of theological statements.

In the context of current discussions of these problems the initiative was undoubtedly taken by Wolfhart Pannenberg and Gerhard Sauter, who have opted, from a concern with problems specifically raised by philosophy of science, for a patently argumentative theology rather than any form of dogmatistic axiomatic theology based on the preconceived and unquestionable certainties so typical of positivism. Pannenberg in particular is remarkably outspoken about systematic-theological models in which, given their total neglect of the critical question of theorizing in theology, a particular concept of revelation may so uncritically and ideologically assume an authoritarian character that it consciously rejects any critical examination or justification.

In any evaluation of Pannenberg's and Sauter's positions, then, the question of the subjective involvement of the theologian in his own reflections and in the type of choices he makes between theories must be vital. Our confrontation with Bartley's critical rationalism has taught us that the problem lies not so much with the theologian's basic convictions or ultimate commitments as with the subtle effect that commitment, already theorized, may have on the shaping of theological views. Here, then, lies the real problem of the nature and limits of a theologian's model of rationality.

Theologians such as Pannenberg and Sauter must, therefore, consider the role the theologian's subjectivity plays in his theological thought and in the theorizing underlying it. The question of the theologian's subjective involvement is in fact the question of the role and function of a personal religious commitment in the theorizing already implied in the methodological premises of theological thought.

In the light of critical rationalism and the implications of Kuhn's paradigm theory, systematic theologians are compelled to answer an exceptionally difficult question: Are they at all capable of thinking from a pretheoretic personal commitment without falling back irrationally and subjectively on certain unquestioned basic convictions as the very premises of their thought? To put it differently: Is it possible to theologize from a subjective, personal religious commitment to Jesus of Nazareth, without falling into the theoretic trap of a fideistic, irrational theological premise?

Our question about the nature of theorizing in systematic theology will ultimately culminate in the question whether theologians' preconceptualized personal religious commitment must function as an immunization tactic when they are confronted with questions on the role of pretheoretic assumptions in the conscious formulation or unconscious manipulation of theological premises. This question must be asked not only of Pannenberg's and Sauter's theologies, but also of our own theological models. Any attempt to answer these problematic questions demands much more than merely adopting a creditable or topical approach in the contemporary debate of philosophy of science; it involves, rather, the intellectual integrity of theology itself—of a rational mental activity seeking to remain dynamic and creative in its attempts to make creditable and valid statements on God and His relationship to the world.

The Universal Nature of Theology

The theological model of the renowned German theologian Wolfhart Pannenberg is of crucial importance to any consideration of the problem of theorizing in systematic theology.[1] This is so especially because Pannenberg asks the pertinent question, What is theology? In doing so, he focuses directly on the problem of the nature of theological theorizing, and thus also on the question of the origins of theological conceptual models.

The fundamental reasons for his broad approach may be found in the earliest development of his thought, long before his well-known book on the nature of theological science (Pannenberg, 1973b). In *Grundfragen Systematischer Theologie* (1967:11-12) Pannenberg already makes the point that systematic theology is always shaped by the tension between two seemingly divergent trends: on the one hand, theology's commitment to its religious source, namely, God as revealed in Jesus Christ and testified to by Holy Scripture; on the other, theology's assumption of a universal character transcending all specific themes in its striving toward truth itself, precisely because it would make statements on God. This universality emanates from the fact that reality, in its all-encompassing totality as God's creation, is not only dependent upon and committed to God but is in its profoundest sense incomprehensible without God (Pannenberg, 1967:11).

In Pannenberg's view it goes without saying that theology is, ultimately, fully and most profoundly concerned with God's revelation in Jesus Christ. Precisely as God's revelation, however, that revelation can be properly understood only if we realize that all knowledge and anything we might regard as true or as the truth must have some bearing on that revelation. As the Creator, God is not only creatively responsible for everything in our reality, but is greater than our present, created reality. Therefore, any aspect of that reality is correctly— albeit provisionally—understood only in relation to God's revelation and His truth.

Given the universality of the concept of God, as logically implied in the concept of creation, Pannenberg has consistently maintained that systematic theology can never fall back on an exclusive and epistemologically isolated revelationist position. It has therefore always been clear to him that theology could never exist purely as a positive ecclesiastical theology, isolated from the other sciences. Although such a ghetto theology might ensure an unproblematic coexistence with philosophy of science and other sciences, it would have a radical impact on the universality implicit in the concept of God.

Systematic theology would ultimately betray its own nature if it were to concentrate entirely on a unique, esoteric task. Above all, theology dare not positivistically narrow down its task to mere scriptural exegesis. In fact, Pannenberg sees such a thematic restriction of theology to exegesis as self-contradictory; for any form of scriptural exegesis directly implies the universality of theological thematics, as founded on the biblical concept of a monotheistic God (Pannenberg, 1967:12). A theology that merely attempts to explain and follow

1. For a detailed discussion of Pannenberg's theological model, see van Huyssteen, 1970.

Scripture is nonetheless still speaking of the world, of people, of history, and therefore, ultimately, of truth in the most comprehensive sense of the word.

In the broad spectrum of theological disciplines, systematic theology in particular is directly concerned with this universal perspective. As such, it is committed to rationality. This not only raises the question of the broad fundamentals that theology shares with other sciences and of what constitutes the unique character of theological reflection; systematic theology also becomes the area in which theology itself must be able to account critically for its own credibility and for the validity of its conceptual paradigm.

In accounting critically for his own credibility, Pannenberg (1973b:8) states that the breakthrough into serious discussion in terms of philosophy of science has not only become the crucial issue of our time but has ushered in a new phase of reflection by theology on its own character. The problems may seem esoteric, but the debate in philosophy of science is not concerned with a flight from the so-called primary functions of science into a kind of unproductive self-contemplation; it means, rather, the involvement of theology—precisely for the sake of its credibility as a rational mental activity—in an attempt to redefine for our time what we mean by science, scientific thought, rationality, and objectivity.

Pannenberg therefore justly emphasizes that the debate in philosophy of science compels any discipline to reflect on its own fundamentals in a broader context and to reformulate anew its own task. Such reflection, however, is of cardinal importance not only to the university, as home of the sciences, but may also have radical implications for theology in particular. Theology's participation in the debates of philosophy of science is therefore vital to its future, since the possibility of theology being regarded as a science can no longer be taken for granted.

For theology such a critical discussion would necessarily imply self-criticism, but then a type of self-criticism that might eventually lead to its rejuvenation as a scientific discipline. In his analysis (1973b:11-17) of the history of the concept of theology, Pannenberg also outlines the close links Christian thought has had for centuries with philosophy. In the current debate between theology and philosophy of science those links are of the utmost importance; for through the close association of Christian thought with the long history of philosophical reflection Christian thinkers have since the second century sought to assert the general or universal truth of the Christian message. Those attempts were of fundamental significance to Christianity at a time when—virtually as a Jewish sect—it first ventured out into the world.

Against this background Pannenberg (1973b:17) may justly say that if theology somehow had to disappear from our universities because most people regarded it as an unscientific, authority-bound, and esoteric activity, it would mean a radical setback for the Christian conception of truth—even if theology were taken over by and kept alive in ecclesiastical institutions. Understandably, then, Pannenberg is strongly opposed to a theology that, content to be regarded as an ecclesiastical theology isolated from the general concept of truth in the sciences, declines participation in any discussion of the question of its own identity. He is also sharply critical of any form of theology that takes its stand on an esoteric conception of truth further founded on an assumed grasp of God's revelation as the so-called immutable premise for a self-sufficient theology. Such a theology would narrow itself down to a ghetto theology, of significance only to initiates. It is understandable that this resistance to any form of exclusively ecclesiastical theology must make Pannenberg (1973b:22ff.) deeply critical of the theological model of Karl Barth in particular.

Specifically for the sake of the truth of the Christian message, systematic theology must take up the task of formulating and founding its concept of science in a confrontation with the perceptions of contemporary philosophy of science, and thus with alternative conceptions of the nature of science. For the sake of its intellectual integrity, theology can on no creditable grounds claim a privileged advantage in its pursuit of truth. If it did try to claim such a privileged position, it would be able to do so only by founding its thematics on arbitrary, irrational, or authoritarian grounds—a tactic that would in turn become the target of renewed criticism of theology itself.

Theology and Philosophy of Science

In his debate with philosophy of science, Wolfhart Pannenberg (1973b:28ff.) not only scrutinizes logical positivism and its pervasive effect on diverse scientific disciplines but also pointedly rejects both the positivist unitary ideal for all sciences and the positivist influence that causes science to be constantly oriented and formulated on the model of natural sciences.

Ultimately, however, Pannenberg's relationship with critical rationalism and with Kuhn's paradigm theory must be crucial to an evaluation of his thought. Although critical rationalism undoubtedly had a decisive influence on his thought and he consistently—as will become clear—reveals links with Popper's thought, it is especially Thomas Kuhn's paradigm theory that has guided him in the later phase of his inquiry. In his reflections on the nature and identity of theology he sought to liberate systematic theology not only from the one-sided demands of a positivist concept of truth, but also from the falsification criterion of critical rationalism, precisely to leave room for scientific validity in theological statements and theories. Whether Pannenberg has in fact succeeded in doing so, and how these various elements of his thought are interrelated, will have to be closely examined.

First, Pannenberg (1973b:43) points out that Karl Popper, in his attempt to find a meaningful demarcation criterion that would transcend the one-sidedness of the positivist verifiability criterion, gave a central place to the falsifiability of theories in his model of philosophy of science. In doing so, Popper was looking not merely for a criterion that would separate science and metaphysics, but also for a broad base on which the social sciences would be able to subject their hypotheses and theories to the falsification test.

Although Pannenberg (1973b:44ff.), having outlined the well-known Bartley arguments, proceeds to discuss further themes from critical rationalism without coming back specifically to the demands of Bartley's pancritical rationalism, it is clear that he is very much concerned with Bartley's sharp criticism of theology, namely, that it too readily falls back on an irrational and fideistic premise as a final base for argument. In an evaluation of Pannenberg's theoretic model we shall have to consider very critically to what extent he has in fact avoided having his own thought definitively structured by the critical-rationalist model. The crucial question will be to what extent Bartley's demand for a commitment to noncommitment has perhaps determined Pannenberg's development of his own answer to the question of the identity of theological science.

These problems will come to a head when we proceed, while examining the sources of theological statements, to ask critical questions about the role and function of the theologian's own conceptualized subjective involvement—in this case specifically with regard to Pannenberg's own theological model. Even at this stage we might formulate our final critical question to Pannenberg: How does he justify the role of the theologian's personal religious commitment in the eventual theorizing in his theology?

Pannenberg (1973b:50) admits particularly that Hans Albert's charge against theology, namely, that it tries to salvage the concept of God by speaking of God as nonobjectifiable, is largely unanswerable—except for Albert's view that not only an obsolete and redundant concept of God but the very idea of God must be rejected together with an outdated worldview. Here Albert (1968:104ff.) uses Popper's argument (the so-called conventional twist or conventional stratagem) which implies that a hypothesis or theory, once falsified, cannot be modified ad hoc to evade further falsification.

Pannenberg (1973b:51) counters this criticism by stating clearly (and in my view correctly) that this principle of Popper's cannot be applied so strictly even in the natural sciences; furthermore, Popper's formulation of the principle in itself does not rule out the possibility that elements of an old theory (for example, the concept of God) might form part of a new one. The only condition would have to be that the new theory must also be exposed to the risks of falsification. Therefore a new theory cannot be formulated merely to immunize a certain preconceived idea against all criticism.

Concerning the thesis of the nonobjectifiability of God, Pannenberg maintains that it must be probable and reasonable to assume that the main motive behind its formulation was to safeguard the concept of God against criticism. That does not by any means, however, imply—not even by the principles of Popper's critical rationalism—that the idea of God is in itself meaningless. Therefore Hans Albert's insistence that the idea of God as such must be totally abandoned makes sense to Pannenberg only as an expression of a patently pre-scientific hostility to theology; it cannot be justified in terms of the principles of Albert's own critical rationalism.[2]

Pannenberg (1973b:51) then quite correctly identifies the crucial question in this inquiry as follows: Should systematic theology be evaluated so decisively by the principles of critical rationalism? That Popper's *The Logic of Scientific Discovery* was originally conceived with a view to the natural sciences raises not only the critical question whether the criteria of critical rationalism have been successfully applied to the natural sciences themselves, but especially also the question whether this principle of critical examination by falsification can indeed simply be transferred to other disciplines in the name of a unitary scientific method. Popper himself, and certainly also Bartley and Albert, would apply the principles of critical rationalism in this comprehensive sense—a procedure which, if accepted as correct and applied, would have radical consequences for theology. What also makes Pannenberg's confrontation with critical rationalism of cardinal importance is not only that he never takes a naïve and dogmatistic stand against the demands of the Popper school, but also that he critically examines those demands and exposes their limitations and even their untenability from the inside, as it were.

In a critical discussion of the possibility of falsification Pannenberg (1973b:52ff.) examines in detail the main demands of critical rationalism. For our purposes—to determine not only the nature of the systematic-theological model Pannenberg adopts but also its origins—it is important to appreciate that Pannenberg follows Popper in his view that inductive reasoning and the principle of verification offer us no solutions to the question of scientific knowledge. A general rule is always applicable to an infinite number of instances: an infinity, however, of which only a limited number can be known at any given time. In Popper's view, therefore, generalizations can never claim absolute certainty, and for that reason the strict verification of postulated general laws is also impossible. At the same time, as we have clearly seen in our discussion of critical rationalism, it is possible in principle to falsify such a generalization, for instance, through a single deviation from the general rule.

The basic propositions that must now act as objective criteria in the process of scientific thought, and in terms of which falsification might be possible, must, however, be testable on an intersubjective level, according to the principles of critical rationalism. Our discussion of critical rationalism has shown that, with Popper, the old positivist ideal of value-free, objective knowledge has been turned into intersubjective correspondence. Objectivity thus becomes the characteristic of a certain group, realized by mutual criticism: a so-

2. Pannenberg, 1973b:51. For Albert's response, see his 1982:158ff.

cial matter that can no longer be founded purely on so-called atheoretic, self-evident facts.

In this sense, basic propositions are data accepted on the grounds of a group's decision or agreement and may therefore also be called conventions (Popper, 1968:106). That Popper could dismiss as fairly harmless the degree of dogmatism arising from such a conventionally determined objectivity is in Pannenberg's view (1973b:5) in itself an underestimation of the problem, since it makes it possible to formulate a principle of falsifiability by which a hypothesis contrary to a given basic proposition need not be ruled out or falsified. The very objectivity operating here as a criterion is, however, dependent on the group that accepts it as objective, and would therefore also be subject to change.

Pannenberg (1973b:56) makes the further point that the implications of this type of consideration make it very difficult to distinguish absolutely between scientific and metaphysical statements. In fact, if the concepts and language in which experiences are scientifically describable are a matter of convention, there can be no compelling reasons for preexcluding the concept of God from the exclusive circle of scientifically admissible statements. For Pannenberg, then, it is clear that Popper's concept of the theory-ladenness of all observation, and his acknowledgment of the conventional nature of so-called objective statements, must ultimately lead to failure in his attempts to draw sharp distinctions between scientific and metaphysical statements. In Pannenberg's view, scientific statements are thus in themselves ultimately founded on general worldviews of a profoundly philosophical and/or religious nature.

Furthermore, Pannenberg (1973b:75) sees this dependence of the linguistic form of basic propositions on the perspective of experience as a reinforcement of the view that the objects of scientific inquiry are not merely individual hypotheses but full-fledged theoretic constructs or contexts. Such a theoretic construct determines, in turn, observations as well as the language in which they are reported. That in itself implies, as Kuhn demonstrated so clearly, that hypotheses cannot be empirically tested within the framework of theoretically neutral observations; that testing must form part of a process Kuhn calls paradigm articulation. In terms of philosophy of science I would put it as follows: the personal involvement of the scientist, and therefore of the paradigm from which he lives and works, always plays a role, not only in the context of discovery but also in the context of justification.

This conclusion Pannenberg reached in his own fashion, and in my view correctly, as far as critical rationalism is concerned. This in fact also shows Pannenberg's (1973b:57-60) spiritual affinity with Kuhn's thought. Kuhn (1970a:192) points out that even in the natural sciences the testing of hypotheses does not normally consist of direct attempts to falsify them but is, rather, a comparison of the abilities of various theories for providing meaningful solutions to certain problems. This clearly shows—for Wolfhart Pannenberg too—that the capacity for integrating and giving meaning to available data, and thus providing solutions to puzzles, is the primary principle in the testing of both strictly scientific and theological hypotheses.

Therefore Pannenberg, partly under Kuhn's influence, opts for a rationality model that must transcend the bounds of critical rationalism to allow for critical inquiry on a much wider front. Whether he thus succeeds in answering the question of the scientific quality and validity of theological statements, or in avoiding critical-rationalistic codetermination of his own conceptual model, will now have to be examined in detail.

Theological Statements as Hypotheses

Pannenberg's debate with critical rationalism had a lasting impact on his own questioning of the identity and nature of theological science. In particular, Bartley and Albert's criticism of theology infuses his thinking on this theme. Albert's reproach that systematic theologians fall back too readily on a supposedly unique and esoteric epistemology as an ideological immunization against criticism, and Bartley's related reproach that theologians evade critical scientific questions by retreating to an irrational position of faith, ultimately become the focal points of Pannenberg's attempt to formulate a creditable theory of theology.

This, together with Pannenberg's (1973b:266ff.) rejection of Karl Barth's revelatory-positivist response to the demands Heinrich Scholz had made of systematic theology, makes him reject out of hand any authoritarian axiomatic theology that uncritically takes its stand on prepostulated dogmatic certainties. Thus Pannenberg (1973b:271) could state that if the reality of God and His revelation or the liberating act of God through Jesus Christ is to function epistemologically as a preestablished datum in theological theorizing—and thus as a theological premise—theology can no longer be concerned with knowledge or science, but merely with the systematic description or exposition of what might be regarded as the true dogma or proper doctrine of a church.

This reproach by Pannenberg is also directed at a type of theology that regards the questions asked by philosophy of science about the nature and structure of its own statements as unnecessary precisely because, as theology, it claims to be an obedient reflection upon God's revelation. Such a conception of theology, as a theology of faith, contains the destructive potential of founding that which forms its unassailable priority, namely, God and His revelation, on a subjective and irrational venture of faith. If the premises of such a theology are finally exposed to criticism it is, ironically, its very conception of God and revelation that stands exposed as a subjective and arbitrary mental construct.

Pannenberg rightly objects to any such reduction of the object of theology to the religious consciousness of the believer. A so-called direct theological premise in God and His revelation offers no escape from this problem. Barth's confrontation with Scholz's philosophy of science demands has already shown that faith in God's revelation is by no means a self-evident alternative to subjectivism in theology. The theologian who appeals directly to God's Word— whether as Scripture, as an ecclesiastical creed, or as an encounter with Jesus Christ—thus remains fully committed to his own subjective and therefore pretheoretic involvement: a subjective involvement that must play a role even in the structuring of his statements on God's Word.

From the above it becomes clear that, for Pannenberg, creditable theological argument is possible only if one acknowledges that no theologian can formulate meaningful statements without being involved, somehow, with the question of criteria for truth. This is so because theological statements also attempt to be meaningful, valid, and comprehensible, and especially to lay claim to truth. This implies, however, that theological statements claim to be testable in principle, even if it does not imply that they must be confined to a specific form of testing (Pannenberg, 1973b:277). For Pannenberg, then, the fact that theological statements claim to be true and therefore (logically) try to exclude untruth implies that such statements must also come within the scope of logical criteria. This directly implies the untenability of any revelatory-positivist position.

This preliminary outline of Pannenberg's criteria for scientifically creditable theological statements shows clearly his intense interest in a type of theological theorizing that would transcend a merely confirmatory, uncritical Christian exegesis. For Pannenberg the concept of hypothesis belongs in this context. Pannenberg (1980:171) sees hypotheses as only those assertions that, as statements on a particular issue, are distinguishable from the issue as such. As he put it: in terms of linguistic analysis, any assertion on something may be seen as a hypothesis, since the logical structure of any assertion is in itself hypothetical.

The hypothetical nature of assertions implies the possibility that a given one may be true or false, and thus also the possibility of checking or testing. Pannenberg (1974:31) maintains that logical positivism was quite correct on this point, except, of course, in its one-sided restriction of examination to a particular type of test, namely, that of sensory observation. It remains true, however, that an assertion which cannot be tested, at least in principle, cannot be a valid assertion on something else.

Theological statements, too—and even statements of faith—are not merely expressions of a certain religious commitment; they contain an element of assertion or reference, which is needed to make such a commitment possible. Even the simple assertion *I believe* makes sense only if there is Someone to believe in. In my view Pannenberg is therefore justified in concluding that, in this sense, all statements of faith have a cognitive core. For Pannenberg it is clear that all theological statements and even pretheological statements of faith must be seen as hypotheses if they are to be taken seriously as assertions, rather than the merely emotive statements of the speaker.

It must also be noted that Pannenberg, in his use of the term *hypothesis* for both theological statements and assertions of faith, is by no means limiting the certainty expressed in statements of faith, nor is he reducing the term to uncertainty. His concern is the structure of a religious or theological statement, rather than the religious commitment in the intention behind such statements. Of course, the person making the statements is not always aware of their hypothetical and provisional structure, since he or she is obviously—also in spontaneous religious statements—seeking correspondence with a particular object. That religious and theological statements made about something are distinct from the person making them implies that the correspondence or truth sought through such statements can not only be held to be true but can in fact also be questioned. Especially in our religious statements—as Pannenberg rightly points out—we are seldom aware of that problematic quality, and it is only on the level of theological reflection that it is often identified thematically and as a definitive problem.

As assertions, and therefore as hypotheses, theological statements about God must, in Pannenberg's view, be logically accessible to some form of rationally responsible testing. And it is in this context that Pannenberg returns to the so-called minimum demands Heinrich Scholz (cf. 1971:221ff.) had put to Karl Barth in 1931. Although that debate has become dated, and although Scholz was arguing on the basis of a positivist unitary ideal for science which would no longer be accepted unquestioningly in contemporary philosophy of science, Pannenberg (1973:329) still finds in Scholz's minimum demands the essential criteria a theological statement would have to meet in order to qualify for scientific credibility. Pannenberg's own development of a philosophical model on the basis of the nature of systematic theology may be seen wholly as an attempt to meet Scholz's demands for theology. Our discussion of Karl Barth's response to a positivist concept of science has shown that the minimum demands Scholz put to theology—as to any other science—if it is to qualify for scientific status are in themselves founded in the logical structure of assertions. Those minimum demands may be summed up again briefly:

1. *the demand of assertiveness and irrefutability:* this is met if a statement is cognitive in nature; in other words, if in claiming that something is true it not only seeks correspondence with what is asserted, but at the same time attempts logically to exclude untruth about its subject.

2. *the demand of coherence:* this minimum criterion demands that any science be directed toward a definitive and coherent object-field—one that must be distinguishable from statements made about it. This follows logically from the hypothetical nature of assertions and implies, furthermore, that various assertions may relate to the same subject. It ought to be clear that this postulate of coherence ultimately forms the basis of Scholz's first criterion, namely, the minimum demand of irrefutability.

3. *the demand of testability:* for Scholz (and also for Pannenberg) this demand follows logically on the preceding ones. If a statement as an assertion constitutes a hypothesis about a certain object-field, it may either hit or miss that object, thus being either true or false. And it should then be possible to demonstrate convincingly, and therefore to test, its claim to truth.

Pannenberg (1974:33) points out rightly that Scholz's three minimum demands merely spell out what is already implied in the logical nature of assertions. The implications of the logical structure of assertions does not, of course, make this an easy task for systematic theology (as was demonstrated by Karl Barth's response to Scholz's demands), precisely because of its commitment to an object as unique as God and His revelation. Yet Pannenberg maintains— rightly—that unless systematic theology would uncritically refrain from any self-criticism, it must examine Scholz's demands more closely. This is important especially because these demands of philosophy of science clearly subject to examination what is implied in theological statements, namely, that they claim to be not only expressive formulations of subjective religious experiences but also real assertions about God and His revelation—an object-field that theology dare not allow to be reduced to mere mental constructs.

It should now be clear that the debate with philosophy of science has confronted systematic theology with profound difficulties. Even Scholz's second demand, that of a unitary area objectively distinct from our statements about it, poses a major problem to the theologian. If, for example, theology defines the Word of God as its object, how can the theologian be sure that his statements are in fact about God's Word, and not merely about a human expression of a supposedly divine Word? Besides, if theology claims that God Himself must be seen as the object of theology, the difficult problem arises of how God might be seen as a Reality, truly distinct from theological assertions about Him. With Pannenberg, the critical theologian, no longer satisfied with an ideologically entrenched axiomatic theology, is then confronted with an unavoidable question: Whether in our time the concept of God is in itself still an accurate depiction of reality or has become a fiction.

Given the logical implications of assertions, as pointed out by Scholz, the questions that philosophy of science has asked about the status of theological statements must culminate in the question of the object of systematic theology. And at this point the question whether theology has an object leads almost naturally to the question of the testability of theological assertions, which for Pannenberg means testability of the claims to truth in theological statements.

Pannenberg (1973b:34) rightly suggests that this question confronts the theologian with the most rigorous demand of all. Conscious of Bartley and Albert's stringently rationalistic criticism, he maintains that the systematic theologian dare not evade this most stringent of all philosophy of science demands by retreating to an irrational religious commitment. Any such immunization of theological premises against criticism must ultimately rebound on systematic theologians with redoubled force, since the very statements they make could then no longer be taken seriously.

The Object of Theology: God as Problem

In reply to Scholz's question about a specific and coherent object-field for theology, Pannenberg (1973b:299-300) could answer without hesitation: Theology is the science of God. In fact, Christian faith obviously depends entirely on God's reality, and therefore no systematic theology could be satisfied with regarding itself as a limited, narrow science of Christianity; to Pannenberg this would be unacceptable in terms of both religious and cultural history. Systematic theology cannot evade the question of the implications of its statements—that God reveals Himself as reality and as such forms the object of theology. It must examine the truth of these statements precisely because they are hypotheses. In view of the universal implications of the concept of God, theology as a science of God has no finally demarcated field of study or object-area. Furthermore, God as object provides the intrinsic structural unity of theology.

A difficult question remains, however: Is it in any way possible to test theological statements, whether as direct or as indirect assertions about God? After all, assertions about God cannot be tested against their immediate object, not only because the reality of God has become so problematic in our time, but also because it would surely contradict God's divinity if He became a present object, accessible to human scrutiny. Clearly, assertions about God cannot be tested against their implied object.

Given the universal implications of the concept of God and the logical implications of the hypothetical structure of assertions, Pannenberg sees clearly that the question of God's reality, and thus also the question of the truth of Christianity, can be posed only within the broader framework of a science having as its theme not only Christianity or the Christian faith but the reality of God Himself. For Pannenberg (1973b:229) this becomes possible in the context of a theology of religions that transcends the narrower bounds of theology as the science of Christianity. Therefore any theologian sensitive to the questions asked by contemporary philosophy of science realizes not only that the concept of God forms the thematic focus of all his inquiries but that God, as a problematic concept, has in fact become the object of a wider critical theology (Pannenberg, 1973b:301).

In Pannenberg's view, a theological science defining God as its problem concept is the counterpart to a dogmatic, axiomatic theology that adopts the reality of God and His revelation as its unproblematic premise. It is clear that Pannenberg, in his formulation of such a premise for systematic theology, and in his identifying an object for systematic theology, consistently takes serious note of Bartley and Albert's critical-rationalist criticism of any subjectivistic, fideistic religious commitment. The critical question that must be put to Pannenberg even at this stage is whether he is convinced that making God as a problem the premise for theology really meets the criticism of critical rationalism. In my view—and this will have to be demonstrated—what we have here is, rather, a concession to Bartley and Albert's criticism (especially to Bartley's commitment to noncommitment): a concession that not only fails to solve the problem of a fideistic axiomatic theology, but also fails ultimately to confront the vital question of the role of the theologian's subjectivity (his ultimate commitment and its theorization) in the theorizing of his theological reflection. These problems play a crucial role in the development of Pannenberg's model for theology and can, in my view, be referred directly to the conflicting influences of critical rationalism and Kuhnian elements in his thought.

We have seen that, for Pannenberg, the conception of God as object of theology links directly with the problematic role of the concept of God in our wider experiential world. For him—at least in the first, broad phase of his theology—God can therefore be the object of theology only as a problem, not as an established datum. But can this problematic concept of God be defined more closely, or does it remain an abstract hypothesis in theology, untestable against the object of its statements? According to Pannenberg, that concept can be defined more closely. The fact that reality—if God is indeed really God—is totally dependent on God is, after all, a minimum requirement for the concept of God. For that reason Pannenberg can give more content to the hypothesis of God, maintaining that if God is real, He must be the all-determinant reality. And although the concept of God can in itself not be tested or verified directly against its object, it is in fact possible to assess that concept in terms of its own implications. Thus the concept of God, which as a hypothesis includes the idea of God as an all-determinant reality, now also becomes testable by its implications for our experience of reality (Pannenberg, 1973b:302).

In Pannenberg's view, the concept of God that would ultimately be most successful and solve most problems in the meaningful integration of human experience would be the one that had shown itself to be true in a valid manner. Assertions about God are therefore testable by their implications for our experience and our understanding of reality. Such assertions are testable by whether their content does indeed give maximal sense and meaning to our present, finite reality. If that were true, it would imply that nothing in our finite reality can be fully understood outside its relationship to the living God. Obversely, one might expect this implied divine reality to have opened up a much more profound understanding of all that exists than would have been possible without it.

To the extent that both these demands could be met, Pannenberg maintains, one might speak of a validation or checking of theological statements.

That verification is done not by criteria alien to the concept of God, but through a kind of proof provided by God Himself. But since our surrounding reality is incomplete and unrefined, and since our experience of it is tentative and ambivalent, the concept of God remains, in terms of philosophy of science, a mere hypothesis. In view of the finite and tentative nature of our theological choices, the concept of God can never be finally verified by our experience of ourselves and of the world.

Pannenberg (1974:36) realizes, of course, that this raises a vital question: How can total reality, as implied in the concept of God, provide a truly practical criterion for the (provisional) testing of theological statements? Whereas Ancient Philosophy attempted to understand the totality of all finite reality as cosmos, and to conclude back from that to the ground or *arché* of this totality, our present experience of reality as a whole is always unfinished and incomplete; so that the sum total of what we experience as reality is by no means the true whole.

And yet, Pannenberg (1974:36) maintains, we can never abandon the (regulatory) thought of an ultimate, all-encompassing whole, because any experience has meaning only in relation to the larger whole to which it belongs. Therefore the idea of an all-encompassing whole reaches out beyond the as yet finite and not fully present reality to a larger whole that would eventually embrace it. For Pannenberg, this as yet only anticipated total meaning of reality is already part of every individual experience, but it becomes explicit, visible, or thematic only in our religious experiences. It is in fact in mankind's religious experiences, and thus in religion(s), that one confronts the question of the basic meaning of one's being.

If, therefore, Pannenberg were asked which experiences indirectly implied God—as a problem—in order that those experiences might be seen as traces of God's presence in our reality, he would reply: all experiences (Pannenberg, 1973b:304). If God is truly God, and therefore to be seen as the all-determinant reality, all man's experiences of himself and of reality must ultimately relate to Him, whether directly or indirectly. And if God is to be seen as the all-determinant reality, and theology as the science of that God, it follows logically for Pannenberg that theology is initially possible only as the wider science of religions. As the science specifically of Christianity, theology is ultimately possible only as a particularized segment, a kind of second phase, of such a universal science of God. This brings us to the essence of Pannenberg's thesis: since in our time access to the concept of God is no longer direct and self-evident, it can be achieved only indirectly, through one's self-concept and one's experiential relationship with reality.

In response to Heinrich Scholz's demand of testability, Pannenberg (1974:36) could therefore argue that the testing or checking of theological statements would have to be done in the context of the historical religions and the history of their development. For it is precisely in the religions that we find an explicit anticipation of the integrated, meaningful totality by which the truth of theological statements ought to be tested. Equally important, moreover, is that in the very changes in religions throughout history one already finds the factual culmination of that which will ultimately culminate in the testing of theological statements. The statements of a religious tradition are practically measured by whether they offer a truly meaningful integration of reality as experienced by believers themselves. If they do not, the statements, concepts, and conventions of that tradition are amended or even replaced by new mental constructs.

In a theology of religions, assertions about God are tested by people's everyday experiences and understanding of them. And in a critical theology of religions the uniqueness and particularity of the theologian's own religious experience would, according to Pannenberg, have to be examined in relation to other religions. By the same token, one would have to ask, considering the changes within one's own religious tradition (for instance, in the history of Christianity), to what extent that religious tradition had succeeded not only in absorbing but also in anticipating shifts in people's experience of reality, so that it might continue to integrate most meaningfully people's experiences and understanding. In view of the infinite nature of reality and the limitations of all human knowledge, a religion can offer hope for the unknown future only if it can achieve that integration.

By this means Pannenberg sought to develop a problem field within which theological statements might be evaluated (hence the so-called context of justification of theology). Assertions about God (for instance, about God as the creator) may therefore, on the one hand, be measured by the handed-down ideas that have accumulated within a certain religious doctrine of creation, and on the other hand these assertions may be tested against the problems confronting such inherited concepts (such as the doctrine of creation) in terms of the natural sciences and philosophy of science of our time.

Seen like this, statements about God can ultimately be measured only by the implications such a concept of God has for man's meaningful experience of himself and of the world. For theology, the area in which to do so is, above all, the religions, since religious experiences provide us with an answer to the question of the meaning of life, and thus to the question of a meaningful integration of experience of oneself and of the world.[3] If such a concept of God is

---

3. For Pannenberg it is clear why there has been and still is such a close bond between philosophy and theology. Philosophical questions, too, are not directed merely at some particular being or narrowly defined area of reality, but are essentially directed at reality as such. This inevitably implies the question: What is there in this reality that gives it its coherent unity? And this is where the question of God also arises for philosophy, precisely because that question is aimed at discovering the determinant of total reality. For philosophy, however, the question of God is an ultimate question; philosophy concerns itself with numerous other themes and can therefore postpone or even evade (albeit with inherent contradictions) the question of God. In theology, however, the theme of total reality is subservient to the concept of God's reality, inasmuch as God alone is conceivable as the all-determinant reality (Pannenberg, 1973b:305-306).

realized successfully, Pannenberg (1973b:313) maintains, it must also be seen as a self-manifestation of God, because the idea of God as an all-determinant reality would surely be contradicted if He were to become accessible by any means but Himself.

I would like to sum up Pannenberg's rather theoretic—even complicated—thoughts on the development of theology as a science of God:

1. Theology can be a science of God only indirectly, through people's experiences of God and of religion in the light of reality as a whole.
2. Total reality, however, does not yet exist in its final form; it is still an incomplete process and therefore accessible only through the subjectivity of mankind's religious experience as an anticipation of that totality.
3. The anticipatory character of religious experiences can ultimately be recognized as a manifestation of divine reality. Individual religious experiences, however, must always be seen in relation to the historical religions and are relevant only in terms of that intersubjective relationship.
4. In its first phase, therefore, theology as the science of God is possible only as the science of historical religions.
5. Christian theology becomes possible only in the next phase, as the science of the Christian religion or of Christianity.

For Wolfhart Pannenberg (1973b:317), this laborious road has one especially important implication: theology becomes truly the science of Christianity only if founded upon a more broadly conceived science of God. In practice, however, and in certain situations, theology may only function as the science of Christianity. To Pannenberg this is acceptable only if the problematic question of God and the questions asked by philosophy of science about the nature, structure, and implications of theological statements are not, for example, ideologically barricaded against critical discussion but remain in principle, at least as questions, relevant and open to discussion.[4]

The influence of Bartley's criticism and pointed rejection of any retreat to commitment is clearly evident in Pannenberg's development of his own conceptual model. For Pannenberg, divine revelation cannot be preannexed by any particular religion, to be set up against others as the only true one. He could therefore say (Pannenberg, 1973b:322) that only a religious option that had in advance immunized itself against all critical reflection could unproblematically identify God's revelation in its own religious tradition, to set it up as an absolute against all other traditions.

This brings us to the most problematic element of Pannenberg's theological thought. Although he shared Kuhn's view of the paradigmatic determination of our thought, he remains caught up in the critical-rationalist demand for a most

---

4. Pannenberg's spiritual affinity with the earlier thought of Ernst Troeltsch is here clearly evident. Cf. also Pannenberg, 1973b:319.

specific type of noncommitment in the evaluation of theories. Ultimately, this provides no means of thematizing, and even less of resolving, the problem of the role of the professing theologian's subjective religious commitment.

On this point Pannenberg (1973b:323) concedes that theology, like all other sciences, does not approach its object without presuppositions or values, as a kind of tabula rasa. Theologians obviously tackle their subject with a certain interest, which also implies opinions and presuppositions, that may relate to the religious communities to which they belong. They may even be Christians, which may either stimulate questioning or act as a restraint on the unbiased evaluation of their object and their own tradition.

Against this background, Pannenberg (1973b:323) could say that theologians' subjective religious commitment may fall in the context of discovery, but definitely not in the context of justification. His conception of discovery is the all-inclusive historicosociological framework that produces a certain science; the context of justification, however, is the theoretic framework within which specific criteria have an explanatory and evaluatory function in respect of theological statements. Confusing the two contexts, for example, by converting a personal religious commitment into the premise for rational argument— and at the same time claiming intersubjective validity for that argument—is in Pannenberg's view a fatal mistake.

This attempt by Pannenberg to claim objective criteria for a scientific theology's context of justification is, on the one hand, a clear echo of Bartley's (1962:217) "people can be engaged without being committed," and thus reveals the lasting effect of critical rationalism on the structure of Pannenberg's thought. Nevertheless, Pannenberg himself had earlier pointed out that this would make critical rationalism untrue to its own principles: basic or objective criteria in terms of which testing—and therefore falsification—becomes possible must surely be testable intersubjectively, according to the principles of critical rationalism. This is why it also became clear that, with Popper, the old positivist ideal of value-free, objective knowledge had been twisted into intersubjective correspondence. In critical rationalism, therefore, objectivity ultimately becomes a conventional matter, no longer dependent on so-called a-theoretic facts. In fact, Pannenberg pointed out that the purportedly objective basic propositions of critical rationalism could be seen as conventions precisely because of their intersubjective determination. He also pointed out (1973b:54ff.) that the implications of that determination made it impossible to draw such sharp critical-rationalistic distinctions between scientific and metaphysical statements.

Thus Pannenberg concedes not only that the nature and origins of scientific statements are rooted in the sociocultural context of the individual researcher (the context of discovery), but that scientific statements as such (the context of justification) are founded indirectly on general worldviews. In my view this is not merely a matter of philosophy and/or religion; ultimately such statements are also deeply rooted in the scientist's subjective religious commitment.

Therefore, in attempting to separate the theologian's subjective commitment from the theoretic context of justification, Pannenberg is not merely abandoning Kuhn's concept of paradigm-articulation, for which he had formerly opted and which now confronts his own demand for a context of justification without personal commitments; he is also evading the truly problematic question—not the question of how the theologian's subjective commitment may be temporarily suspended, but the question of how the theorizing implied by that religious commitment may be laid bare and accounted for, precisely to prevent its becoming an uncritical and irrational immunization tactic in critical reasoning.

But to return to Pannenberg's argument: in the context of justification of theology as a science of God, the unique and special character of Christianity and its conception of truth must become problematic, even if theologians may be subjectively convinced that the truth and uniqueness of Christian faith will eventually emerge from their theological inquiries. Apart from the problems arising—as we have seen—from this line in Pannenberg's thought, it is at least clear that he is consciously attempting to abandon any form of confessional or fideist theology. For Pannenberg, a specific Christian theology cannot be founded merely on recourse to specifically Christian commitments, any more than a specifically confessional theology can be founded merely on certain immutable confessional traditions.

Here Pannenberg would be obliged to take into account the radical differences that might be shown to exist between the problems posed by a confessional tradition elevated, as a context of justification, into an authoritarian critical structure, and the consciously methodological problem of accounting critically for the theological theorizing that has already established itself in the theologian's own religious commitment. To put it differently: a pretheoretic commitment cannot simply be equated with irrational religious choices. On the contrary, the form in which that commitment manifests itself in religious statements and viewpoints must be exposed to critical argument. If that is done, the question of the relationship between our religious statements and theological statements again becomes the focus of our inquiry. Only thus will it eventually become clear that a personal religious commitment does not necessarily—to answer Bartley and Pannenberg—imply unscientific or irrational thought.

In his reaction to the way the concept of revelation is formulated and abused in most forms of confessional theology, as immunization against criticism, Pannenberg tries to follow the wider program of a comparative theology of religions. He even maintains (1973b:326) that such a theology is ultimately based on the tradition of biblical Christianity. A definitive, final justification of theological statements is unattainable, however, and is in any event sharply distinct from the nature of pretheoretic religious certainty. Nevertheless, a provisional justification of theological hypotheses may be attained inasmuch as they may lend—at least provisionally—maximal meaning and clarity to our experiences. In my view, however, that provisional justification of theological statements and theories is possible only if we can think from a paradigm that enables us to handle such criteria. This may also be founded on a paradigm choice that cannot be suspended temporarily and theoretically but refers consciously to a critically responsible basic conviction or religious commitment.

The Scientific Nature of Theological Reflection: Critical Evaluation

So far we have seen what Wolfhart Pannenberg means by theology as the science of God, and how, in the context of the questions posed by philosophy of science, he has tried to find answers to Heinrich Scholz's three minimum demands for theological scientific thought. From the above it has become clear that theological science inevitably develops in two phases: first as a broader theology of religions, which may form a basis for the second phase, its development into a specifically Christian theology as the science of Christianity.

For Pannenberg, our Western conception of theology mainly as such a special theology of Christianity is attributable purely to extrascientific interests, such as the broader community's piety for the Christian faith, the influence of churches on the training of ministers, and the dominant interest of theologians in directing theological questions toward the clarification of their own faith. Pannenberg (1973b:327) also makes the point that such a concentration on Christian theology can maintain its credibility only if it takes into account that the scientific thematics of theology embraces much more. If, then, systematic theology restricts itself to the theology of Christianity as the hermeneutics of Christian revelation, it should be borne in mind that one vital decision—on the truth and the absolute character of Christian faith—has already been made provisionally, an assumption that may become a recurring problem in the broader methodological structure of theology.

Pannenberg himself opts for a wider theological course in which the actual theme of theology—God and His revelation—is by no means abandoned but is in fact consciously and critically chosen as a means of deconfessionalizing theology. What remains problematic is that in this process of deconfessionalizing, Pannenberg, by setting up an uncommitted and objective theoretic framework as the context for a scientific theology of religions, has still not examined the relationship between that context and the life and religious commitment of the individual theologian—a relationship in which deconfessionalizing can by no means, not even theoretically, simply be assumed.

Pannenberg (1973b:328) maintains, furthermore, that a specific theology of Christianity—as practiced by most Christian theologians—demands at least a sound theoretic basis in fundamental theology, which would then determine the typical and unique character of Christian revelation. Only through the identification of the specifically Christian in Christian faith does the reasoning of such a special theology of Christianity become accessible to and, to some extent, testable by others. That, according to Pannenberg, is what Heinrich Scholz demanded of Barth when he called for an identifiable criterion for the evangelical in an evangelical theology. Obviously—and here Pannenberg is right—the contents of such a criterion would remain contentious. That does not, however, affect its function, namely, to make the reasoning and theorizing of a certain Christian theological model accessible and acceptable to others as well.

For this reason, Pannenberg maintained, a creditable Christian theology could never function on the basis of presupposed confessional contrasts between Christian churches but should have an essentially ecumenical direction. A Christian theology must, for example, always function hermeneutically through the words and events of Holy Scripture, never dogmatically from confession.

With regard to the two essential phases of systematic theology, Pannenberg (1973b:330) could therefore make the following points: *Theology* focuses on the historical religions and tries to ascertain to what extent the reality of God, as the all-determinant reality, is revealed in their traditions. *Christian theology* is directed at its own particular tradition, but with the same aim. In this process—which Pannenberg also calls the hermeneutics of Christian revelation—theology must, however, constantly remain aware of and take into account the relationship between Christianity and other religions in the process of religious history.

And when—as claimed in theology's hypothetical statements—God's reality manifests itself as the all-determinant reality in finite reality through our experiences of ourselves and of the world, Pannenberg sees in it the way to answer Scholz's demand of testability. Scholz had already seen that this demand in fact constituted theology's major problem, since the demand for testability of theological statements stood in sharp contrast to the authority of God, which theology had always found in Holy Scripture and which had related directly to ecclesiastical doctrine.

God's authority, however, does not come to us so unproblematically through Scripture or church doctrine, precisely because our conceptualizing and theorizing are peculiar to our conceptions of Scripture and doctrine. Therefore Pannenberg maintains that the question of that authority cannot be answered uncritically and dogmatically; in theology—and therefore also in Christian theology—it must be treated as problematic. If theology failed to do that, it would no longer be able to demonstrate convincingly that its statements actually constituted assertions about reality, distinct from the theologian making them. Such a theological language would then be no more than the expression of a specific religious thinker's subjective convictions and choices.

In my view that would remain true even if such convictions and choices were supported by an established tradition or paradigm. Insight into the fallible and provisional nature of theology leads logically to insight into the human nature of our conceptions of Holy Scripture. For Pannenberg, the authority of Scripture—and thus our conception of Scripture as God's Word—therefore becomes in itself an assertion of which the contents must remain open to verification. The demand for testability of theological statements cannot be evaded, since testability is implied in the logical structure of assertions about an object.

Although, as we have seen, theological statements cannot be tested directly against their object, statements about God as all-determinant reality can nevertheless be evaluated indirectly in terms of our experiences of ourselves and the world. Not only does this indirect testing become the key to understanding the scientific rationality of theology (Pannenberg, 1973b:335), but it is also clear that faith and religious experience provide Pannenberg with an experiential and therefore an empirical basis for theological science (Pannenberg, 1980:176). This important element of Pannenberg's thought could also be formulated as follows: theological statements become provisionally testable through their experiential referents, and thus through their capacity for providing meaningful explanations within the scope of a larger paradigmatic context.

If asked what that experience comprised, Pannenberg would answer that it was not confined primarily to specifically religious or even to Christian experience but included people's more general everyday experiences—and thus the ultimately essential relationship between such experiences and religious experience (Pannenberg, 1980:176). Only if the Christian religious awareness bore a positive relationship to reality could it also become the premise for significance in the contents of experience, by positively attributing normal, everyday experiences to that God toward whom our Christian religious expectations are directed. In my view we can in principle agree with Pannenberg on this point, but then only if he conceded that attributing significance to human experiences in itself implied a commitment, which might not be rationally explicable but of which the pretheoretic basis could in fact be exposed by argument and dedogmatizing to achieve eventually an evaluation of that commitment. This insight, however, that the sources of theological theorizing may be traced to the way believers experience their reality, rules out the structuring of a systematic-theological context of justification (as Pannenberg demanded under the influence of critical rationalism) outside the theologian's religious commitment. From the above it will follow that the theologian's personal commitment, if rightly understood and credibly accounted for in terms of philosophy of science, need not stand in the way of a scientifically acceptable model of rationality.

Against this background, Pannenberg could claim that theological statements, like other scientific ones, belonged in the framework of clearly definable theoretic contexts or paradigms. It also follows that theology ought to devote itself to the explicitly systematic and deliberate designing of theoretic models. By their nature such models—and statements about them— already have a hypothetical quality. Pannenberg maintains rightly that every theological statement ultimately gains a multilayered, hypothetical structure. Whereas normal, everyday experiences anticipate reality's total significance only implicitly, religious experiences (and thus also statements of faith) imply an explicit awareness of that total significance, be it ever so indirectly. The theologians' critical statements on what claims to be the manifestation of God in our religious experiences are already hypotheses of the third order: for Pannenberg (1973b:336), theological statements are, therefore, hypotheses on hypotheses on hypotheses.

If questioned about the testing of such hypotheses, Pannenberg (1973b:338)—despite his earlier critical-rationalistic demand for an uncommitted context of justification for theology as a science of God—can say with Kuhn that deciding whether a particular statement has been tested depends on the paradigm from which that statement is judged. In contrast to logical positivism's demand of verification and critical rationalism's demand of falsification, Pannenberg therefore sides with Kuhn in opting for a theory's capacity for solving particular problems as effectively and meaningfully as possible. In this regard, hermeneutical and natural science theories are comparable in all respects (Pannenberg, 1973b:339). In Pannenberg's view, a theory—also one about God—has proved itself if it has succeeded in maximally solving and meaningfully integrating problematic data and mankind's experiences of reality.

In theology, as in philosophy, one finds what Kuhn has called paradigm-precisioning. In theology, however, the totality of experienced reality is examined in terms of God's reality, in such a way that the question arises of how awareness of that reality has emerged in the history of religious experiences. Apart from theology's links with philosophy, the historicity of religious experience as a theological datum also gives it direct ties with historical science. For Pannenberg, the evaluation or testing of theological statements is therefore possible only with direct reference to those two disciplines. Theological statements are, however, concerned not only with specific religious experiences and historical phenomena but also with the way those phenomena—for instance, texts or documents, like Holy Scripture in Christian theology—reveal God as an all-determinant reality embracing not only the past but also the present and the future. Therefore theologians, when critically examining a certain historical event or text, are in fact asking to what extent it may illuminate and integrate their own experience of reality, in order to establish—also for our time—the claim to truth in particular statements.

We have thus seen that, philosophically, theological theories imply hypotheses and ought to be judged by the same criteria as philosophical statements. Theological theories, however, always relate philosophical perspectives to a religious dimension of human experience, and theology's examination of the religious dimension in history creates a bond between theological statements and historical and hermeneutical criteria (Pannenberg, 1973b:344), especially because such reflection implies the process of tradition in specific religious experiences. Pannenberg states rightly that Christian religion, too, constitutes such a comprehensive complex of traditions. It is as a traditional process, therefore, and not as a system of doctrine and myths, that Christianity must become the object of inquiry.

Apart from the influences of Heinrich Scholz, of critical rationalism, and of Thomas Kuhn, we also note the influence of H.-G. Gadamer's hermeneutics on the development of Pannenberg's theological concepts. For Gadamer, the historicity that plays such a central role in Pannenberg's thought implies the presence of the past through tradition, and the manifestation of the past in the present through tradition must be understood hermeneutically as a merging of horizons in which mankind ultimately comes to recognize itself.

Whereas theological science has to reckon with philosophical, hermeneutical, and historical criteria, Pannenberg identifies a further cluster of criteria in the history of theological theorizing as such and in the degree of problem-consciousness attained through it (Pannenberg, 1973b:345-346). Through interpretation and criticism, theological theorizing must be directed at both the tradition and the conceptual and life-forms of its own time, if it would eventually confront contemporary problem-consciousness with the current truth and relevance of the tradition.

In the light of all relevant criteria, Pannenberg therefore concludes, theological statements are ultimately fully open to evaluation. But since we are not yet able to attain a total grasp of our reality we are also not able to form a final assessment of theological hypotheses. Traditional statements, however, like reformulated contemporary theological ones, can prove themselves provisionally by being capable of revealing the overall sense of our experiences of reality more meaningfully, and thus more convincingly and illuminatingly, than other traditions or statements.

In Pannenberg's view, the very concept of God becomes justifiable if it integrates and illuminates someone's view of life in such a way that all that person's experiences gain maximal meaning. And for Pannenberg this is a question neither of merely irrational, existential religious certainty, nor of a final, logical, theoretic certainty. Such a maximal gain in meaning does, however, enable one to demonstrate provisionally to what extent theological assertions may be held to be true or untrue.

Therefore Pannenberg (1973b:348) could arrive at the following criteria for checking theological theories. Theological hypotheses can be considered unsound if:

1. They claim to be hypotheses on the totality of the Israelite-Christian faith, yet are not demonstrably successful formulations of the true implications of biblical tradition.
2. They do not reveal an involvement in the totality of reality, thus also failing to relate to the present status of philosophical problem-consciousness.
3. They do not succeed in integrating experience, especially if they make no attempt to give maximal meaning to human experiences.
4. Their capacity for meaningful illumination and problem solving has not yet reached the level of the most recent theological problem-consciousness, and if they make no attempt to transcend the limits of previous theological theories.

I should like to suggest positive forms for these four criteria, which Pannenberg offered as checks and therefore as the context of justification:

1. Theological statements must demonstrably and testably express the essence of the biblical message.
2. Theological statements must emanate from a universally conceptualized theology, must examine the relationship between God and reality, and must therefore correlate closely with the level of problem-consciousness in modern philosophy and philosophy of science.
3. Theological statements must integrate human experiences as meaningfully as possible.
4. Theological statements must be fully cognitive of the status of problem-consciousness in modern theology.

In Pannenberg's formal definition of the crucial problem of the scientific status and identity of systematic theology he has in my view not only emphasized the universal nature of theological thematics but at the same time shown irrefutably that theology has a commitment to rationality—a commitment for the sake of the awareness of truth in Christian faith.

For this reason alone one values Pannenberg's resumption of theology's debate with philosophy of science. His acute recognition of the fact that Scholz's minimum demands are still relevant to inquiries into the nature of theological statements also shows that he is prepared, for the sake of intellectual integrity, to hazard the existence and identity of his own field of study by sincerely questioning the scientific quality of theology. Closely linked with that sincerity is the way Pannenberg attempts to show—rightly—that systematic theology is concerned with reality as a whole, as accessible through our everyday and religious experiences. Thus reality as a whole is in all senses related to God, and Pannenberg rightly resists any diminution of that concern with reality in modern theology.

In reply to our thematic questions about the nature, structure, origins, object, and testability of theological statements, Pannenberg thus opts for a rationality model that shows strong correspondences with Popper's critical rationalism and Kuhn's paradigm theory. The theological model developed by him, however, shows clear signs of his close ties with critical rationalism. The principal consequence of that bond is that Pannenberg sees the concept of God as a hypothesis that has to be justified; a justification, however, that—under Kuhn's influence—is bound up with its capacity for meaningful explanation and problem solving.

Our discussion has also shown that Pannenberg, in opting for a rationality model that had to transcend the limits of critical rationalism, could not escape having his thought structured by critical rationalism. These two clear lines remain irreconcilable in Pannenberg's thought: on the one hand, the critical-rationalistic demand for an uncommitted, areligious, and objective context of justification for theology; and, on the other, Kuhn's conviction that the so-called objectively scientific criteria are paradigmatically determined and as such rooted in the researcher's sociocultural context. We have seen repeatedly that Pannenberg clearly defined but failed to resolve the problem of a fideistic axiomatic theology, because he failed to face the crucial question of the theologian's personal commitment and the theorizing implicit in it.

Pannenberg's concession to critical rationalism—by adopting a stand in which God's existence is made a problem in philosophy of science—is in itself highly problematic. While writing about God as a problem in the context of a theology of religions, he could also (from the Christian tradition!) cite 1 John 4:11, that no one had ever seen God. One might ask not only whether Pannenberg's own pretheoretic religious commitment remains consistently parenthetical, as demanded by his critical-rationalist premises, but also whether he does not perhaps after all—given the implications of his own unacknowledged commitment here—consistently maintain a veiled Christian concept of God.[5] A rationally justified common concept of God (for various religions) is in fact a critical-rationalistic remnant in his thought, irreconcilable with his ultimate attempt to structure that thought in Kuhnian terms.

This highlights yet again the crucial problem of Pannenberg's debate with philosophy of science. His reduction of God, the object of theology, to a hypothetical, all-determinant reality in terms of philosophy of science implies clearly that our theological statements must ultimately be hypotheses on hypotheses on hypotheses. Nowhere in his *Wissenschaftstheorie* does Pannenberg question the relationship between this theoretically admissible datum and the fact that, for the believing theologian, God does exist and is the object of faith.

The reason for that failure can lie only in the critical-rationalistic demand for noncommitment, which engages Pannenberg throughout the development of his conceptual model. Despite a so-called areligious context of justi-

---

5. Cf. also H. Hempelmann, 1980:172; and, provisionally, van Huyssteen, 1970:214-243.

fication, Pannenberg's own religious commitment intrudes repeatedly into this context of justification. This problem permeates the very structure of, and raises questions about, his entire theology of religions.

Pannenberg's criterion for the eventual justification of a concept of God centers on the question whether our experience of that concept does indeed reveal God as the all-determinant reality. One might well ask whether the idea of God as the all-determinant reality is not in itself oriented toward Christianity. If that is the case, one could hardly speak of justifying the concept of God (Hempelmann, 1980:173). Finally, Hans Albert (1982:162), too, is justified in stating that anyone who thus anticipates reality as total meaning has already opted for theological interpretation. The ambivalence in Pannenberg's thought lies in his failure, on the one hand, to admit openly that theological interpretation based on personal commitment does not necessarily imply unscientific thought or irrationality, while on the other hand, to cling to the critical-rationalistic demand for an areligious context of justification—a demand, as he himself has shown, that cannot be sustained in terms of critical-rationalistic criteria, and that has therefore already put a question mark over Popper's distinction between scientific and metaphysical statements.

Instead of consistently pursuing his incisive criticism of critical rationalism, Pannenberg at this point opts for irreconcilable elements from the rationality models of rational criticism as well as Kuhn's paradigm theory. One would like to see Pannenberg critically examining his eventual deliberate choice of the Christian faith—a choice based on rational factors, but not on rational ones alone—and at the same time attempting to show that a commitment to the God of Christianity need also not imply, in terms of philosophy of science, an irrational immunization tactic.

Despite Pannenberg's criticism of this facet of Popper's thought, however, he himself (Pannenberg, 1973b:323) opts for a theology of religions of which the so-called context of justification excludes the theologian's personal religious commitment. To justify that, Pannenberg would have to assume equal levels of thought and reflection in each of the great religions. Attaining such levels, and thus providing for transcultural and transreligious criteria, seems to me an impossible and illusory task. Apart from that, Pannenberg's questioning of the various religions' concepts of reality, as well as his final formulation of criteria for theology (cf. in particular his first criterion: Pannenberg, 1973b:348), clearly reveals his identification with Christianity.[6] His attempt to examine the various religions' truth in terms of a common, transcultural concept of God also contradicts the criteria and implications of Kuhn's paradigm theory, since Kuhn had already pointed out that the incommensurability of paradigms made it impossible to arrive at a valid and creditable judgment of one paradigm on the strength of another.

6. Also H. Hempelmann, 1980:172.

The problem of the theologian's religious commitment and basic convictions thus surfaces once again in Pannenberg's thought, inasmuch as he finds himself compelled to vacillate between the world of faith on the one hand and the world of critical thought on the other. And even his reference to Gadamer's hermeneutical understanding does not always succeed in countering the theoretic alienation that sometimes marks his conceptual model.

Bartley's critical-rationalistic reproach of a retreat to commitment thus exerts a subtle influence throughout Pannenberg's answer to the question of a scientific rationality model for systematic theology. Although Pannenberg does not account for the role of the theologian's personal religious commitment in theological theorizing, his incisive and highly original debate with contemporary philosophy of science enables us to pursue this discussion with greater confidence and credibility.

7

Theology as a Critical-Argumentative Science: Gerhard Sauter

The language of faith is made of precisely the same stuff as our ordinary human language is made of, language as a life-form and as a social reality. There is no special ghetto language of faith.

    E. Schillebeeckx, "The Crisis in the Language of Faith as a Hermeneutical Problem," in *Concilium*, 5/9 (1973):34.

Darum gilt: an ihrem Verhältnis zur Sprache entscheidet sich das Schicksal der Theologie.

    E. Biser, *Theologische Sprachtheorie und Hermeneutik* (Munich: Kosel, 1970):15.

Systematic Theology as an Argumentative Theology

Like Wolfhart Pannenberg, Gerhard Sauter has become well-known in Germany for his concentration on the question of the scientific status of theology. For Sauter (1971a:16), too, it is imperative that the systematic theologian answer affirmatively questions such as the following: Is theology in fact a science? Should it have a place at our universities? Can it maintain its position at universities? At the same time, however, that affirmation of the scientific status, and thus of the rational credibility of theology, should not be founded on mere presumption; Sauter insists on rational proof that theology is scientifically concerned with a creditable, specific pursuit and method. The validity of that method will hinge on the question of the sources of theological knowledge and the medium in which it is conveyed. For Gerhard Sauter (Daecke, 1974a:63), then, the question of the scientific quality and reliability of theological statements will be intimately bound up with the question of methodological progress in theology, and thus ultimately with the question of a specific object area in systematic theology.

In examining the essential nature of systematic theology, Sauter seeks to demonstrate that the professing theologian is capable of rationally responsible, and thus scientific, reflection. This ideal brings Sauter close to Wolfhart Pannenberg, but it will eventually become apparent that their theological models differ both in their points of departure and in their emphases.

Like Pannenberg, Sauter seeks to demonstrate that systematic theology can meet the criteria for a science and yet remain true to its unique object. Therefore—again like Pannenberg—he opts for an argumentative theology rather than an axiomatic one which typically takes its stand on preconceived and untested certainties. For Sauter, too, confrontation with the problems engaging current philosophy of science is the only creditable course for a theology in pursuit of its own theoretic and structural identity. Above all, he has sought to make the results of the present discussion in philosophy of science intratheologically fruitful (cf. Hempelmann, 1980:183). In this context he advocates an argumentative theology with an analytic-theoretic line of thought that might not have the range and comprehensive quality of Pannenberg's model but is equally sincere in its examination of the factors that determine theorizing in systematic theology.

Sauter (1973:9) points out—in my view correctly—that Protestant theology has always been markedly reserved and even hostile in its attitude to the concept of theory. In fact, the unique nature of its object has always led theology to regard any examination of theory as adverse and too abstract for the vital relationship that sustains it. Such a conception of theology is usually founded on the fear that confrontation with philosophy of science might subjugate theology's special and unique character to the criteria of a secular conception of science, alien to revelation.

But Sauter maintains that dialogue with philosophy of science can only be beneficial to systematic theology. It would not only help theology to formulate valid, formally correct, and relevant statements, but would also inspire theologians to examine the scientific status of their own pursuit without reservations. Dialogue with philosophy of science also highlights the essential distinction between scientific and prescientific (everyday) language. That distinction is not only vital to theology but also highly problematic, precisely because it is by no means easy to distinguish between ordinary statements of faith and scientific statements in theology. In consequence of the theologian's religious commitment, the two language modes overlap very easily.

In the context of Sauter's own theological model it is clear, too, that he is not attempting, through a confrontation of systematic theology with philosophy of science, to achieve a superficial modernization of theology. For him that confrontation is above all an attempt to define the scope or significance of theological statements. What he is examining is not only the scope of particular theological statements in relation to their object, and whether they can in fact be seen as hypotheses, but also the testability of theological statements.

His concern is not only the relationship between faith and knowledge, or between experience and revelation, but also the question of the relationship between theology and the other sciences. In his approach to that question, Sauter (1973:13) is not trying to revert to the positivist unitary ideal. Instead of such an artificial unity, contemporary philosophy of science provides a forum in which various and divergent sciences can present their conceptual models, objectives, and methods for examination.

And it is in fact the question of the aim, method, and object of theology that has become highly contentious in our time. What Sauter (1973:21) maintains about dialectical theology is also true of Protestant theology in general: that it is normally taken almost for granted that theology is fundamentally, and not only in its object and method, distinct from other sciences. That position has been and is still founded on the fact that theology's task and mission are bound to the church, which in turn—as a social phenomenon—cannot be related to other social structures. Faced with such an introspective privatization and isolation of theological thematics, theology might draw on philosophy of science to ascertain precisely what science demands of it as regards its methodology, its objectives, and the factors bearing on its theorizing.

To Sauter it is clear that such a critical-argumentative approach offers theology not only control of its methods but also the insight that no science can ever operate without presuppositions. By becoming the theme of theological reflection, the question whether theology is a science becomes fundamental to theology, since it focuses specifically on the principles of theorizing in theology. In facing that question, however, the theologian can never fall back on a purely confessional justification for his conceptual model. On the contrary, the confessional diversity of Christians and their churches ought to serve as a problematic point of departure for theologians (Sauter, 1975b:166).

Five Basic Problems in Theology

We have seen that, for Sauter, the question of the scientific status of theology is a question of the possibility and justification of a specific theological epistemology—one that can also creditably meet the criteria of modern philosophy of science. But the pursuit of a creditable theory for theology in itself confronts the systematic theologian with an acute dilemma: on the one hand, theology's attempt to make lucid and testable statements commits it to rationality; on the other hand, theology, as a science of faith, involves the explication of a highly distinctive and rationally impenetrable conception of truth. This dilemma becomes especially acute when theology is called upon to defend its very exclusive claim to truth—a claim usually in sharp conflict with the demand that no scientific statement or claim be held without its being tested.

As a rule, theology's response to this apologetic dilemma (Sauter, 1973:213) is to argue that whereas nontheological sciences are concerned with present reality and can therefore make statements only on truly objectifiable facts, theology's concern is not a limited object-field but God as the all-encompassing Truth—a truth which, in any event, is not objectifiable. This division of labors, however, leads inevitably to mutual suspicion between theology and the other sciences. This usually means that theology, for its part, can found its sweeping claims to truth only on a subjective choice, and thus on an irrational one—an untested premise of such magnitude that theology must forfeit any claim to scientific status.

Sauter also maintains—in terms that evoke Bartley's *tu quoque* argument—that theology often tries to bridge the dilemma by arguing that the other sciences are no less authoritarian and ideological in their approach; for they too must hold similar untested presuppositions about life and reality. Sauter (1973:214) correctly typifies this difficult problem by pointing out that the mutual suspicion between theology and the other sciences is always premised on a dogmatic distinction between authority and rationality. Faced with these alternatives, theology has little choice but to claim the role of an outsider, a critic of other sciences.

If theology can take its stand on no more than exclusive, authoritarian statements, inaccessible to any testing, it must always be in competition with other sciences—or it must function, at best, as an ancillary worldview following the conclusion of true scientific debate. As Sauter rightly maintains, this dilemma is aggravated by the real possibility that theology, caught in the tension between the alternatives of authority and reality, may eventually vanish from the sciences' field of vision.

Sauter thus warns against an aggressive no from theology to dialogue with philosophy of science as well as a pseudoscientific adjustment of theology to current philosophy of science concerns. In both cases theology would be making an exclusive decision on its identity and then confidently presenting its conclusions, regardless of whether they in fact constitute scientifically creditable results. Theology would even be intensifying the dilemma of rationality versus authority if, on the one hand, it employed current historical, hermeneutical, and linguistic methods while, on the other hand, uncritically and dogmatically ignoring the problem of the nature and quality of theological statements. Not only is that dilemma highly problematic; in subtle and barely discernible forms it is often also implied in the very fact that theology—faced with the alternatives of authority and rationality—is dependent on a tradition whose validity has long been inaccessible to rational explanation, and which is therefore all the more susceptible to authoritarian abuse.

Against this background, Sauter's search for a theological theory is not a matter of self-explication or explaining his own faith; what he is attempting is to examine the validity of theology's statements about its own theory. Only a valid theological theory can save theology from vacillating aimlessly between obscurantism and pseudoscientific fashionability (Sauter, 1973:218).

For Sauter it is also vital that the question of theology's scientific status should not be debated in pure abstraction. It is interesting that on this point Sauter (1973:221-222), unlike Pannenberg, rejects Heinrich Scholz's minimum demands, which he regards as positivist and as dated, seen against the more recent debates in philosophy of science since Popper. In advocating analytic-theoretic reflection Sauter also warns that meaningful theological theorizing would not be possible as long as theologians, as often happens, based their conceptual model on both existential and pseudoscientific premises. It is significant that Sauter also adopts the well-known conceptual distinction that philosophy of science has drawn between the context of discovery and the context of justification in his attempt to establish the position and direction of a theoretic justification for the professing theologian's theological statements.

We shall eventually have to examine precisely how these two contexts are related in Sauter's thought, but at this stage two points are pertinent to that contextual distinction. First, Sauter maintains that theology must distinguish between, on the one hand, the Reality about which theologians make statements and, on the other, the objects or themes of theological language as such. That language is the object of a theory of theology, by means of which it will eventually be possible to describe theological reflection. In terms of philosophy of science, the objectification of theological language is of primary importance. For Sauter, therefore, a theory of theology would first and foremost comprise the criticism and analysis of language. Second, it is clear to Sauter that scientific knowledge originates in and grows inter alia through consensus on the functions and results of research. Consensus affects not only scientific work but also the people dependent on the results of that work. For Sauter, the concept of social commitment plays a crucial role.

One obvious implication of Sauter's stand is that the relationship between the church and theology is vitally important to him (Sauter, 1973:226) in his examination of the nature and scientific status of theology. When he finally faces the question of the specific structure of the contexts of discovery and justification, his conception of the church as a point of orientation for theology plays a decisive role. That conception will eventually enable Sauter to call for analysis of the theorizing hidden behind crucial theological concepts such as revelation, reconciliation, church, history, mankind, and Holy Scripture: a task he identifies correctly as the prerequisite to conceptual clarity in theological theorizing.

In attempting to formulate a theory of theology, Sauter identifies five basic problems directly confronting theology—problems that could raise serious theoretic and structural difficulties if not handled responsibly:

1. The degree to which theologians can truly communicate the Reality on which they make their statements: the question of the rational limits of theology.
2. The describability of theology.
3. The relationship between history and the present: the hermeneutical problem.
4. Theology's capacity for truly creative, innovative thought and creditable problem solving.
5. The object of theology.

(1) For Sauter, the question of the means by which Truth becomes concrete in theology—for instance, how God, as the all-encompassing Reality, may have meaning for our concrete existence—is not merely a hermeneutical problem but also a structural one; for behind that question lies the problem that whereas the theologian speaks of a definitive revelation of God giving meaning to mankind and its history, there seems to be no evidence of that revelation manifesting itself in or coinciding with the course of history.

The degree to which theologians can make truly creditable statements on God is, of course, closely bound up with their own commitment to the Truth they profess. Sauter rightly warns that ethics in science can never be deduced unproblematically from religious commitment; nor can a systematic theological methodology be founded on purely existential grounds. Attempts to do either might lead to the notion that the mere concurrence of like-minded theologians or believers constituted the essence of theology: a kind of intersubjective consensus that might easily negate the rational limitations of a theological conceptual model.

If theology and faith, or theological statements and religious experience, are linked so uncritically, theological reflection is itself reduced to merely another expression of our faith. Sauter rightly cautions against this misleading notion of theology; for although the intention behind such a model, namely, to honor the theologian's personal religious commitment, may have merit, it is a model that fails to distinguish adequately between what Sauter calls the pretheoretic source and the theoretic objectives of theology. In such a theological model, practical distinctions might be drawn between church and university, but the danger remains of an authoritarian axiomatic theology in which the theologian's subjectivistic convictions become the only true theological model. And in such an axiomatic theology the victim is, ironically, the relationship between theologians and the Truth they claim to convey, since they will have exchanged the rational limitations and provisionality of their own statements for a positivistically structured personal stand presented, with large claims to truth, as the only possible one. Such theologians would be forgetting that their task is to speak of the object of theology, not of themselves.

Sauter (1973:234) could therefore make the telling point that systematic theology can make meaningful statements in spite of their rational limitations, provided the basic problem of the incompleteness and inadequacy of theological language did not become an existential problem to theologians by turning the tentativeness of their own insights into a personal threat. Faced with the eschatological tension between revelation and history, theologians must therefore remain prepared to make limited statements.

Sauter thus opts for a rationality model in which it must be possible to objectify and describe the language of theology without making that the basis of our faith. Ultimately, then, his aim is to make nontheorizable faith comprehensible by bringing to bear on it the precision of philosophy of science. Instead of a theology that could be seen as merely a synthesis of personal convictions, Sauter opts for a theological theory in which the limitations of our theological language are consciously recognized in an attempt to define the quality, validity, and range of theological theories and concepts.

(2) If theological thought is to meet the criterion of relevance, and thus also of intersubjectivity, it must become describable. In other words, theological language must be objectifiable in one way or another. Sauter maintains that this is the only way theology itself can make statements on theology. A theory of theology would enable us to define the possibilities of language used to make statements about God. In addition to theoretic statements about theology, such possibilities would include doxological and professional ones: statements of faith as a form of assertion, as spontaneous, affirmative answers made from faith in God. Sauter (1973:237-238) sees the capacity of theological language for actually making statements about God as the primary problem of modern systematic theology. Therefore theology must first objectify its own language in order to ascertain whether it is in fact capable of making such statements.

In the strictest sense, then, Sauter is examining the essential structure of a language act in a theological statement—a scrutiny that eventually again raises the question of the theorizing implicit in theological statements. In his view, the inadequacy of theological language for actually making statements about God and His revelation lies at the heart of the problems surrounding the describability of theological statements. This basic problem, as Sauter sees it, is not merely a matter of the difficulties the theologian faces in speaking of God in human—and thus fallible—terms; it is, rather, the extreme difficulty of ascertaining, given the limits of our rationality, whether theology is overstepping its bounds while claiming to be relevant.

For Sauter, this implies that theology's ultimate aim is to speak about a real, living, and manifest God—be its statements on that God ever so provisional and limited. He maintains that theoretic theological formulations must never be allowed to obstruct the presence of God (Sauter, 1973:239). Correctly construed, then, the question of the objectification of theology does not divert us from the question of the object of theology. On the contrary, it ultimately helps us to formulate that question even more sharply.

(3) In view of the long tradition of thought behind both Christianity and theology, history has naturally become a framework of orientation for theology (and thus an essential part of its context of discovery). That history must now—as meaningful to theology—be made hermeneutically fruitful. This brings theology to the division between past and present—to the hermeneutical problem in its full complexity. For Sauter, this is in an important sense a problem of where in history we have encountered God, and of what that encounter means to us now.

That basic problem, which may also be defined as the problem of God and His relationship with history, is an indication of where we might in fact encounter God; in other words, an indication of why our theological statements about God could indeed be possible and meaningful. At the same time, however, God can never be equated with history; nor can God ever be directly and unproblematically deduced from a historical experience.

It becomes increasingly clear, then, that Sauter would in fact seek an empirical basis for theology in religious experiences. Whether the presence of God can indeed be discerned in certain events may, of course, be defined as another basic problem for theology. For Sauter (1973:242), formulating that problem precisely—and not burdening it with false questions—is one of theology's most daunting and yet most meaningful tasks. The question of God's past and present reality is of the utmost importance not only to theology but also to Christians, who find themselves confronted with it in their daily religious experiences.

Here it becomes important to Sauter that theology must ensure methodologically that God's freedom is maintained in our theological statements. If God were finally pinned down in any of our formulations, theology would no longer be speaking of the true God. In Sauter's view, the freedom of God in relation to the world and history supports any biblical pronouncement on Him. The fundamental problem of God and history must therefore be made fruitful and lucid for systematic theology as a methodological problem in terms of the theory of science. Until that basic problem has been included as a structural one in theological theorizing, no systematic theologian can hope to make statements that are creditable both theologically and in terms of philosophy of science.

(4) For Sauter, the fourth basic problem of theology is closely bound up with the hermeneutical problem. It may also be stated as follows: How can theology in every new situation invoke the novelty of the gospel in a new and cre-

ative manner? This leads to the question whether theology is indeed susceptible to true progress. Is there in fact progress in our knowledge of God when interpretation makes the truth of God in Jesus Christ accessible in our present-day situations, or is it merely a reiteration of the message of Christ in a new or different context? Ultimately it will have to be shown that theology, while conceptualizing tradition, is not just blindly following a tradition of reflection on God but is interpreting the tradition so creatively that it may help to solve the problems currently engaging us. Not only the so-called relevance of theology but also its quest for lucidity and clarity thus becomes a criterion for progress in systematic theology. And valid theorizing in theology then demands, in addition to a traditional historical focus, orientation on practical problems.

(5) To Sauter (1973:262) it is clear that our statements about God must indirectly be made through our experience of the world and of humanity, since God is neither part of our reality nor a point of view on all that is real. Here the basic problem is, of course, the precise relationship between our statements about the world and people and our statements about God. This problem may be further defined as the question whether our theological statements have any cognitive quality. After all, truly theological language can never be seen as an evocation of reality; its task is in fact to lead us to the conceptualization of that reality. It is of course exceptionally difficult to define the problem as a structural one for theology, since any mention of objectivity directly implies some form of testing. Sauter rightly warns that the so-called nonobjectifiability of God might here be misused to evade the problem of the factors governing theological theorizing.

The Origin of Theological Statements

In the light of his five basic theological problems, Sauter sees the specific question of the possibility of formulating a systematic theological theory that would be both meaningful and acceptable from a philosophy of science point of view as the central task in any philosophical reflection on the scientific status of theology. Thus he opts argumentatively for a theoretic analysis of theological modes of thought, which would make it possible—precisely because the question of theorizing is asked within theology—to practice a positively critical theology.

Sauter (1971b:299) counters the dogmatic authoritarian mode of dialectical theology, in particular, with his own analytic-theoretic model. By this means he seeks to pave the way for a theory of theology that would not merely produce *ex cathedra, indisputable* statements but would pertinently and specifically confront the question of creditable justification. In his view, then, critical theology must not merely explicate but also reason; it must not merely speak out and profess in faith but in fact also speak about faith and the language of faith. For the sake of God and His revelation, a critical theology would no longer unquestioningly and uncritically assume faith and revelation as premises for theological statements; faith and revelation—and our statements about them—would become the objects of critical examination.

With Sauter, therefore, the intimate link between faith and theology figures much more prominently than it did—initially—with Pannenberg. In his quest for criteria for theorizing Sauter is not attempting to alienate faith from theology; on the contrary, his aim is to reveal by way of theory whatever is experienced in faith and expressed in theological language. Religious experience and formulations must ultimately be justified in the theological context.

It must be noted that, for Sauter, the theologian's commitment is of the utmost importance precisely in respect of theorizing. The theologian is a theologian because he is directly committed to and concerned with the truth he seeks to express. Sauter warns, however, that theologians—including systematic theologians—should not uncritically measure their methodological approach by that commitment. What he finds totally unacceptable is a type of epistemological naïveté in which the mere citing of biblical texts purports to justify theological statements. He points out rightly that even the Reformed *sola scriptura* principle as a method of scriptural exegesis could easily lapse into exegetical positivism with kerygmatic pretensions (Sauter, 1970a:36; 1971b:300). Instead, Holy Scripture, as the authoritative text for theology, must be explored hermeneutically and critically to discover any binding and relevant statements it might still contain for us. It is all the more important, then, that systematic theologians should realize that their statements are sociohistorically determined and cannot be universally valid simply because they are about God and His revelation.

Sauter sees systematic theology as the provisional result of reflection on the contents of Scripture as well as the historically developed conception of those contents, with the exclusive object of making them accessible and relevant also for present times. Moreover, theology as a critical discipline becomes possible only if it sees itself as a particular moment in the history of Christianity and remains methodologically conscious of its pretheoretic origins. For Sauter, all these factors will ultimately play a decisive role in questions about the origins of theological statements, about the object area presupposed by such statements, and about the material drawn on in the actual formulation of theological statements.

Sauter (1973:301) therefore answers the question of the origins of theological statements—the context of discovery for theological statements—as follows: systematic theology's context of discovery is not merely the theoretic context on which systematic theologians draw for their questions and problems; as a context, it includes all factors involved in the shaping of theological concepts. Thus it includes not only the contents of Holy Scripture and the historically developed reflection on Scripture but also the broader history of Christianity. In Sauter's view the context of discovery refers not only to the sociohistorical orientation of theologians and their thought, but also to the fact that only the church can form the ultimate point of orientation for theologians. In the shaping of ideas, too, theologian are therefore bound to the church and its tradition of reflection.

Sauter points out, furthermore, that theology's context of discovery plays a fundamental role in the theorizing behind every central theological concept, such as revelation, history, church, God, or mankind. He emphasizes rightly that analysis of that conceptualizing and theorizing must be the ineluctable function of any theory of theology. The religious commitment of theologians to the object of their reflection, however, goes beyond the theorizable and remains fundamental to our statements of faith—which, as we have seen, Sauter also typifies as assertive (affirmative or confessional) statements. Here we shall have to examine critically whether Sauter has adequately accounted for the theorizing or theory-ladenness implied in assertive pronouncements. This question is crucial to an understanding of the problems surrounding theological theorizing, since statements of faith—as assertive statements—also fall in the context of discovery of theological statements. If the sources of theological statements are traced to such statements of faith, inter alia, the theorizing implied in statements of faith must also determine the eventual formulation of theological theories. Whether Sauter explored this consequence for his own conceptual model will have to be examined critically.

It is clear, in any event, that Sauter advocates a positive assessment of assertive statements as the specific language mode of prescientific religious experience. Assertive speech is not a mere expression of blind convictions; it expresses victory over any doubts about God's existence. For Sauter, then, statements of faith, as assertive statements, have nothing to do with problems of authority; they are concerned with the positivity of living faith. Systematic theologians formulate their statements in relation to such statements of faith. As such, theological statements are, for Sauter (1973:288), answers to questions asked in the language context of the living Christian faith.

By critically thematizing the close ties between religious experience and theological reflection, Sauter attempts to demonstrate that theology need not opt for theoretic thought at the expense of religious experience in an attempt to salvage its so-called rationality or scientific status. Christian faith itself and the way it is experienced provide grounds for and lead to rational reflection, since that faith is expressed above all in statements on faith, which it links together in an argumentative structure. Our religious experiences are in fact concerned with conceptual clarity and, ultimately, with structured communication.

Since our religious experience is inevitably present in statements on our faith, it is imperative that our faith should be described, and also that its description should be separated from the pretheoretic and extratheoretic sphere of original and authentic statements of faith. In Sauter's view (1975b:172), that delineation leads theology into the process of scientific communication and makes it relevant for theology to call for consensus—a consensus of believers that will not simply determine the eventual theological consensus but rather the origin and purpose of that consensus. Theology will, however, achieve that kind of consensus only if it becomes theory-conscious in a radically new sense. Sauter (1970b:37) maintains—in my view correctly—that the present Protestant systematic theology has on the whole so far failed to take account of the concept of theory and the problems that concept poses.

The failure to accommodate theory is patently detrimental to systematic theology and is a direct cause of the reduction and impoverishment of theological debates and discussions into a mere front for widely divergent premises—premises whose theoretic origins are not critically examined, but which nonetheless contribute to a final structuring of criteria by which the truth or falsehood of all theological statements must be tested. Such an axiomatic theology also tends to narrow down theology's task of exegesis and of explicating Scripture into a quite specific task and function for the church. As such, theological statements of this kind are placed beyond any form of theoretic testing.

To interpret Sauter's conceptual model properly, one has to note that, while emphasizing the close links between church and theology in his analysis of the origins (context of discovery) and testing (context of justification) of theological statements, he also firmly rejects any reduction of theology to a type of ecclesiastical doctrine. If that happened (Sauter, 1970b:37), the concept of theory would remain a blind fellow-traveler of church and theology. Consciousness of theory, and therefore reflection on the concept of theory, naturally leads the systematic theologian to question whether theology is a science and who the people are who practice theology, and ultimately to the critical question of the origins and formulation of theological theories. Moreover, the systematic theologian must be aware of the fact that these difficult questions cannot be answered in isolation. Even the most tentative reflection on the concept of theory leads theology into a discussion with philosophy of science, since theory as such is a basic concept in that philosophy.

Sauter maintains, therefore, that theorizing must necessarily be exposed to epistemological scrutiny, since systematic theologians, in their theological contact with reality, produce descriptions—descriptions which, as statements or assertions, are no manifestations of truth but rather hypotheses anticipating that truth. It will have to be clear, then, that theological theories are not dogmatic, conclusive premises but rather provisional, tentative constructs. The question of theological theorizing is ultimately a question of theology's ability to formulate theories truly capable of solving problems. For Sauter (1971b:58), then, the question of theorizing is not solely a matter of theology's objectives (theology is in fact concerned with much more than the problem of theorizing), but rather of its problem area.

Here theory must be distinguished from method: on the one hand, Sauter sees theories as constructs designed to provide a meaningful explanation of some problem; on the other hand, he regards theories as methods once they have proved themselves in a particular sense and have therefore become converted into a specific, acceptable basis or modus operandi (Sauter, 1971b:59). This distinction is important inasmuch as systematic theology, if it fails to reckon with the problems surrounding the concept and formulation of theories, must also be random and unreflective in its methods. Critical awareness of the factors bearing on theological theorizing is in fact an essential prerequisite to critical evaluation and precisioning of the questions asked about method in systematic theology.

A theological theory may eventually be seen as a cluster of hypotheses. Here Sauter (1980:163) distinguishes between hermeneutical and language-analytical conceptions of the term *hypothesis*. In a hermeneutical construction of that term, it may be said that no statement can ever be tested conclusively, since all statements are historical and may therefore be modified by new experiences. In terms of language analysis, certain statements are defined as hypotheses inasmuch as they might in principle be or not be susceptible to confirmation. The confirmation or justification of such a hypothesis must of course also be formulated in terms of statements, but its status differs from that of hypotheses. As confirmed and conclusive statements, theses lead to the formulation of further hypotheses. Sauter's interest in the nature of hypothesis centers on the relationship between these two conceptions, and especially on the transition from one to the other in theology. As far as the theological application of the concept is concerned, Sauter's interest is not so much the question of certainty as the problem of formulating truly binding theological statements.

His use of the concept of hypothesis once again clearly shows his interest in a kind of theological theorizing that would transcend merely affirmative Christian statements. What remains problematic, however, is that Sauter regards confirmed, conclusive theological statements (for example, statements about God, such as ones about the Trinity doctrine) as no longer hypothetical. They might lead to new hypotheses and thus provide a basis in the context of justification, in contrast to other provisional and prescriptive theological statements. Sauter sees the latter type as concretizations of universal statements (for example, the transition from dogmatic to ethical statements), as prescriptive statements of limited scope, and therefore as still hypothetical.

Wolfhart Pannenberg (1980:169) has pointed out that Sauter, by drawing these distinctions, pointed the way to theological productivity. But I find it problematic that Sauter, despite his repeated appeal for critical analysis of the factors affecting theorizing in theology, still adheres to the framework of a rigidly traditional conception of the conclusiveness of dogmatic statements. He is correct in his view that tradition provides the source for the theologian's productivity in the present. Only theology's efforts to achieve that productive formulation of theological themes can determine to what extent and why that very tradition, and with it certain dogmatic models, remains binding in our time.

But conclusive dogmatic statements must surely also become the object of the critical questioning of theorizing that Sauter demands for other theological hypotheses. In that sense we are faced with the fact that dogmatic and ecclesiastically binding statements are hypothetical and thus constantly open to critical reinterpretation. Pannenberg (1980:171) has shown convincingly that this does not imply a lapse from certainty into uncertainty or provisionality in statements of faith. As any analysis of language shows, however, pretheoretic statements of faith also contain assertions, and without that hypothetical structure all theological statements—including dogmatic, authoritative ones—would be meaningless.

The Justification of Theological Statements

In analyzing the factors bearing on theological theorizing, Sauter has clearly shown that the systematic theologian must inquire into the gradual formation of theological statements, into the object area presupposed by such statements, and into the material drawn on in the formulation of theological theories. It has become clear that Sauter does not regard theological science as an isolated, specialized discipline, but rather as a research field with a broader, theological-ecclesiastical responsibility. He therefore sees theologians as persons facing questions from their *Umwelt*—questions they themselves must formulate precisely and correctly in order to answer them theologically.

Within the context of a system of responsible theological criteria, Sauter wishes to evaluate and define the questions that the believer—and the professing theologian—faces and communicates in statements of faith. For Sauter, however, this implies lucid reflection on the relationship between theological truth and theological statements—reflection in which the clear distinction between the two must not be obscured. That means evaluation or justification in theology must not be pushed to its positivist extreme, which calls for rational or historical universality.

The question of testing or justifying theological statements within a certain context of justification cannot be met by referring to an empirical or quasi-empirical criterion for meaning. It would therefore be impossible to see peace or conciliation or brotherly love or humaneness, for example, as a final criterion for true Christianity. That such acts or attitudes may be motivated by true Christian faith can at best be asserted with strong conviction; it cannot be justified conclusively. No more can the question of the justification of theological statements be met by postulating a uniquely theological concept of verification. Sauter (1973:266-267) sees such a verification concept in Gerhard Ebeling's statement that we are ultimately verified by God. A unique concept of verification, through which theologians forfeit any communication with other scientists, is postulated when the scriptural theologian argues that theological statements are justified simply by referring to biblical texts. Faced with the incisive challenge of hermeneutical questions, theologians have to justify their statements with more than mere reproduction and analogy.

Gerhard Sauter's warning on this point may be extended to any situation in which theologians might be tempted to tie their reflection to Scripture or might persist in theologizing biblically and directly from Scripture while remaining totally oblivious of the problems surrounding theological theorizing. A stand on the authority of the Bible, for instance, is not proof against criticism simply because it corresponds with certain biblical texts; such a stand is in fact structured by my preconceptions about proper authority. Thus not the Bible but my conception of it becomes authoritative. My theological statements are therefore not biblically justified or tested; they have merely been tested against my subjective conception of proper scriptural authority. Sauter (1971b:302) puts it as follows: the justification or testing of theological statements must surely be more than and different from mere exegesis.

From Sauter's approach to the difficult question of the justification of theological statements it is clear that the question of the testability of such statements is also the question of their bearing on reality or their degree of realism. From this, Sauter developed a special means of justifying or testing theological statements. For him (Sauter, 1971b:305), testing is bound up with the function of theological statements, since they function as regulators of ecclesiastical pronouncements. To put it differently: the status and quality of theological statements is, in Sauter's view, bound up with their origin and testing in the specific context of the church. For him, the question of the empirical quality of theological statements is thus converted into the question of communicative involvement within a context of communal religious convictions.

Within the arena of the church, theological statements function as rules for dialogue. This is especially true of theological statements that have gained a certain conclusive or universal stature against the background of tradition, scriptural reflection, and theological discussion (for instance, the doctrine of the Trinity, Christ's divinity, and the authority of Scripture as the Word of God). As rules of dialogue, they demarcate an area within which new statements must be critically tested and integrated. For this theoretic context, Sauter chooses the term *context of justification.*

In speaking of the justification or evaluation of theological statements, Sauter means their vindication or rejection within the bounds of a dialogic method of control. His concern is not so much the empirically verifiable but rather the reliability of a statement that has to be confirmed within a certain context of justification. That—mostly confessional—context of justification is in his view comprised of such universal postulates or *Ist-Sätzen,* which in the theological sense may be seen as promises, but epistemologically rate as hypotheses of unlimited scope. The concretization of these universal proposals ultimately gives theology its scope for productivity. Sauter (1971b:303) therefore regards as the context of justification not only the Christian tradition, Holy Scripture, and the Christian confessional writings, but also and especially intersubjectivity of consensus within the church's communicative field. The latter, in turn, forms part of a broader problem consciousness, namely, the context of present-day philosophical inquiry.

Theological truth is now no longer defined only abstractly or tested only empirically. Theological statements, however, being oriented toward concrete problems, are formulated and tested within the scope of the church, against certain rules of dialogue. In Sauter's view, theological statements are thus not merely deduced uncritically or dogmatically; they are derived from a process of dialogue. And the rules of dialogue, as context of justification, are derived especially from the canons of Holy Scripture, the church's doctrine and confessional statements, and—what I would call the overall paradigmatic context—broad paradigmatic or interpretative rules regulating theological thought, such as the Reformed *solus christus* or *sola scriptura* (as, rightly, Hempelmann, 1980:186).

Such a context of justification is, therefore, never a mere fabrication; it is constituted consciously by those using it to arrive at further statements, to test such statements and—if need be—to correct them. In total contrast to Wolfhart Pannenberg's concept of a theological context of justification, Sauter posits a context based on spontaneous, tradition-backed religious language which, as assertive speech, must be pneumatologically founded.

From the above it is clear that theologians cannot justify their statements by mere critical comparison with those of a particular theological tradition, or by a kind of biblicist exegesis. Theological statements are justified by examining their intersubjectivity within a particular (Christian) problem consciousness. As such, those statements then function as regulators of ecclesiastical language: they are rules of dialogue, demarcating a theological area of discussion, and therefore always part of a particular theoretic context.

In answer to the important question of the relationship between human consensus, on the one hand, and access to truth, on the other, Sauter (1980:164) answers that one can speak of testing or justifying theological statements only in the context of the rich tradition of theological consensus. But consensus, or intersubjective agreement, is in itself no guarantee of truth; what it does is to point the way to truth. In that sense truth—also the truth of theological statements—is a social phenomenon, binding on a particular group.

A clear distinction must be drawn between the truth of God and the truth of theological statements. In Sauter's view, as we have seen, systematic theology speaks relevantly and scientifically as long as the problem of the autonomy or the inconclusiveness of theological statements does not become an existential problem, and as long as theology, confronted with the eschatological tension between revelation and history, remains prepared to make limited and provisional statements.

By this means Sauter sought to establish that his concern was not so much to justify faith rationally, but rather to make nontheorizable faith comprehensible with the aid of theoretic precisioning. For him, therefore, the transition from religious experience to theoretic description in theology does not mean a shift from irrationality to rationality. He would argue, rather, that the theoretic praxis of theology must be separated from what remains pre- and extratheoretic. In that process, theology itself must become describable, since the question of the objectivization of theology does not divert us from the question of the object of theology; instead, it enables us to restate the latter question even more sharply.

The specific feature of theology's concern with reality is, therefore, that theology produces descriptions designed to expose mankind to a new reality. At the same time, such theological descriptions or statements have a hypothetical character; therefore Sauter could suggest that theological statements, instead of directly manifesting truth, merely offer us an avenue to truth. This naturally also raises the question of the correctness or reliability of such statements. And here, in the question of consensus or concurrence within the context of justification as conceived by Sauter, systematic theologians are once again faced with the question of theorizing. This implies, above all, that they have to account methodologically for their relationship with the Word of God, and thus also for the way they invoke biblical evidence. For Sauter, this leads to a theory of theology which specifically examines the remarkable fact that Christian theology has always construed the Word of God as a definitive revelation.

An Analytic-Theoretical Model of Thought for Theology: Critical Evaluation

Gerhard Sauter's attempt to establish an argumentative theology with an analytic-theoretic mode of thought within the context of theology's close ties with church and confession merits attention from anyone who is critically concerned with the question of theorizing in systematic theology. Although Sauter did not, like Pannenberg, engage in direct dialogue with various viewpoints in contemporary philosophy of science, he did succeed in making some of the major concerns of present-day science theory fruitful for systematic theology and its conceptual apparatus. We have also seen that Sauter—unlike Pannenberg, who sought to expose problematic statements on God and His reality, as axiomatic data, to a philosophy of examination in order to gain a scientifically creditable theology—preferred to examine a philosophy of inquiry within theology, in order to achieve, by analytic-theoretic means, greater clarity and distinctness in the process of theological reflection as such.

To a large extent Sauter's model succeeds in its aim of being rationally founded, especially because he so pointedly rejected any form of uncritical, dogmatist axiomatic theology. As a theologian he wishes to reason, not merely to declaim. Thus all theologians studying his works are directly challenged to an analytic-critical examination of their own position and therefore of their own inquiries. By this means Sauter also confronts us with an incisive critical consciousness of the factors bearing on the process of theorizing in systematic theology.

Sauter is adamant that the question of theology's scientific status cannot be discussed in mere abstraction. Throughout, he rightly opposed any positivist scientific ideal that might usurp the essence of theology. For that reason he rejected Heinrich Scholz's then dated minimum demands for science, maintaining that they had been superseded by the philosophy of science debate since Popper and Kuhn.

Here Hempelmann (1980:187), however, rightly points out a problematic feature of Sauter's model: although he rejects Scholz's minimum demands, he cannot avoid reverting to them indirectly. Scholz's examination of the cognitive quality of theological statements is consistently present in Sauter's inquiry into theology's capacity for valid statements. Sauter also examines the demand for a coherence of theological science. Furthermore, Scholz's demand of testability of theological statements is one of the main themes in Sauter's discussion of the structuring of a context of justification as a testing ground for the question of truth in theological statements.

Sauter maintains that the systematic theologian cannot ignore the question of theology's scientific status, but he rejects Scholz's criteria as positivistic. Yet he invokes those very criteria in his examination of the nature and scope of theological reflection. At this point one might ask whether Sauter should not rather consciously take up and examine Scholz's minimum demands for a scientific theology, as Pannenberg in particular did in his own manner. After all, Pannenberg had already pointed out that the three minimum demands were still valid, despite their historical orientation, since they in fact concerned the assertive character of theological statements.

In spite of these problems, Sauter warns that critical theorizing in theology becomes impossible if theologians, as often happens, base their statements on purely existential or pseudoscientific grounds. And although the twin concepts context of discovery and context of justification are themselves no longer generally accepted in philosophy of science, they do help Sauter to put strong emphasis on the question of the origin of theological statements (and the factors bearing on theorizing) as well as the question of the truth and reliability of such statements. It is also to Sauter's credit that he sought to make the philosophy of science inquiry fruitful within theology, and that he argued as a professing theologian from the outset. In doing so, Sauter conceded that the theologian's personal commitment was a primary factor in both the context of discovery and the context of justification, and should therefore be taken into account. He also warns that direct ethical claims can never be deduced unproblematically from that religious commitment, nor can theological models be founded unproblematically on the theologian's own commitment. Such an approach, as we have seen, may have the result that mere consensus among like-minded theologians or believers becomes elevated into the essence of theology.

Whether Sauter has reflected adequately on the theoretization and conceptualization of the theologian's personal commitment remains a question. In my view Sauter never critically examines the theorizing implied in the theologian's own religious experience—a factor that surely emerges from his inquiry, in the context of discovery, into the origins of theological statements. His distinction between theological statements, on the one hand, and statements of faith as assertive statements, on the other, would also be convincing only if he did not stop at spontaneous assertive statements in his inquiry into the origins of theological statements. Assertive statements, no matter how spontaneous and pretheoretic in their relationship with and origin in religious experience, already reveal the hypothetical structure of assertions and have already been theorized and conceptualized by the background and environment that constitute the theologian's context of discovery.

Whether Sauter is adequately aware of the theory-ladenness of theorizing implied in a pretheoretic religious commitment is not therefore a question of the certainty of faith; it bears, rather, on the fact that we have faith only in terms of statements on and out of faith. But in themselves statements of faith already show a theoretic structure, and that structure has to be analyzed and examined critically. Failing that, the structure and content of religious statements may have an uncritical and dogmatic impact on the later formulation of theological statements. Of this, it seems to me, Sauter is not critically aware, although it is in fact implied in the extrapolation of his critical model.

I would agree with Sauter's final conclusion (Sauter, 1973:239) that theological formulations should not stand in the way of God's presence in religious experience. The critical question remains, however: What form of theorizing is already present in whatever is experienced as the presence of God? Sauter is also convincing when he argues that theology must remain methodologically aware of its pretheoretic origin, but he does not inquire critically into the way that pretheoretic origin—in the context of discovery—has already been experienced in a theorized form and conceptualized in statements. And this is of the utmost importance to any examination of theorizing in theology. Since the origin of our theological statements is related to—inter alia—statements of faith as assertions, the theorizing implicit in statements of faith in fact codetermines the eventual design of theological theories and conceptual models.

Sauter's (1973:288) claim that assertive speech, as the specific medium of faith, has already overcome any doubts about God's presence and is therefore totally unrelated to the problem of authoritarian pronouncements, I find highly problematic and epistemologically naïve. Statements of faith have a definite origin and have been so conceptualized by their sociocultural orientation that, on their level too, a positive religious experience can surely be no safeguard against dogmatism. It seems, then, as if Sauter, contrary to the intent of his model, cannot escape the charge of uncritically and undogmatically attempting to deduce statements of faith from the theologian's commitment.

I find that a pity, because Sauter is in fact attempting to examine the close ties between faith and theology and thus to demonstrate that theology need not choose between the alternatives of theoretic reflection and religious commitment, precisely because Christian faith offers grounds for rational reflection. Sauter has rightly shown that such grounds may be found in the fact that the critical theologian's faith is also evident in statements about that faith. And such statements point the way to conceptual clarity and scientifically creditable, accessible communication.

Another important critical question about Sauter's model for theology as a science touches on his handling of the difficult but important issue of the testing of theological statements. Here the crux of the problem is not only the way Sauter—against the background of what he considers the context of justification for theological statements—makes consensus or intersubjective correspondence the final criterion for reliability in theological statements, but also the way he incorporates church and confession in that consensus.

If certain ecclesiastical or confessional statements, or a certain theological tradition, became the exclusive context of justification for theological statements, such a context of justification would function merely as a regulator of ecclesiastical pronouncements. A one-sided emphasizing of the consensus aspect of truth (which is apparent especially in Sauter's earlier writings) may, however, lead to extreme ecclesiastical conventionalism, of a type that might make the ecclesiastical language of a particular time or place the basis of the justification of systematic theological statements. Given the nature of its object, however, confessional ecclesiasticism cannot be accepted uncritically as a basis for theology. After all, systematic theology is essentially ecumenical; it cannot, therefore, take its stand on the (confessional) discrepancies between Christian churches. Sauter's choice of consensus as a concept of truth—in contrast to, for instance, correspondence—may ultimately be seen as his attempt to evade the problem of verification through empirical testing (cf. Hempelmann, 1980:188).

Intersubjective consensus naturally contains an important element of truth—we concede the truth of something only if we agree on it. One might critically ask Sauter, however, whether the truth of a matter can indeed be established only argumentatively, through dialogue. Quite apart from whether consensus can indeed be achieved by this means, the question remains whether a statement of consensus ultimately does correspond with its purported object. Here Wolfhart Pannenberg has demonstrated convincingly that the question of correspondence eventually follows logically from the structure of theological statements as assertions. If that were not so, there would be no means of ascertaining whether theology was concerned with reality or with illusion. In itself, any conception of truth as consensus presupposes the conception of truth as correspondence. Sauter (1980:161) concedes that he has so far not given adequate attention to this problem. He correctly identifies the crucial problem, namely, to what extent certain theological statements can be shown to correspond with or even provisionally anticipate truth. He agrees, moreover, that a consensus truth merely points the way to truth, without fully revealing that truth. We might also ask whether such an ideal communicative society does in fact exist, to provide a safeguard against any form of positivist dogmatism or traditionalism. The church, with its history of conflict and schism, is by no means such a community (cf. Hempelmann, 1980:189).

It is also clear that Sauter's criteria for a context of justification constitute a theological paradigm that in itself calls for critical examination—especially of the theorizing hidden behind the rules of dialogue which Sauter relates directly to tradition and Holy Scripture.

Even pneumatological justification by intra-ecclesiastical testing does not absolve theology of conceptualizing and theorizing, nor from theorizing the way that pneumatological element itself is experienced and formulated. It is true that personal faith cannot refer to its own origins for its final justification. But theological statements, if they claim to be valid in philosophy of science terms, cannot be justified merely by referring to such faith, or to the pneumatological basis of such a commitment. This is, of course, bound up with the fact that the essential nature of the personal act of faith can also be defined satisfactorily only with reference to its eschatological structure. The critical exposure of the inevitable theorizing implied in the theologian's personal pretheoretic commitment will therefore have to take into account the *skandalon* character of the Christian gospel. The *skandalon* is a fundamental issue that will and must be a conscious methodological and epistemological problem for systematic theology. Correctly understood, however, it need not become an irrational theological premise; instead, it might offer insight into the hypothetical, and therefore provisional, nature of religious, confessional, and theological statements, at the same time giving us a sense of the inevitable plurality of the Christian religious experience and Christian statement about God in our time.

PART III

SYSTEMATIC THEOLOGY: A CRITICAL-REALIST PERSPECTIVE

8

The Nature of Theological Statements

Theology, by the very nature of the kind of fundamental existential questions it asks and because of the nature of the reality of God upon which theology reflects, must develop public, not private criteria and discourse.

David Tracy, *The Analogical Imagination: Christian Theology and the Culture of Pluralism* (New York: Crossroad, 1981):xi.

To nobody, O Illustrious One, can you communicate in words and teachings, what happened to you in the hour of your enlightenment.

Hermann Hesse, *Siddhartha* (London: PAN Books, 1973):28.

Introduction

The indisputable interrelatedness of philosophy of science problems and fundamental-theological questions must by this stage have made one dominant and liberating impression on any systematic theologian who feels intensely concerned with the problem of theorizing in theology: there are no convincing arguments for the acceptance that our theological reflection has a merely marginal or peripheral existence, outside the broad context of intellectual and scientific activities. In fact, any theologian who has taken note of contemporary philosophy of science inquiries is now confronted with the challenge and responsibility of creatively articulating the valid claims of systematic theology in a creditable model of rationality.

In the preceding chapters I have tried to develop a specific theological approach to these daunting but fundamental problems. In the course of that reflection I have repeatedly raised the same crucial problems, which I should now like to express more finally as follows:

1. What type of rationality models operate in specific theological traditions and in the intellectual frameworks of strongly individualistic theological thinkers?
2. By its nature a philosophy of science illumination of the origins of and differences among rationality models confronts theology with the vital question of the new nuances of meaning that have become possible for basic concepts such as objectivity and rationality. The final part of this chapter will concentrate specifically on that question.
3. These specific problems can, however, be discussed only after examining, in the first part of the chapter, the nature of our theological statements.

Meanwhile it has gradually become clearer that the actual contextuality of systematic theologians and their field of study must always loom large behind the apparently esoteric, theoretic problems outlined above. After all, the theologian is a believer reflecting from a total commitment to Jesus Christ. And that nonnegotiable commitment is not only in the fundamental-theological sense a further basic problem for the theologian's appeal to insight and rational comprehensibility; in the end the problem must also be brought home, with an equally forceful appeal, to the religious experiences of other believers.

Religious Experience and the Language of Faith: The Origin of Theological Statements

In the light of the above the crucial problem of theological statements may be formulated as follows: What precisely happens during theorizing, when our religious language is apparently transformed into theological concepts and conceptual models that might indeed make a valid appeal to both our intellectual insight and our religious experience?

Any theory of theology seeking to provide a meaningful answer to that question will have to be highly attuned not only to the special relationship between the theoretic language of theology and the original, mostly pretheoretic language of religious tradition (cf. Tracy, 1978:149), but also to the relational nature of all religious language. In attempting here to reveal a relational structure in the language of our spontaneous religious experience, I am specifically concerned with the way believers (like professing theologians) draw on the basic commitment of their religious convictions to make committed statements about a Reality outside themselves. This rules out the risk of any attempt at objectivistic and the inevitably resultant subjectivistic thought. Like other sciences, theology uses relational language to form, in terms of metaphors and models, theories about the unknown that are at least approximately true, albeit only provisionally.

It will eventually become evident that the language of our spontaneous religious experience is, in the most profound sense, the origin of our theological language. But prescientific language cannot be assimilated uncritically and unthinkingly into the vocabulary of systematic theology. In some way or other the metaphoric language of our religious experience must be transformed for maximal conceptual clarity, and to that end a theory of theology—in the sense of fundamental-theological reflection on the nature of religious and theological statements—is indispensable.

In this regard our discussion of Gerhard Sauter has led to certain important conclusions. A valid theory of theology will not only safeguard systematic theology against aimless vacillation between a kind of irrational obscurantism and pseudoscientific fashionability; any theory of theology, any fundamental-theological reflection on theological metaquestions, is first and foremost a form of linguistic analysis. And the critical evaluation of theological language is essential because only objectification of religious and theological language can reveal the process of theorizing behind the sources of theological statements. It has already become apparent that the limitations and describability of theological statements are among the most basic problems to be dealt with in any theory of theology.

To the above should be added that it is nowadays by no means taken for granted that the language of our religious experiences is meaningful—especially not the acceptance of only certain definitive constructions of the many facets of our religious language (cf. McCormack, 1984:431). Theology must therefore account in some way for the meaning of our religious language according to criteria for meaning, validity, and truth that would be acceptable in terms of current confessional, theological, and philosophy of science inquiries.

It thus becomes clear once again that systematic theology can no longer adopt a ghetto-like privatistic confessional stand, and that a so-called fundamental theology cannot confine itself, a-contextually and in theoretic isolation, to esoteric inquiries into axiomatic questions. The question of valid criteria for an evaluation of meaning in religious and theological statements, as well as the question of a creditable rationality model for systematic theology, ultimately leads all systematic theology into the sphere of a new context of apologetic debate and communication. Theologians who concern themselves on a fundamental-theological level with the basic questions directed by philosophy of science at theology are no less authentically occupied than those who have opted for a confessional approach. Their authentic involvement is simply from a different perspective; they are concerned with the same problems and founded on the same basic conviction.

Regarding the origin and nature of our systematic-theological statements, I should like to formulate the central theme of this section as follows:

> *The way the theologian, as a Christian believer, experiences his or her faith and the nature of the ensuing religious language are mutually determinant of the status of theological statements, both in theology itself and in philosophy of science.*

This statement is given a particular profile by two basic convictions which have consistently figured in this text—whether explicitly or implicitly. I should now like to formulate them in simple terms, before further discussing them from various perspectives:

1. No religious experience is prelinguistic or pretheoretic.
2. All relational religious language refers directly or indirectly to God; as such, religious language is never merely expressive but also contains a cognitive core, as revealed in its explicatory or referential structure.

(1) Thomas S. Kuhn has already taught us that all sciences, and therefore also systematic theology as an intellectual activity, are sociocultural forms of reflection and as such contextually determined, both in the wider and in the narrower sense of the word. Our religious experiences, too, can therefore never be seen as prelinguistic, since they are governed by the language and tradition of the specific group(s) to which we belong. In this sense the ecclesiastical-confessional implementation of a certain theological model may come to determine even the way some believers experience their religion. Faith itself thus becomes a comprehensive interpretative framework within which believers live. Anthony O'Hear (1984:2) has clearly summed up this inevitable conclusion: "Faith, indeed, for the religious believer is not a belief or a set of beliefs alongside scientific beliefs, historical beliefs, psychological beliefs and the rest. It is something much more like an all-encompassing set of attitudes to human life and the world, a context in which one's whole life, including one's cognitive life is set. Faith is that which men live by."

It should now also be clear that what Kuhn, on a philosophy of science level, showed up as the sociocultural contextuality of all conceptual models has opened the door for systematic theology to a sociology of knowledge broadening of the question regarding the origin of our religious, confessional, and theological statements. This is important, because the origin and nature of the multilayered types of statement ultimately play a role in any attempt to formulate meaningful criteria for a creditable model of rationality. Therefore the way the Christian believer experiences his or her faith, and the nature and structure of the ensuing religious language, eventually help to determine the status of theological statements, both in theology itself and in philosophy of science.

All Christian statements about God are primarily founded on the way believers' religious experiences are recorded in the Old and New Testaments, and for nearly two thousand years since then, on the religious experiences of Christians in the multidimensional interpretative framework of Christian tradition. This makes the Bible itself the most fundamental, albeit not the only, expression of Christian religious experience (Tracy, 1978:44). In the broader paradigmatic context of the Bible and Christian tradition, religious experience has always been seen as experience of God, and thus as a personal religious encounter (cf. Hempelmann, 1980:272). As an encounter in which God is experienced as a personal reality, this form of religious experience still defines the most essential religious dimension of contemporary Christian experience.

It would be fatal, of course, if the systematic theologian, in a kind of total hermeneutical amnesia, were to deduce the nature of theological statements directly and precritically from the nature of religious statements. Such a model of scriptural exegesis would be literalistic or naïve-realistic (Peacocke, 1984:40), or even mimetic (Bosman, 1987). In such models the biblical text is seen as a mirror or mimetic reflection of historical events and theological convictions, and the reader is supposed to find historical fact and theological truth directly and unproblematically in the text. Such a positivistic derivation of binding religious and even theological statements from the religious experiences of people long ago, based on supposedly direct access to the reality of the text and totally negating both hermeneutical criteria and the metaphoric nature of religious language, deserves no further comment.

Systematic theologians seeking to construe their own conceptual model as a form of critical accounting for their faith are, however, compelled also to question their self-conception as theologians. In this hazardous balancing act between the demands of creditable intellectual insight and authentic religious experience, neither the religious experience of biblical believers, nor that of subsequent ones in Christian tradition, nor the theologian's own religious experiences and convictions can serve to guarantee the creditability and validity of theological argument. What gives meaning to the long process of religious experience is not only that theologians find the origins of their statements in the rich history of religious experience and the corresponding relational religious language. What that process also reveals is the nonnegotiable fact that every religious experience since the earliest biblical ones has always been regarded as referential and, as a religious experience, directly or indirectly an encounter with God.

In the profoundest sense, this constitutes the purported cognitivity of all religious language. And in the process of creative conceptual construction the systematic theologian must therefore find a model that will most adequately express the essential religious dimension of our experiences and the language in which we articulate them.

(2) In the wider Christian interpretative framework all religious language refers directly or indirectly to a type of experience that Christians through all ages have come to call an encounter with God. And it should be noted that in any religious experience the salient feature was not only that something had been experienced, but also the question of precisely what had been experienced. This makes the very specific way people experience their faith meaningful in content too, to such an extent that religious experience is in itself enough substance for rational reflection. In this sense religious experiences and the language pertaining to them are never merely expressive; they also have a disclosing or referential structure which—closely analyzed—may be seen as the cognitive or realist element of religious language.

We have seen that, since Kuhn, it has become possible to relativize the positivistically inspired question of demarcation and to opt for a wider and more flexible rationality concept that would give a new and valid relational profile to the question of subjective involvement as well as objectivity. A creditable rationality model for a systematic theology seeking to make a valid appeal to both experience and insight would therefore have to take into account that the question of the cognitive or referential quality of religious and theological statements includes the question of the theologian's basic convictions and subjective religious commitment. From this perspective, the question of the origins and nature of our theological statements becomes a question of the opinion-making role the subjective religious convictions of theologians play in their decision to identify with a particular model—a choice that will not only determine the way they experience religion but also definitively structure their theological statements.[1]

In fact, our discussion of William W. Bartley has clearly shown that the personal religious commitment of theologians, always already conceptualized and theorized, often contributes subtly to the final form of their theological views. Here we can see the ultimate theological consequence of the fact that no religious experience can be called prelinguistic, since it always occurs within a comprehensive interpretative framework that has been determined traditionally, confessionally, and personally. In fact, our prescientific and pretheological religious experiences have a dimension of conceptualization which, as a submerged and theory-laden model, ultimately helps to define any criteria theolo-

---

1. "This then is our liberation from objectivism: to realize that we can voice our ultimate convictions only from within our convictions—from within the whole system of acceptances that are logically prior to any particular assertion of our own, prior to the holding of any particular piece of knowledge" (Polanyi, 1962:267).

gians might wish to formulate. This fact was the crux of our criticism of Wolfhart Pannenberg's attempt to construct a rationality model for theology. At the same time it has become clear that recognition of a personal or subjective religious commitment can no longer be equated with opting for irrationality or taking an unscientific stand.[2]

This insight demands that critical theologians make their personal religious convictions explicit, to take a hand in their shaping, and ultimately to maintain them responsibly and creditably. Theologians who appreciate that systematic theology is a process of creative conceptual construction and who, mindful of the factors bearing on the theorizing in their own thinking and reasoning, hold responsibly to the beacons of insight and experience, are ultimately teaching themselves to hold on to their own basic convictions, and therefore also their religious convictions, with both dedication and insight.

Even more important is the fact that a subjective commitment thus becomes the only way to intersubjectively valid knowledge that may lay claim to a certain objective or cognitive quality. Wolfhart Pannenberg has also shown us that every statement may be seen as a hypothesis at least in terms of linguistic analysis. And it is the assertive element in such a statement that ultimately makes it possible to be committed to a particular model or interpretative framework. This assertive element, or the referential nature of all religious and theological statements, also determines the hypothetical and eschatological structure of all theological statements.

In the light of the above it should be increasingly clear how valid Mouton's (1985:17) standpoint is from a philosophy of science point of view. In theology, too, the quest for a creditable rationality model will ultimately mean that objective thought implies committed thought, since the criteria for validity in some research subjects imply a high degree of subjective empathy. As criteria of rationality, reliability, and validity are always contextual, so is the criterion of objectivity; that is, it is dependent on the type of intellectual reflection and its objectives. This will be discussed more fully in the last part of this chapter, but what is now becoming clearer is why well-known theologians such as David Tracy, Gerhard Sauter, Harry Kuitert, Wolfhart Pannenberg, Gordon Kaufman, and Sallie McFague maintain consistently that theology—given its own nature and the nature of its Object—is committed to rationality.

In the light of the above I should like to make the following point: In the intellectual reasoning of systematic theologians, their personal and subjective religious commitment does not signify imperfection in their knowledge; it is, rather, an essential component of all rational cognitive development. A rationality model that fails to take that into account is not only unsuitable for theo-

---

2. "The attribution of truth . . . is a fiduciary act which cannot be analyzed in noncommittal terms." In the same context Polanyi speaks of the fiduciary rootedness of all rationality (Polanyi, 1962:294, 297).

logical reflection but also suspect and even invalid from a philosophy of science point of view.[3]

It becomes clear, then, that theologians who see their pursuit as a critical accounting for their faith have by no means exchanged their religious commitment for critical, theoretic alienation from their beliefs. It is in the nature of critical theologians' pursuit that they should experience some tension between their long-standing beliefs and a critical approach to those beliefs. Moreover, the presence of such tension signifies that theologians are not only authentically but also critically involved in their subject, since that critical tension will in itself lead them to new questions (cf. Kuitert, 1977:12).

The personal commitment of systematic theologians ultimately governs their formulation of statements about God. The relationship between God and believer forms the basis of the referential element in religious language and also constitutes, in the most profound sense, its relational nature. Furthermore, it is typical of the statements by theologians that they take cognizance of that relational quality, since they are most profoundly interested in the objectivity or realist nature of their references. Through religious language, religious experiences in all their complexity are in fact fully dependent on the truth of what is asserted in our religious statements. Failing that, it would also become impossible to distinguish in our beliefs between fantasy and whatever Christian believers experience and conceptualize as revelation.

The question of the nature and origins of theological statements is, therefore, the question of the structure of our religious statements and the question whether such statements refer to a reality that might give them a creditable cognitive core.

Religious Language as Metaphoric Language

The way the question of theorizing in systematic theology has developed so far has shown up more and more clearly the central role played by language—here specifically the language of faith—in the process of theorizing. I have a number of times referred in passing to the metaphoric nature of religious language— a central dimension of religious statements that merits pertinent attention at this stage of our quest for a creditable rationality model for theological reflection.

The language we use to articulate our most immediate religious experiences is not only the ultimate basis for confessional and theological language, but is usually also—precisely as an expression of our religious experience—

---

3. M. Polanyi formulates this strikingly, albeit from a different perspective, when he says: "Commitment offers to those who accept it legitimate grounds for the affirmation of personal convictions with universal intent" (1962:324).

figurative or metaphoric in a very particular sense. The metaphoric nature of all religious language also highlights the provisionality or limitations of that language. In this sense metaphoric religious language might also be described as limit-language (Tracy, 1978:108): a language consisting of limit-questions and limit-answers about the crucial limit-situations of life. The metaphoric nature of religious language constitutes its essentially religious dimension. The language of religion is the ordinary language of mankind, and its metaphoric nature does not reveal a supernaturalistic world; it opens up a limit-dimension for the benefit of this world, this experience, and this language. This quality of religious language eventually also points to its most essential characteristic, namely, that it never has a merely expressive function but rather a relational, reality-depicting, or referential character.

Throughout its long tradition Christian reflection has always been markedly conscious of the provisional and limited nature of our religious language, and thus also of the necessity for figurative or metaphoric language.[4] In the previous paragraph we saw that the referential element forming part of the provisional and metaphoric nature of religious language enables us to commit ourselves to that which is asserted. Even the various biblical authors found an encounter with the Reality referred to in religious language so overwhelming that it was totally impossible for them to speak of it neutrally, reflectively, or with "objective" detachment. And since it lies in the relational nature of religious language that it can never be seen as a mere expression of religious engagement, religious language is also most specifically concerned with the object of that engagement (cf. Hempelmann, 1980:272). And it is the disclosure of that object by metaphoric means that constitutes the essential structure of all religious language.

What Is a Metaphor?

For the moment the following basic definition of metaphor will suffice: a metaphor is normally a word or expression used in an unusual context to lead us to new insights. A good metaphor, which figuratively helps us to understand the unknown in terms of the known, ultimately makes us see our ordinary, everyday world in novel and unusual ways (TeSelle, 1975:4, 29, 34). What is impor-

---

4. Cf. S. McFague, 1982:2: "It is no accident then that the mystics in all religious traditions have been the most perceptive on the question of religious language. Aware as they are of the transcendence of God, they have not been inclined to identify our words with God: in fact, their tendency is more often to refuse any similarity between our words and the divine reality." And: "The mystics have also not restricted their language about God to biblical or traditional imagery, for the experience of God, the certainty and immediacy of it, has been the basis for new and powerful religious language."

tant is that a metaphor is a way of knowing, not merely a way of communicating (Botha, 1984:29-30). And since the nature of our theological language about God is essentially a linguistic problem (which has often grown out of a more deep-seated experiential problem), and as such is also a hermeneutical problem, it will eventually become clear that metaphor and metaphoric speech are the origins and heart of our theological reflection.

The Bible, in both the Old and the New Testaments, is exceptionally rich in metaphor in all its literary forms. Since the Bible in virtually all its genres comes to us in narrative form the metaphoric and relational character of biblical religious language becomes all the more explicit.[5] In fact, the Bible's analogical language in terms of metaphor already provides the key to relevant and creditable statements about God (cf. C. du Toit, 1984:3). But metaphor is more than a mere literary or poetic device; TeSelle (1975:44) states rightly that "metaphor follows the way the human mind works." In that sense, metaphoric speech is as fundamental as thought.

It is pertinent to the quest for a creditable rationality model for systematic theology that metaphoric speech is currently again at the center of philosophy of science and literary studies. In theology it offers exciting possibilities for examining our religious language as a direct expression of our religious experience. Moreover, when Max Black (1966:237) says that "metaphorical thought is a distinctive mode of achieving insight," and Sallie TeSelle (1975:38) says that "assertions are always implicit in metaphors," metaphor is seen as offering us a key to the theological cognitive process as well as material for the ultimate formulation of adequate criteria for a creditable systematic-theological conceptual model. At the same time it becomes clear that any theory reducing metaphor to mere comparison, verbal transference, or linguistic ornamentation can offer no satisfactory or valid models for meaningful statements about God. It would be equally impossible to answer the question of metaphoric truth in direct, literalistic, or positivistic terms (cf. McFague, 1982:40).

For a sound grasp of the role of metaphors and models in theology it is essential that we now consider the question of the nature and function of metaphors and models in science. A thorough and comprehensive study of this aspect of metaphor was recently done by Elaine Botha (1984:29-63), who maintains that the role of metaphors and figurative speech in the creative process of discovery and in the accumulation of knowledge has been known in the Western intellectual tradition since pre-Christian times.[6] If metaphors and metaphoric

---

5. What S. TeSelle (1975:35) says so strikingly about the New Testament is in my view equally true of the Old: "It is fortunate that the New Testament writers were endowed with rich imaginations, for otherwise the New Testament would hold little chance of being revelatory."

6. Botha, 1984:29. Cf. also McFague, 1982:37ff.; and C. W. du Toit, 1984, Chapter 4 (which examines the intellectual-historical development of the concept of metaphor from Aristotle through Thomas Aquinas up to and including contemporary authors of standard works, such as M. Black, P. Ricoeur, and P. Wheelwright).

thought do indeed play such a crucial role in the acquisition of knowledge, it is understandable and illuminating, especially from a philosophy of science point of view, that metaphoric language must have a strong bearing on the formation of scientific knowledge.

Metaphor is a form of figurative speech in which something (the unknown or lesser known) is seen in the light of something else. It is in fact a mode of speech in which language itself is stretched, as it were, to gain new insight, to understand something which was previously incomprehensible. This characteristic quality of metaphor might also be described as its *it is and is not* quality (McFague, 1982:13), or its *as if* quality (Botha, 1984:37). That element of tension, as well as the context in which the living metaphor functions, is vital to an understanding of the metaphoric nature of all religious language, as will shortly become clear.

What makes metaphoric language liberating is that it communicates or opens up insights into aspects of our world that cannot be articulated in literal language (cf. A. van Niekerk, 1984:67). This underlines not only metaphor's fundamental role in the expansion of language and knowledge, but also the fact that metaphor is ordinary language. And if we were finally to ask why religious metaphors are especially powerful, the answer would be that this type of speech is in line with the level on which we think in ordinary language. And here metaphor, in its simplest sense, means seeing one thing as if it is something else.

For the role metaphoric language eventually plays in the constitution and development of theological knowledge, a statement by Sallie McFague (1982:15) is illuminating: "Thinking metaphorically means spotting a thread of similarity between two dissimilar objects, events or whatever, the one of which is better known than the other, and using the better-known one as a way of speaking about the lesser known."

This statement underlines even more clearly the tension inherent in the nature of metaphor—the ability of maintaining in metaphoric reference the first or everyday perspective side by side with the new perspective suggested in it. This creative faculty of double vision, which metaphor makes possible, could also be called stereoscopic vision (cf. McFague, 1982:136; Botha, 1984:31). A centuries-old Christian tradition of analogical speech, and thus of using old and new metaphors, would here form an outstanding example; consider, for instance, the traditional distinction drawn in nearly all Christian religious language between God's transcendence and the finite nature of the created reality. In fact, this basic model of the Christian religious paradigm[7] not only enables

---

7. I am using the term *paradigm*—as I do throughout this book—in the sense of a general worldview or interpretative framework, but I am fully mindful of the fact that Kuhn himself later refined this complex concept by distinguishing between a disciplinary matrix (as a comprehensive scientific worldview encompassing the commitment of a particular group, and thus providing the conceptual framework for a scientific theory) and a narrower type of scientific paradigm which he called *exemplars*. For a lucid and thorough exposition of that conceptual refinement, see Botha, 1984:45-46.

us to use metaphoric religious language but is also indispensable and inevitable. The basic biblical model of God as a personal, transcendent Creator and Savior also forms the comprehensive basis of all further theological models and metaphors purporting to articulate our religious experience (such as transcendence–immanence, *analogia entis,* pantheism, incarnation, etc.). The necessity of metaphoric language—owing to a transcendent God who is at the same time invisible—also offers fascinating possibilities of comparisons with other sciences working with invisible entities such as atoms, values, and intelligence, for whom metaphor is therefore also indispensable. A further argument for metaphoric language in theology is of course the analogous way other religions describe the reality of what they believe: not in literal but in metaphoric language. Chryssides (1985:145-146) could therefore write:

> Adherents of most religions typically claim that there is something of which they are aware which is far greater than their own knowledge is capable of grasping—whether one calls it God, Allah, Brahman, the buddha-nature or the Tao. And when one attempts to describe that object of awareness one finds oneself using language which, if construed literally, would lead to all sorts of absurd conclusions and entailments. For example, as Wittgenstein pointed out, the Judaeo-Christian believer will talk about the 'eye of God' but will be unlikely to infer that God's eyes are accompanied by eyebrows. Literal discourse is therefore likely to be totally inadequate for expressing what the religious believer really wants to express.

In ordinary as well as religious language a metaphor therefore functions as a filter used—often subconsciously—as an organizing principle to widen one's vision[8] and at the same time also to redescribe one's world. This has an important bearing on our earlier identification of relational religious language—now more closely defined as metaphoric religious language—as the origin or source of our theological statements. In the same sense in which Old Testament religious language was relational because it consistently focused—in metaphoric terms—on the Covenant between God and Israel, so too is the language of the New Testament relational religious language. In terms of numerous metaphors—and in the case of Jesus of Nazareth often through parables as extended metaphors (cf. McFague, 1982:42ff.)—it sought to redescribe a world in which love of God and love of one's fellow human beings would be the essence of humanity. Against that background one could say that religious metaphors are concerned not only with what can be known provisionally about God, but also with the fact that what we learn from them may become a new way of living our ordinary lives through faith.

---

8. The idea that metaphors can die through literalization (Botha, 1984:33) or become senile (McFague, 1982:40) cannot be pursued here. What does become pertinent, and is discussed later, is the growth of ideologies, authoritarian standpoints, and idolizing in the context of religious and specifically theological language.

Since metaphor thus forms the basis on which both ordinary and scientific knowledge is gained for the creative shaping of new meaning, it is pertinent to the ultimate question of a philosophy of science and theologically creditable model of rationality that TeSelle (1975:41) states: "But if new meaning is always metaphorical, then there is no way now or ever to have strange truth directly."

Inasmuch as metaphor redescribes reality in a relational context it ultimately transforms both our language and our perspective on the redescribed reality. And this, in the most fundamental sense, constitutes the referential or cognitive quality of metaphoric speech. By this means the classical antithesis of subjective and objective thought, as well as the ensuing question of the objective nature of religious language, is superseded by a more relational conception of truth.[9] The metaphoric mode of thought unlocks the reality of that which is referred to in religious language, in a constructive manner that—true to the nature of metaphor—imparts new knowledge *(it is . . .)* while at the same time protecting and preserving the mystery *(it is not . . .)*. This insight will ultimately have both liberating and far-reaching consequences for our theological knowledge. If metaphoric thought characterizes human knowledge, all human knowledge—thus also theological knowledge—must be tentative, dynamic, historical, and relational. It also becomes clear, however, that a rationality model which does not account for the form of knowledge that transcends final conceptualization (cf. Strauss and Visagie, 1983:3) is not only one-sided but also unfit for expressing the meaning of theological reality.

From Metaphor to Thought Model: The Nature of Theological Conceptualizing

The preceding section has clearly shown that metaphoric speech—also in religious language—is essentially explicatory and relational. This insight is of the utmost importance to theology: whether our religious language, and also our statements about God, has any cognitive reference to reality is closely bound up with what we might now call the ontological creative function (cf. A. van Niekerk, 1984:67) of metaphoric language. In our use of language—as also in our religious statements about God—we are not simply describing realities that are equally accessible by other means. Language does not merely represent or reflect reality; it also constitutes reality. In this sense metaphoric

9. Cf. W. van Huyssteen and B. J. du Toit, 1982:10-15, 57-62. Of the epistemological problems surrounding the extremes of objectivism and subjectivism, TeSelle (1975:59) writes: "The main difficulty with post-Cartesian epistemologies is that they do not figure in the figurer; they split mind and body, reason and imagination, subject and object, nature and history and end with something other and less than human knowing."

language opens up to us, both creatively and exploratively, the reality of which we speak, since what we see as reality is to a large extent creatively and exploratively determined by the metaphoric potential of the language in which reality is articulated.[10]

It is also important to note that in theology, as in all other sciences, metaphoric speech gives rise to models which enable us to formulate certain theories or networks of theories. From the earliest biblical times, for instance, the metaphor *Father* has in ordinary religious language provided a dominant model for Christian statements about God. It could do so because the Father model offered Christian believers an explanation for what they experienced in their relationship with God, namely, love, protection, discipline, care, etc. This also applied to theological models such as the Trinity, or a theological theory such as the theory of inspiration, which developed from the original metaphor of inspiration into multifaceted and divergent theories. Thinking in terms of metaphors and models is therefore an essential characteristic of the development and discovery of all scientific knowledge. An essential link exists between metaphors and models, since both produce creative and exploratory proposals for new designs or interpretations (cf. C. W. du Toit, 1984:112). In this sense, models founded on metaphors are established or designed in order to get a grip on and explain the structure of complex phenomena in science (Botha, 1984:56).

Since some metaphors in our language have for some reason become popular and exceptionally useful in the structuring and organizing of our experience of reality, such metaphors develop into models. As Sallie McFague (1982:23) puts it: "The simplest way to define a model is as a dominant metaphor, a metaphor with staying power."

It is also essential to realize that models thus become a further step along the way from metaphoric to theoretic language. If a metaphor becomes a model, it not only presents a comprehensive organizational structure with great interpretative potential but also retains, as a model, its metaphoric roots, and thus its typical metaphoric qualities. Among the most notable metaphors in our religious language which became so dominant in the Christian tradition that they have finally become models and are already reaching out, while retaining their metaphoric roots, for the typical qualities of theoretic thought, are the well-known biblical references to God the Father, or to Jesus Christ as the Redeemer or the Savior. Like metaphors, models—albeit more comprehensively and consistently—help us to think about the unknown in terms of the known. As such, a model may be typified as a filter enabling us to say something we could not have said otherwise,[11] and therefore models may be said to function as extended and systematized metaphors in terms of which things are explained.

Models, more comprehensively even than metaphors, provide a means

10. On the realist character of metaphors, see M. E. Botha, 1984:53-56.
11. For a detailed discussion of the function of models in language, see Black, 1962:219-243.

of speaking about the unknown. Good models not only provide a network of language enabling us to understand; they also maintain a fascinating balance between simplicity and detail, thus creating links that make further suggestions possible. Models naturally play a central role in the formation of new scientific ideas, since their metaphoric roots provide scope for creative imagination.[12] On the way from metaphors to theoretic concepts, models are hypothetically infused with structures and relationships, from the known to the lesser known.

As a special blending of metaphor and theoretic concept, models play an important role in the context of our Christian religious tradition for the very reason that they are, in a sense, midway between the metaphoric nature of our religious language and the theoretic nature of our theological language. As dominant metaphors, models emphasize the priorities of a particular religious tradition. As systematized organizational principles in the rich network of such a tradition's figurative language, religious models consistently lead us to systematic thought and theorizing; as comprehensive interpretative networks they also form the center of theological questions about their referential quality—and thus about truth and the depiction of reality. As metaphors, models control and regulate the way we reflect on God and humanity, and on the multifaceted relationship between God and humanity, precisely because tension is implicit in the *as if* quality of metaphors.

As in scientific models, theological models naturally demand a form of total commitment (cf. McFague, 1982:90-91). Botha (1984:28, 63) rightly cautions us against a too direct identification of the role of commitment in science with commitment in terms of basic religious convictions, but she also makes the pertinent point that a metaphoric approach to scientific theories ultimately provides scope for the accommodation of both forms of commitment. (Unless the contrary is specifically stated, I myself consistently use the term *commitment* in the context of basic religious convictions.)

In theology there is indubitably also an intellectual commitment to particular paradigms. In fact, the theologian can hardly avoid thinking and working in terms of paradigmatically determined models, whether in wider theological traditions or in specific models consciously chosen, by certain definitive criteria, as the most successful and meaningful ones in a particular tradition. We shall later see that the absolutizing of certain models inevitably leads to dogmatism and ideologizing in theology, since it implies the negation of the dynamics and tension inherent in their metaphoric roots.

In theology, as in other sciences, models as conceptual frameworks (Mouton and Marais, 1985:141)—specifically in the form of creeds and dogma—provide a systematic network for explication. It is interesting to note, however, that theological models are much more prone to permanence—and

---

12. On models in science, cf. Black, 1962:219ff.; but especially also S. McFague, 1982:67-102; and Barbour, 1976:29ff.

thus to the danger of ideologizing—than other scientific models, perhaps mainly because the dominant models of certain theological traditions may become so all-encompassing that certain models may begin to function as virtually immutable and permanent basic metaphors.[13] Moreover, the use of models in liturgy, for example, often entrenches them as a permanent and essential component of the truth of a certain religious tradition (cf. McFague, 1982:95).

The permanence of theological models naturally provides essential and meaningful continuity in certain religious traditions, but that permanence may have the adverse effect of certain theological models' being ideologized virtually to the point of becoming unchangeable and ageless icons, at the inevitable expense of all the provisional, referential, and open qualities of metaphors. At this stage it is clear that our thought vacillates constantly between metaphor and theoretic concept, a process in which conceptual models play an essential and indispensable role. We use our concepts to interpret metaphors and to preserve them from ideologizing through literal interpretation. Since theoretic concepts never lose their metaphoric roots, we need metaphor to understand them, to explicate them meaningfully, and thus to preserve their tentative openness.

To understand the process of conceptualizing in systematic theology we should now perhaps refer to what was said at the beginning of this chapter about the preconceptualizing of all religious experience (and therefore also the theologian's). In the case of theologians, that structuring or conceptualizing of religious experience would be reinforced by their commitment to a certain model or network of theological models, which may function subconsciously as submerged or hidden models and thus as organizing principles on the experiential as well as the intellectual level. In dealing with such a commitment, for example, to the model or models of a certain theological tradition, it is essential to realize that these—often submerged—models are sustained, in theology too, by an even deeper commitment to the root metaphor of that religious tradition.

Writers such as Black (1962), Barbour (1976), McFague (1982), and Botha (1984), who attempt to explain the structure of science with the aid of metaphors and model formation and therefore advocate a new epistemological approach in which the theory-ladenness of all scientific language is taken into account, point out that in the scientific formulation of both models and concepts a clear link—although also a distinction—exists between broader kinds of philosophical, worldview, or root metaphors and narrower models and metaphors (cf. Botha, 1984:45).

What makes this so important for theological conceptualizing is that the essence of a religion such as Christianity might be seen as its basic or root metaphor. Such a basic metaphor would of course be open to divergent interpretations from various perspectives and Christian traditions. But whether the root metaphor of Christianity is seen, for example, as liberation through Jesus Christ

---

13. On basic metaphors, see Botha, 1984:45.

or as the advent of God's Kingdom (thus McFague, 1982:27), that basic metaphor constitutes not only that which distinguishes the Christian faith from other religions but also explicitly that without which the Christian faith would lose its essential character and thus cease to qualify as Christian in any sense.

The basic metaphor of our Christian faith—which I myself would call salvation in Jesus Christ—thus develops from the complex biblical language, through the numerous dimensions and meanings of a long-standing tradition of Christian reflection, into models and eventually into theological concepts, which become accessible through faith and various devotional forms (including creeds, liturgies, and confessions) and thus in turn direct the religious experiences of Christian believers. What is of cardinal importance is that, in the ultimate formulation of theological concepts and the clustering of theological statements into theories, that reflectional theoretic language must remain true to its metaphoric sources and their links with a certain basic metaphor. If it does so the metaphoric tension inherent to all language—and therefore also religious language—is preserved throughout the lengthy process of the development of theological language and reflection.[14]

A meaningful distinction can be drawn between the pretheoretic language of faith and the theoretic language of theology, but they can never be separated rigidly. Metaphoric religious language and the precision of theological language are essentially interdependent. We have seen that the origins of religious language lie in religious experience, and that experience—even if it always occurs in terms of submerged or conscious religious or theological models—is first and ultimately an encounter with God. Such religious experiences, articulated in metaphoric language, sustain theological reflection and the forming of theoretic concepts. McFague (1982:119) is therefore correct in calling that interdependence a symbiotic relationship, in which metaphors provide food for theoretic concepts while the clarification sought through theoretic concepts lends vision or perspective to the metaphor.

The two basic needs of human cognition, namely, the metaphoric articulation of our experiences and the conceptual organization and theoretic clarification of those experiences, come together in the models of our theological language. Concepts may now also be defined as linguistic constructs with which we classify our reality (Mouton and Marais, 1985:58ff.). In systematic theology concepts are therefore primarily the instruments enabling us to understand our religious reality and to sort and organize the often unsystematized contents of our religious experiences. And such concepts can gain meaning—or even new meaning—only in certain broad or global paradigmatic contexts, not only because metaphor and theoretic concept fuse creatively in the model but also because theological concepts are theoretic concepts or constructs.

14. Cf. McFague, 1982:127: "Theology begins with a root-metaphor and ends in an ordering, comprehensive system, but even the system, while different from the metaphors that found it, is or should be a continuum with them."

Since systematic theology covers such a broad spectrum of meaning, theology and the history of theological reflection offer a multitude of theological models striving constantly to redescribe, in metaphoric terms, the reality referred to in the basic metaphor of our faith. In our eventual construction of a creditable model of rationality for systematic theology we shall therefore also have to formulate criteria that are, from a philosophy of science point of view, both valid and theologically capable of enabling us to make relevant and responsible choices between models, to arrive at radical reinterpretations of existing theological models, and even to discover new models.[15]

Understanding the formulation of theological models and their role in systematic-theological theorizing is therefore essential and indispensable for an understanding of theological conceptual language. Theological models are always a unique combination of metaphoric and theoretic language, providing us with filters to interpret the essential implications of the basic biblical metaphors. The theological doctrine of the Trinity of God, for example, is not a conceptual construction designed to describe God's essential being in an absolutist literal and final sense; its purpose is to unlock the essential implications of the basic biblical metaphor with the aid of a number of further metaphoric models from the Bible (Father, Son, Holy Spirit).

Contrary to naïve-realist or fundamentalist models that see dogma in theology, for example, as precise, literal replicas of basic biblical metaphors, the metaphoric basis of theological models and theoretic concepts now enables us to open up the meaning of that which is referred to in theological language, and to do so critically, creatively, and exploratively. For this approach, in which the scientist and therefore also the theologian attempts to say something about a reality beyond our language by means of provisional, tentative models in terms of human constructs, the term *critical realism* might be fruitful.[16] A critical-realist approach to theology now becomes feasible because metaphors and models play such a decisive role in all cognitive development—also in theology. A critical-realist stand is realistic because in the process of theological theorizing this concept enables us to recognize the cognitive and referential nature of analogical language as a form of indirect speech. It is also critical, however, because the role of metaphoric language in theology would teach us that models should never be absolutized or ideologized, but should retain their openness and provisionality throughout the process of theorizing.

15. From this perspective I find highly problematic C. W. du Toit's (1984:118) view that theology develops differently from the natural sciences, for example, because God's revelation is concluded and the gospel is an eternal truth—even if he leaves room for a possible rejuvenation of existing models. Du Toit is probably (and rightly) referring to the nonnegotiable nature of the basic biblical metaphors, but even then—given the multidimensionality and multisignificance of biblical metaphors (as well as those that have since become dominant metaphors)—we cannot escape the theorizing nature of and hermeneutical problems surrounding these central metaphors.

16. Cf. also, although from a particular reformist-feminist point of view and with a characteristically personal epistemology and parabolic Christology, S. McFague, 1982:133.

9

Criteria for a Critical-Realist Model of Rationality in Systematic Theology

*The problem is that each type of theology is embedded in a conceptual frame-
work so comprehensive that it shapes its own criteria of adequacy.*

George A. Lindbeck, *The Nature of Doctrine: Religion and Theology in a Postliberal Age* (Philadelphia: Westminster Press,
1984):113.

Introduction

A heavy responsibility rests on any systematic theology that would now pursue
its theological reflection within a comprehensive conceptual model in which
theology is first and foremost a form of critical accounting of faith. The models
such a theology uses, reinforces, or explores in the process of conceptualizing
must not only remain true to Christian tradition, and thus to the essential or basic
metaphor of that tradition, but must also make a valid appeal to our perception
of reality and current scientific concerns. A systematic-theological model that
fails on any of these crucial levels jeopardizes our Christian religious paradigm
and would therefore have to be replaced by another, better, and more valid conceptual model. To be able to make the hazardous kind of evaluation such a sub-
stitution demands, however, we shall need clearly formulated criteria.

In discussing William W. Bartley's critical-rationalistic confrontation with theology we could already, from a fundamental-theological point of view, formulate the dilemma and problem of the systematic theologian as follows:[1] Is it at all possible for theologians to advance reasons for their mostly conscious choice of a particular systematic-theological model, or are they inevitably doomed to an inexplicable and irrational commitment to a certain line of theological thought? Owing to the radical transformation and broadening of the concepts of rationality and objectivity since Thomas S. Kuhn, however, we could abandon that line of questioning as an unreasonable and therefore invalid polarization.

For precisely that reason, neither the strict scientist nor the critical-realist theologian need see any hazard in admitting the correctness of the following statement by Michael Polanyi (1962:322) in respect of scientific and religious convictions: "Our believing is conditioned at its source by our belonging." But the quest for criteria for a valid rationality model for theology is by no means suspended when the theologian gains the freedom of committed, metaphoric, and relational thought. And theology will have to move beyond the Kuhnian model if it would formulate both philosophy of science and systematic-theological criteria for a model that might guide it rationally as well as contextually to a new credibility, once it has found, through the metaphoric roots of its language, the key to cognitivity and contextuality. Theologians must be able to show why they believe their statements to be true to reality, and why those statements are indeed relevant and topical in their own sociocultural context.

Theology is an attempt to reflect as authentically and creditably as possible on whatever we have, through our religious commitment, come to know and experience as God's revelation. Theology is therefore a form of reflection in which we use the formulation of models to transform our metaphoric religious language into lucid and explicit theoretic concepts, thus striving for a tentative articulation of our provisional but nonetheless certain knowledge of God. That is why, in my view, theological reflection may be seen as essentially a process of creative conceptual construction. And since the long-standing tradition of Christian thought has produced various and divergent interpretations of that tradition and its basic metaphors, current theological interpretation of the essence of our Christian faith must also be diverse and multifaceted. For systematic theology it is therefore inevitable and even self-evident that we should now have various and even divergent conceptual constructions in the form of a plurality of theological models.

This once again leads us to the central question of criteria for a creditable systematic-theological model. No systematic theologian, given the universal claims of theology's central thematics, can ever be reconciled to an esoteric conceptual model that provides, in ghetto fashion, its own intratheological criteria for truth. We have seen that the question of rationality leads theology

---

1. Cf. in detail Chapter 4 above.

directly to the question of criteria that would also be valid from a philosophy of science point of view. Similarly, the question of the origins of our theological statements may lead us to supersede and broaden the rationality question with a wide-ranging examination of the historical, hermeneutical, and sociology of knowledge criteria for a creditable systematic theology.

From the outset, however, this book has been concerned with the exploration and rediscovery of the concept of rationality for theology. Although our inquiry has shown the value and validity of a wide range of theologies from a philosophy of science point of view, the theologian remains committed to finding criteria by which various conceptual models might criticize and supplement each other. By this means theologians from divergent contexts or traditions might eventually help each other toward greater coherence, consistency, and loyalty in respect of the core of the Christian religious tradition.

A theology that sees itself as a critical accounting of faith could thus be enabled to bring new insights to bear on its ecumenical task in current theological inquiries, precisely because such a theology would be looking for criteria that would be intersubjectively illuminating, both from a theological and a philosophy of science point of view. A critical theology that has thus learned to see its reflective processes as a creative conceptual construction will never be able to proceed from established confessional contrasts between churches, but should be essentially ecumenical. In my view, confessional differences and variety ought to be one of the systematic theologian's first concerns, since he will have learned to live and think hermeneutically, from both the Bible and the long tradition of theological reflection since the Bible, and never dogmatistically from tradition alone. At the same time, however, it is the very content of theological reflection, as well as theology's own critical scientific nature, that also leads it beyond church and confession to a concern with the issues engaging our times. Thus systematic theology is given a transconfessional dimension that has at the same time a scientifically and ecumenically liberating impact on theorizing.

The question of theorizing in theology, as of plausible criteria for a systematic-theological conceptual model, ought to be pursued on that supraconfessional level. It is vitally important, however, to emphasize that fundamental-theological inquiry on a supraconfessional level need not lead to the deconfessionalizing of theology, but should ultimately lead the theologian to reconsider, with new insight and commitment, certain specific confessional problems. In view of that background, and in opting for well-founded criteria for credibility, a theology that sees itself as a critical accounting of faith need never run the risk of becoming a-contextual.[2] On the contrary, contextuality— whether experiential, confessional, sociopolitical, or historicotheological—

---

2. This misgiving about theoretical alienation in my approach to theology is to be found in John W. de Gruchy, 1985.

will have to be an essential component in the formulation of criteria for a valid theological model.

In the previous section we noted that the key to the question of the nature of our theological statements lay in the process by which theories are established. The key to finding criteria for a creditable theological rationality model lies in our conclusions on the nature and origins of theorizing in the formulation of our theological statements. The archetypal sources of our religious language lie in religious experience; in religious language, as a metaphoric limit-language, we could discover the origins of our confessional and theological models. In those models, as a blending of metaphor and theoretic concept, we could find the creative basis for the pursuit of conceptual clarity. In our theological concepts we could find material for the clustering of theological conceptual language into hypothetical theories seeking to formulate—from a consciously considered religious commitment, and with the retention of the metaphoric roots of all theological language—a tentative statement on God's reality for this world and for our present-day experiences.

The process of theorizing in systematic theology is lengthy and complicated, as we have seen. But then, God's message of redemption through Jesus Christ also came to us through a Person and events of long ago. The way Christian believers have for nearly two thousand years experienced that event in faith, and have reflected on its claims to truth, is the reason why it will never be enough simply to keep telling the story of Jesus of Nazareth. To be able to contextualize that ancient story for our time we need theological reflection, and in that sense Jesus of Nazareth in fact provides theology's only right of existence.

That rich source of all forms of theological reflection also commits systematic theology to rationality. And the formulation of criteria that may lead— also from a philosophy of science point of view—to a valid rationality model for systematic theology will also be a testimonial to a theology that wishes to see itself as a critical accounting of faith. The criteria listed below[3] also try to take into account the plurality of the South African theological context and the diverse perspectives emerging from the complex and problematic South African experience; they will therefore have to be broadened further through sociology of knowledge and otherwise.

I should now like to propose the following criteria for a valid systematic-theological model of rationality:

1. The reality depiction of theological statements.
2. The critical and problem-solving ability of theological statements.
3. The constructive and progressive nature of theological statements.

If a theology that sees itself as a critical accounting of faith has become aware of its own reflective processes as a form of creative, conceptual

---

3. For an earlier (and hence provisional) identification of the three minimum criteria for systematic theology, cf. my "Teologie en Skrifgesag," in van Huyssteen and du Toit, 1982:41-63.

construction and can show, moreover, that its theological model appeals to both insight and experience because of its reality depiction, and if, furthermore, such a theology can critically identify and attempt to solve problems and can show creative progress, then that theology has in my view succeeded in establishing a comprehensive and valid rationality model for a creditable systematic theology.

The Reality Depiction of Theological Statements

Instead of the concept of reality depiction as one of the minimum demands or criteria for establishing the rationality of theological statements, we might also have chosen to speak of their realist or referential nature. In the context of this theological realism, *reality* refers primarily and specifically to the reality of God as posited directly or indirectly in all theological statements. In that sense we speak of the reality depiction as cognitivity, implying not only the Reality anticipated in our theological language but also the role of the subjectivity of the theologian making those relational theological statements.

In another sense, reality depiction may be defined as contextuality. We shall then have to examine the concrete and actual sociocultural context or contexts in which theology has to find, identify, and try to solve its problems. In a special sense, the contexts of religious experience, the church, and theological reflection itself will have to be examined.

Reality Depiction as Cognitivity

From the outset our primary problem has been whether theology can justly claim to be a valid form of scientific thought. We have consistently tried to structure a rationality model for systematic theology that would avoid all forms of privatism by developing, on an intersubjective level, the claim to truth of our valid, albeit provisional, theological statements. It has become clear that in theology, too, a valid form of committed or relational thought is to be found, and that the question of as well as the criteria for objectivity are contextually determined.

It was above all in the metaphoric nature of religious language, as the source and origin of theological language, that we found the key to the fact that religious language transcends itself by referentially anticipating the Reality referred to in that language. The relational nature of religious language is ultimately founded on the fact that it is never a mere expression of religious feelings but is in fact referential. In that sense our religious language is the only valid line of access to the reality of God to which we are committed through faith.

As we have seen, relationality ought to be of crucial interest to systematic theology, since it is most profoundly concerned with the objective quality, with the reality behind the reference. Here we have yet another definition of reality depiction as cognitivity. When that Reality is theologically translated into God and that which believers have learned to experience as His revelation, it becomes even clearer that a theology committed to incisive, intersubjective reasoning can no longer afford to run the risk of undisciplined theological reflection, which often lurks behind the concept of theology.

In philosophy of science, post-Kuhnian thought has developed a fascinating parallel inquiry into the reality depiction or referential quality of scientific statements—a recent development or school of thought that has become known as scientific realism.[4] The Kuhnian stress on the way scientific knowledge develops has led not only to a radical redefinition and broadening of the concept of rationality but also to greater sensitivity to the role of theoretic constructs in the paradigmatic shaping of the scientist's ultimate objectives. Thanks to Kuhn, theology has at last developed sensitivity to the historical contextuality and paradigmatic determination of all its conceptual models. In the process theology has regained a liberating insight into its own theorizing.

Theologically, but also in the broader scientific sense, the question of the reality spoken of has, however, remained vague, at the inevitable risk of the relativism Kuhn was so often accused of. After Kuhn, in philosophy of science circles, there also developed a form of anti-realism with regard to the ontological status of the realities referred to in theories.[5]

With Kuhn's ongoing influence, however, remains the fact that his perspective led to socially contextualized views of scientific theories: a new emphasis on the sociological factors that influence the development of science and the application of the sociology of knowledge specifically to the nature of scientific knowledge. For theology, in the light of the realization that scientific knowledge can apparently never be stable in meaning, because it is never independent of social context, the status of the so often directly implied truth claims of its propositions within the Kuhnian paradigm becomes more urgent than ever before. If it could indeed be finally asserted that scientific as well as theological assertions are thus socially created, it would seem highly likely that the ways of both science and theology to reality have been firmly barred. This in return would create special problems for the truth claims and the validity of all human knowledge, for if all scientific and thus also theological knowledge are pure social constructs, there could be no way in which reference or reality depiction could be claimed for their theories. If neither science nor theology can claim some sort of valid knowledge about existing realities, what could prevent them from becoming mere social ideologies?

4. For an introduction to scientific realism, see Jarrett Leplin (ed.), 1984.
5. Ernan McMullin (1984:25-26) further distinguishes between types of anti-realism, namely, general and limited anti-realism, strong and weak anti-realism.

It is against this background that the recent development of different forms of qualified scientific realism, after decades of positivism and the ensuing constant threat of a paradigmatic relativism, can definitely be seen as one of the most remarkable and welcome features of scientific thought in the twentieth century (cf. Burnham, 1985:28). When it comes to reflecting on the reliability of scientific and theological knowledge, the concept *realism* could indeed be called the catchword of the 1980s (cf. Peacocke, 1984:11). As we will see, scientific realism is so called because it makes a proposal about the reliability of scientific knowledge as such, and is therefore basically a philosophical position. For all philosophers of science who advocate realism, it forms an important alternative to the Kuhnian critique of scientific progress: without losing the validity of the fact that all human knowledge is always socially contextualized, realists with good reasons claim cognitive reference for their proposals.

Especially for those systematic theologians struggling to salvage the respectability of theological claims, realism therefore forms an important new intellectual challenge. Frederic B. Burnham (1985:27) therefore convincingly states: "Now we are beginning to recognize that the common issue for both science and religion at this moment in time is not the origin of the universe, the validity of evolution or the existence of God, but the basic principles of epistemology: how do we human beings come to terms with 'reality,' that which is."

One of the most basic philosophy of science questions of our time is therefore: To what extent do scientific and theological terms refer? And asking this question is asking, To what extent do theology and science respectively describe reality, or certain domains of reality, in an epistemologically valid way?

Hilary Putnam's now celebrated statement (if the objects to which scientific theories refer, do not really exist at all, then the success of science can only be seen as a miracle; cf. Putnam, 1984:141) undoubtedly and inevitably confronted philosophers of science with the claims of scientific realism, which indeed seems to be the only philosophy that does not make the success of science a miracle. That especially the natural sciences succeed in making many reliable predictions and also devise better ways of controlling nature is an undoubted empirical fact. It is precisely this success that is central to the realist argument.

A scientific realist is therefore not someone who for some or other reason believes that all knowledge worthy of the name is necessarily part of science as such. Scientific knowledge, however, certainly forms an impressive part of human knowledge, and what scientific realists do agree about is that the scientific endeavor has indeed been remarkably successful. What this success consists of, how it is to be explained, and what the role of realism is in this explanation do, however, cause much disagreement among realists themselves.

The real issue of scientific realism could perhaps best be described as follows: the nearly invincible belief of scientists is that we come to discover more and more of the entities of which the world is composed through the constructs around which scientific theory is built (McMullin, 1984:9). The reliability of this belief is now being debated vigorously by philosophers of science. The Kuhnian "revolution" in philosophy of science has had the effect of focusing all attention on the basic dilemma caused by the underdetermination of theories, and thereby on scientific change rather than on the traditional topic of justification. This led to the emergence of different forms of anti-realism which are, however, no more a single coherent position than is scientific realism.

Jarrett Leplin can therefore with good reasons state: scientific realism is a majority position whose advocates are so divided as to appear a minority (Leplin [ed.], 1984:1). Realists in philosophy of science are therefore divided on some of the most important realist claims, for instance:

1. The best current scientific theories are at least approximately true.
2. The central terms of the best current theories are genuinely referential.
3. The predictive success of a theory is evidence for the referential success of its central terms.
4. The approximate truth of a scientific theory is sufficient explanation of its predictive success.

What realists do, however, have in common (cf. Leplin [ed.], 1984:2) are:

1. The conviction that scientific change is progressive.
2. The conviction that science makes possible knowledge of the world beyond its accessible, empirical manifestations.
3. The conviction that reliable knowledge does not require truth by correspondence as in a naïve-realist or positivistic paradigm, but stems from the inner logic of the realist argument itself.

It is also important to know that some philosophers of science defend a convergent type of realism in which successful scientific theories are not only approximately true but in fact are more true than earlier theories (cf. Mouton, 1985:12ff.). Advocates of this position are philosophers of science like Newton-Smith and Richard N. Boyd. This becomes apparent when Boyd (1985:59), dealing with the dilemma of the underdetermination of theories in science, argues that the reliability of theory-dependent judgments can only be satisfactorily explained on the assumption that the theoretic claims embodied in the background theories which determine those judgments are approximately true, and that scientific methodology acts dialectically so as to produce in the long run an increasingly accurate theoretic picture of the world.

In theology any form of convergent realism will be virtually impossible to defend. But, as we will eventually argue, progress as such need not at all be defined in the sense of a gradual growth toward truth. Even if the history of at least some of the natural sciences shows progressive approximation to truth in the physical world, the realist position could never depend on "achieving truth" as such. As opposed to a convergent realism, Ernan McMullin defends a more restricted form of realism. Because I am convinced that this model most clearly indicates what the possibilities and limitations of scientific realism are for theology, I shall now focus the remaining part of my discussion of scientific realism mainly on McMullin's views.

By now it must be clear that the basic realist claim is that the scientist is in a creative way discovering the structures of the world. Realism therefore has to do with the existence implications of the theoretic entities of successful theories (cf. McMullin, 1984:13). Realist claims should, however, be made with great caution, for, as McMullin (1984:14) justly warns, "imaginability must not be made the test for ontology." Against this background it becomes very important to know what kind of philosophical position is implied in scientific realism. Of this McMullin (1984:16) says: "The qualifier 'scientific' in front of 'realist' should not be allowed to mislead. It is used to distinguish the realism I am discussing from the many others that dot the history of philosophy. 'Scientific realism' is scientific because it proposes a thesis *in regard* to science."

This important definition is followed by an equally important warning, which should at all times be heeded by realists—also by any eventual so-called critical realists in theology: *realism is not a blanket approval for all the entities postulated by long-supported theories of the past.* On the contrary, the sort of theory on which realists ground their argument is one in which an increasingly finer specification of internal structure has been obtained over a long period, in which the theoretic entities function essentially in the argument and are not simply intuitive postulations of an "underlying reality," and in which the original metaphor has proved continuously fertile and capable of increasingly further extension (cf. McMullin, 1984:17).

I shall return shortly to the important role of metaphor in obtaining reliable scientific knowledge. What at this stage is very important and will eventually prove to be equally important for theology is that realists should at all times realize that the ontological claims they make are at best tentative. Thomas Kuhn was very successful in pointing out some surprising reversals that have occurred in the history of science, but then again the nonreversals in the history of science require some form of explanation too. It is precisely this explanation that is made possible by the realist argument.

If the surprising shifts in scientific knowledge, the under-determination of theories, and the nonreversals in the history of scientific thought eventually form a special challenge to theological thought, the tentativeness of all ontological claims will surely be an extremely important factor in determining the nature of theological reflection. To these challenges should be added the fact that success, as was pointed out earlier, is central to the realist argument. The only reason for believing that scientific statements actually refer is tied to the success of a specific theory. What makes this so important is that McMullin (1984:21) also states specifically: "There is a special class of theoretical entities whose *entire* warrant lies in the theory built around them."

The reason for this, I believe, is fairly obvious: there are important entities to which some scientific statements refer whose reality claims are complicated because they happen to be unobservable (cf. electrons, genes, etc.). To guarantee his or her claim to reality for these entities, the realist will have to provide a theory of reference that will be able to secure a continuity of reference in regard to these theoretic terms. This ties up with McMullin's important analysis of scientific realism when he argues that it is because the history of science testifies to a substantial continuity in theoretic structures that we are led to the doctrine of scientific realism at all. Were the history of science not to do so, then we would have no logical or metaphysical grounds for believing in scientific realism in the first place (McMullin, 1984:22).

For a theologian the realist argument now becomes even more fascinating: not only did Boyd (1984:59) specifically mention an assumption that the theoretic claims embodied in background theories are approximately true; McMullin himself here explicitly speaks of metaphysical grounds for believing in scientific realism. How this relates to the problem of commitment as an existential commitment, a theoretic commitment, or even an "ultimate" faith commitment will hopefully become clear later.

This does, however, bring us back to the basic claim of scientific realism: there is reason to believe that the theoretic terms of successful theories actually refer. McMullin (1984:26) now points to four important qualifications built into this basic claim:

1. The theory must be successful over a significant period of time.
2. The explanatory success of the theory gives some reason, though not a conclusive warrant, to believe it.
3. What is believed is that the theoretic structures are *something like* the structure of the real world.
4. No claim is made for a special, more basic, privileged form of existence for the postulated theories.

In this argument for ontological reference two important factors now emerge:

1. The explanatory success of a theory is a structural type of explanation, which means that in many parts of the natural sciences there has been, over the last two centuries, a progressive discovery of structure. This ontological claim obviously implies that something can be inferred about real structures that are at present out of our reach. What I find a further and fascinating implication at this point is that the realist's claim that there are reasons to believe that the terms of successful theories refer, obviously—and with good reasons—lead to an existential commitment to scientific realism as such.
2. For McMullin the criterion of fertility plays an important role in all scientific explanations. Fertility in structural explanations not only im-

plies the capability to make new predictions but also the heuristic function of theories to suggest new modifications or imaginative extensions to existing models (cf. Mouton, 1985:27). McMullin (1984:30ff.) therefore directly links the criterion of fertility to the use of models and of metaphors in science.

The way in which metaphors are now linked to the very center of scientific thought is of the utmost importance, not only for understanding scientific realism but also for eventually evaluating critical realism in theology. The direct implication of this important fact is that the language of the scientist is not so direct and "literal" as it was once thought to be. Not only are even the most literal-sounding terms "theory-laden," but since they are always to a certain extent provisional they must be regarded as metaphoric (cf. McMullin, 1982:37). To regard certain concepts as metaphoric is not to say that they are not precise, or that they are always ambiguous. On the contrary, McMullin (1982:37) states it well: metaphors are not normally ambiguous, yet at crucial moments in the continuing development of science, they do generate ambiguity, just the sort of fruitful ambiguity that permits a theory to be extended, reshaped, rethought, etc.

Therefore, "The metaphor is helping to illuminate something that is not well understood in advance, perhaps, some aspect of human life that we find genuinely puzzling or frightening or mysterious. The manner in which such metaphors work is by tentative suggestion" (McMullin, 1984:31). The role of metaphor in scientific thought is also the scientific realist's answer to Kuhn's well-known thesis of the incommensurability between paradigms, and therefore often also between theories, in science. As for the problem of continuity when the scientist moves from a rejected theory to a new theory, what provides the continuity is the underlying metaphor or metaphors of successive theories. Thus one may find that in scientific thought one aspect of an original or older theory may eventually be dropped, while others are thought through again and creatively retained. Even in a total "paradigm switch" it will be only the metaphor(s) that constitute the continuity. For McMullin (1984:33) this is the fertility of metaphoric language, and this kind of fertility is a persistent feature of structural explanations in the natural sciences over the last three centuries and especially during the last century.

In our understanding of the world—also our scientific understanding—metaphors therefore play a significant if not central role. In fact the explanatory power or success of a theory depends on the effective metaphors it can call upon. For this reason I would call the epistemological model that scientific realism offers us a relational model. The scientist as subject, the metaphor-maker (McMullin, 1982:37), is now recognized as an inseparable part of the scientific endeavor. Of this McMullin (1982:37) says: "Yet this in no way lessens the *realism* of science, the thrust of the scientist to grasp the 'irreducible X' before him. It is, indeed, precisely the quality of a scientific theory as fruitful metaphor, as lending itself to further development, that most commends it as *good science.*"

A theory in science is a good theory when it provides good explanations. In this process metaphor plays a key role. Precisely this idea will have to be followed up for theology, and in my own interpretation of realism in theology it will eventually be fundamental and decisive for the epistemological status of theological reflection.

From the central role of metaphors in scientific thought, it follows logically that the acceptance of a theory in science does not imply the belief that this theory is literally true. In this sense one could indeed say that the aims of science have been scaled down (so McMullin, 1982:37), and because of the power of partial disclosure that lies within metaphor, a scientific theory can be thought of as truth bearing. Science therefore aims at fruitful metaphor and at ever more detailed structure, and in this process the concepts and models of the scientist progress and develop in an approximation of truth.

The realist would therefore not use the term *true* to describe a good theory. He would, however, suppose that the theory will give us some insight into the reality of that which is being studied. His assurance that there is a "fit" (cf. McMullin, 1984:35; 1982:32), however provisional, between the structures of the theory and the structure of the reality it is groping for comes not from a comparison between them—he has no independent access to this reality—but from the inner logic of the realist argument itself. In this way the realist argument shows convincingly that our only access to the reality on which the scientist focuses is through the scientific concept. Since this concept is part of a conceptual network, the theory, which in itself is open to change and even radical reformulation, has to be regarded as provisional (cf. McMullin, 1982:32). For the scientific realist the theoretic language of science is therefore theoretic explanation of a special sort. It is metaphoric and thus open-ended and ever capable of further development. The precise metaphoric basis of all scientific language gives this language resources of suggestion that are the most immediate testimony to its ontological worth.

Against this background it should now be clear why scientific realism has developed into one of the most important positions in the current philosophy of science debate: it not only highlights the role of metaphoric reference in scientific theory formation while honoring the provisionality and sociohistorical nature of all knowledge,[6] but it also enables us to retain the ideals of truth, objectivity, rationality, and scientific progress in an exciting and reinterpreted

---

6. The relational nature of scientific theories, but also the fact that they are in principle always provisional, is clearly evident from the following statement by McMullin (1984:35): "The realist would not use the term true to describe a good theory. He would suppose that the structures of the theory give some insight into the structures of the world. But he could not, in general, say how good the insight is. He has no independent access to the world."

way. It is therefore not at all surprising that the realist challenge has at present been taken on in the humanities, especially the social sciences but also theology. I am fully convinced that, because of the important relational analysis and the accompanying interpretative and thus hermeneutical dimension of all knowledge in the realist paradigm, this venture can in no valid way be seen as a return to the positivist ideal of the uniformity of all scientific knowledge.

The classic realist paradigm, in spite of its often pluriform manifestations, did of course originate in direct relation to the natural sciences, and it now becomes the task of scientists from other fields to evaluate what the inherent creative epistemological possibilities of this position might be for the other sciences. Important work on realism in the social sciences is at present being done by philosophers of science like Roy Bhaskar, Russel Keat, John Urry, and Andrew Sayer (cf. Mouton, 1986:5-32). Within this field, issues like structural explanation, reference, the underdetermination of theories, and the whole idea of success form a very special challenge.

We must now turn our attention to the very complicated problem of the reliability and epistemological status of theological knowledge. Theology, as the very specific reflection on Christian experience and the relationship thereof to the religious dimension of our culture, certainly has a rather unique nature which sets it apart from most other forms of scientific reflection. This creates special problems for the status of its propositions and their claim to reality. I am convinced that scientific realism, in the form of a qualified critical realism, has tremendous resources for supporting the reliability and validity of theological assertions.

For some theologians the meaningful retention of a redefined post-positivistic concept of rationality in order to claim validity and reliability for the process of theological thought has become a major issue. Closely related to this issue is the strong conviction that the quest for ultimate meaning in life cannot take place within a dichotomy between faith and knowledge, but only within their creative interaction. With this in mind, I think it is fairly obvious why a few theologians have recently begun to grasp the enormous potential of scientific realism for theology. Important works have been published by theologians like Sallie McFague (1982), Arthur Peacocke (1984), and Janet Martin Soskice (1985) on what has come to be known as critical realism in theology.

I think that anyone considering the possibilities of scientific realism for theology should be extremely wary of an uncritical, superficial transferring of the realism of science to the domain of religious belief, and to theology as the reflection on the claims of this belief. I also think Philip Hefner (1985:32) quite correctly questions the somewhat doctrinaire sense in which the term *critical realism* is sometimes used in theology: it is indeed not yet quite an established theory of explanation but rather a very promising and suggestive hypothesis, struggling for credibility while being at the center of discussion. At the basis of the reasons for using this term is the conviction that what we are provisionally conceptualizing in theology really exists. This basic assumption and the good reasons we have for it make it possible for theologians, like scientists, to believe they are theorizing in a valid, progressive, and therefore successful way.

The strength of the critical-realist position certainly lies in its insistence that both the objects of science and the objects of religious belief lie beyond the range of literal description (cf. McMullin, 1985:47). I think this eventually represents a major advance in our understanding of what not only science but also theology can achieve. To put it in Arthur Peacocke's (1984:51) words: the scientific and theological enterprises share alike the tools of groping humanity: words, ideas, images that have been handed down, which we refashion in our own way for our own times in the light of present-day experience. Science and theology, for the Christian, can therefore only be seen as interacting and mutually illuminating approaches to reality. What exactly is meant by "reality" in this context will of course have to be carefully analyzed. In regard to this issue of reality in science and theology, I think Peacocke is correct in warning against a form of discrimination when we attribute "reality" as such. Indeed, there is no sense in which subatomic particles are to be regarded as "more real" than a bacterial cell for a human person or, even, social facts or God (Peacocke, 1984:36).

When Peacocke proceeds to relate these realities to different levels of reality, a cut through the totality of reality, it does become more problematical. It could imply that realism should then apply in a similar way to the fields of both science and theology, which, as we will see, would be highly problematical. I think McMullin (1985:39) pinpoints the problem by underlining the fact that there is no way that science and theology could deal with the same reality, and rather than saying that there are different "levels" of reality, one should realize that science and theology for the most part deal with different domains of the same reality. He states it very clearly (McMullin, 1985:40): "Science has no access to God in its explanation; theology has nothing to say about the specifics of the natural world."

Where I do think the two overlap, however, is on the level of reflection or human knowledge: each has something important to say about two very different but also very important domains of reality. For myself this is very important: it is on this level, the problem of the reliability of theological knowledge, that a theory of critical realism will have to be put to the test and not at all in the sense of "proving" that the Reality theology is talking about really exists or could be only a "useful fiction" for helping people to lead better lives. In this sense, if I interpret him correctly, McMullin (1985:39) also sympathizes with the claim that both science and theology could be regarded as "realist," that is, as making reliable truth claims about domains of reality that lie beyond our experience.

When defining theology, Arthur Peacocke (1984:37) underlines the important fact that theology is to be seen as the reflective and intellectual analysis of the religious experience of mankind and in particular of the Christian experience. Because believers regard themselves as making meaningful assertions about a reality that human beings can and do encounter in faith experiences, religion and religious experience has always been and still is regarded as a "way to Reality," that is, as referring to a reality beyond our experience.

While agreeing with this, the logical and important next question for me should now be: What—within the context of the Christian faith—ultimately evokes genuine faith experiences? It seems to me that this will bring us back to the central and foundational role of the biblical text as the classical religious text of Christianity. Peacocke, however, unfortunately disregards this question and instead asks the following, equally essential question: Can religious experience, which is so intimate and personal and deep within the individual psyche, ever find a communicable language that could not only be socially effective but also manage to refer to God? (Peacocke, 1984:39). This is a valid and important question that will take us directly to questions regarding the status of theoretic terms in theology, and thus also to an assessment of the role of models and metaphors in theology. For it is through the role of metaphors and models that the relationship between science and theology, on the one hand, and the different realities they are claiming in their respective assertions, on the other, becomes clear.

Critical realists—also in theology—take their theories to be representations of the world as a reality. They thus hold that their theories are valid and provisionally true as well as useful. To the critical realist science is discovery and exploration as well as construction and invention (cf. Barbour, 1976:37). Unlike the naïve realist, and along with the instrumentalist, the critical-realist model of rationality recognizes the importance of human imagination in the formation of theories. In this way critical realists try to acknowledge both the creativity of their thought and the existence of structures in reality not created by the human mind. Concerning the role of models in scientific theory, critical realism will be defending a position between literalism on the one hand, and fictionalism on the other hand. In this sense theoretic models now become valid but provisional and limited ways of imagining what otherwise can never be truly observable.

The most fundamental claim of realism—as we have seen—is therefore that while all theories and models are partial and inadequate, the scientist not only discovers as well as creates, but with good reasons also believes that his theories actually refer. This of course now brings us to the central question: If all serious users of models believe that their models in some or other way refer to reality, in what way do they refer? (cf. McFague, 1982:133). In the answer to this question the correspondence between models in science and in theology is indeed remarkable: models, as metaphorically based screens or "grids," indirectly redescribe reality. That means that something new and valid is being said about reality which the user of the model believes describes it better, more appropriately, than other competing views. Any realist position therefore rightly stresses that there is no uninterpreted access to reality and that in the process of interpretation the role of metaphor is central.

In theology, critical realism will imply, on the one hand, a model of rationality where theological concepts and models are indeed provisional, inadequate, and partial, but, on the other hand, also necessary as the only way of referring to the reality that is God, and the reality of His relation to humanity. In spite of important differences, I do believe that in both science and theology our models actually refer and are as close as we can get to speaking accurately of reality. These models are therefore not literal pictures, but they are also more than useful fictions (cf. Peacocke, 1984:42). The metaphoric language of the biblical text, as well as the dominant models we have formed from this, represent aspects of the reality of what Christians believe are in no way directly accessible to us. As such they are to be taken seriously but not literally, for although they refer in an ontological or cognitive sense, they are always partial and inadequate.

We earlier saw how, in scientific realism, metaphor was linked to the concept of fertility. McMullin (1984:31) stated that metaphor helps to illuminate something not well understood in advance and that it does this by tentative suggestion. Metaphors are therefore never to be seen as only ornamental or as mere literary devices. In fact, because metaphors are distinctive modes of achieving insight (cf. Black, 1966:237) and because they always imply assertions (cf. TeSelle, 1975:38), they are epistemologically indispensable (cf. Botha, 1984:29f.) and in this sense follow the way the human mind works.

Not only for evaluating the possibilities of a critical realism in theology, but especially for determining the epistemological status of the Bible in theological thought, one must realize the fundamental importance of recognizing that the Bible—as the classical text of Christianity—has provided the Christian tradition with metaphors so basic to this faith that they are indeed indispensable, not only for the models and theories they eventually generate for theology but also for determining the status of the Bible in theological thought.

Some of these well-known metaphors are the following: God is often described as Father, Creator, King, Shepherd, or Judge; Jesus is seen as the Christ, Messiah, Son of Man, Son of God, Redeemer, Savior, Good Shepherd; and the third person of the Trinity as the Holy Spirit, Comforter. The Bible itself is viewed as the "revealed Word of God" and as such as a very special and "inspired" book. Some of these metaphors have of course grown into dominant models that have generated theological theories that, although theoretic and conceptual, have never and can never lose their metaphoric roots. Peacocke (1984:41) therefore states correctly that these models are so deeply embedded in Christian language that it is extremely difficult to form theories and concepts entirely devoid of metaphor, for even abstract words like "transcendent" and "immanent" partake of spatial metaphors.

Now, if metaphors always work by tentative suggestion and always imply assertions, it is only in an instrumentalist position that the problem of ontological reference can be avoided, and then only temporarily. Thus the most interesting metaphors in theoretic language are those which suggest an explanatory network and therefore are vital at the "growing edges" of science, and hence also of theology (cf. Soskice, 1985:101). What could therefore never be consistent is the sort of "hybrid position" in which some theologians continue to speak of the cognitive use of metaphors and models in theological language when only implying the evoking of meaningful religious experience, and thus do not consider the problem of reference or reality depiction at all. Soskice (1985:106) is thus completely correct in stating: "The conclusion that theistic models are descriptive and representational, but what they describe and represent is the human condition, is not only disappointing when it comes at the end of a comparison of models in science and religion, but makes the whole comparison a nonsense." Realist assumptions have of course always been an essential part of Christian belief, and if there is to be any meaningful comparison between models in science and religion, it would have to be one that takes this realist assumption and the faith commitment implied by it very seriously.

The traditional similarities and differences between models in science and models in theology have been discussed at length by McFague (1982:103ff.), Peacocke (1984:41ff.), and Soskice (1985:107ff.). For the purpose of this argument I want to concentrate very briefly on two additional issues, which I think are of importance to critical realism in theology.

The Role of Religious Commitment in Theological Reflection

Hopefully it is clear at this stage that for the realist, models in both science and theology are metaphoric, and as "candidates for reality" are as close as we can get to speaking accurately of the respective domains science and theology are dealing with. As such the formulation of models in both science and theology partakes of the nature of discovery and of increasing intelligibility (cf. Peacocke, 1984:42). In science it is the entities and structures of the natural world that are successfully discovered and rendered intelligible. In theology it is mankind's search for ultimate meaning in terms of Christian faith that is rendered intelligible. But this faith refers to God, and it is this Reality which is such a decisive factor in establishing the reliability of theological reflection.

As I have pointed out earlier, the issue of critical realism in theology could never be to provide "proof" for the existence of God. On the contrary, theological reflection—in the Christian sense of the word—takes place within the context of an ultimate faith commitment to God as a personal but transcendent Creator. In this sense theology, and the domain of theology, differs profoundly from that of the other sciences: even an existential commitment to theories or to a certain paradigm of thought cannot be compared to the ultimate commitment evoked in the response of faith. This basic assumption, strengthened by the critical-realist argument, makes it possible for theologians to believe they are theorizing in a valid, progressive, and therefore successful way. This commitment is inevitably related to the referential power of the classic religious texts of Christianity. In my own concept of critical realism in theology, this will eventually become a decisive factor.

What is important, however, is that on the level of theoretic, theological reflection this ultimate commitment does in reality function in the same way as does the realist assumption in the other sciences. In this sense an ultimate religious commitment, like an existential commitment to the theories of scientific realism, becomes part of the realist argument and not an irrational "retreat to commitment." Therefore, when Hefner (1985:33; cf. also Russell, 1985:54) asks the difficult question: Does the realist argument open up a way for us to know or assert confidently that the entities referred to in scientific concepts, or the God referred to by theologians, really exist, or do we have to take a "leap of faith" to assert that reality?—we will have to answer by stating:

1. The realist argument opens up a way to reliable and valid assertions about the Reality to which we are ultimately committed (cf. Trigg, 1977:42) and which we have come to call "God."
2. We will also have to acknowledge the basic "need for faith" or the role of a faith commitment in the Christian theologian's attempt at the realist argument: an ultimate commitment that is, however, no irrational retreat to commitment.

But in this attempt we will have to realize that we are not involved in "proving" the reality of God: instead, we are trying to give reasons why as theologians we reason and theorize in the way that we do, and to show that this is not so different from what other scientists are doing. I shall return later to the fact that even an ultimate faith commitment is always already conceptualized and theorized. What is important at this stage is that whatever the difference between a religious commitment and an intellectual commitment to theories might be, in practice both function as already conceptualized background theories on the level of theoretic reflection.

The Explanatory Nature of Models in Theology

In our earlier analysis of scientific realism it became clear that explanatory success was regarded as one of the most important arguments for the realist position. In evaluating the possibilities of critical realism for theology, the important question will obviously be whether models and their resulting theories in theology can also in a meaningful way be regarded as explanatory and thus as progressive and successful.

Soskice (1985:108ff.) showed convincingly how extremely problemati-

cal this issue could become for theology if models in science, as structurally explanatory, were to be wrongly opposed to models in theology as merely evoca-
tive and affective. Such a viewpoint stems obviously from a noncognitivist thesis which draws its strength from an overemphasizing of the emotive character
of religious imagery. Taking the metaphoric nature of theological models into
account, one could never see these models as either explanatory or descriptive,
or as merely affective and compelling commitment. Because of the referential
character of metaphors and models in theology, Soskice (1985:109) is very
much to the point when she says: "A model in religious language may evoke an
emotional, moral, or spiritual response but this does not mean that the model
has no cognitive or explanatory function." In fact, precisely the reverse is true:
the model can only evoke affective religious response because it explains something. This cognitive function of theological language to me is primary and as
such forms the basis for all affective and also contextual claims in theology.
Therefore, if we want to maintain that there are certain important structures in
theological reflection which we legitimately call models—for example, referring to the Bible as the "Word of God"—we will have to take these models seriously as also being explanatory in a very important, valid, and therefore metaphoric way.

This will indeed later become very significant when I argue that progress in a critical-realist theology is of central importance, but then not in terms
of success as in the natural sciences, but in terms of the fact that some theories
in theology can with good reasons claim to be better theories than other competing theories, since they provide better explanations, because of the specific
epistemological status of the biblical text, as well as the nature of the reading
and interpretation this text requires. Soskice (1985:112) is therefore so right
when she says: "although the basis from which a model may claim to depict reality differs between religious models and scientific ones, their application as
explanatory is not as different as has been suggested." This point, of course,
gives rise to a very important problem for a critical-realist theology, and one
which I shall eventually try to answer: what will be the criteria by which an interpretative community selects some theological models as better or more adequate than others? (cf. also Barbour, 1985:112).

In conclusion, the metaphoric language of theological models and theories can therefore be seen as referential and as reality depicting. This can be
achieved without falling back into a naïve-realist, unrevisably descriptive position (cf. Peacocke, 1984:45), and theological models in their own way share this
realist character with models of the other sciences. Therefore when we as theologians speak of God as "Father" or of the Bible as the "Word of God," we are
speaking of an actual or real relationship of God to humanity that cannot be indicated in any other way. In this sense we can hope to speak realistically of
God—in an explanatory and progressive way—through revisable metaphor
and model. A theology that can define the nature and cognitive quality of its re-

alist commitment, that can identify valid contextual problems by critical analysis and attempt to solve them in terms of creditable theological criteria, and that can by this means show creative and inventive progress in its development of knowledge is already at the center of the process of scientific activity with which scientific realism is so specifically concerned in its quest for committed, relational knowledge.

Not only has the basic metaphor of Christianity maintained itself in the long history of Christian theological reflection through the creative insight and religious experience of believers, but the maximal meaning that metaphor has given and is still giving in answer to existential questions has provided sound and adequate grounds (albeit never final, positivistic *proof*) for believing what is directly or indirectly alleged in our theological statements about God. And what is, from a philosophy of science point of view, valid and acceptable about a commitment in the scientific realist sense is, analogously, true of an even deeper commitment in the religious sense. It is assumed, namely, that our theological constructs are something like, or in an anticipatory and provisional sense disclose something of, the Reality for which our metaphoric, relational theological language reaches out. This, and the fact that theology can gradually get to know more about God by making more epistemologically valid statements about Him, is what I have tried to define as reality depiction in a cognitive sense.

Adopting a realist theological stand does not therefore by any means demand some kind of empirical proof of the existence of God. The community of Christians all over the world—and therefore also of theologians—share in the same basic ultimate commitment by accepting the reality of God's existence. In fact, it would even be irrational of a theologian in the Christian religious paradigm *not* to accept the reality of God's existence. Since theology is the intellectual study of the religious dimension of our reality, it would be highly problematic to keep speaking of *theology* once the theologian had ceased to accept the Reality referred to in that religious dimension. In the light of the above it seems to me that theology, given both the ultimate religious commitment of the theologian and the metaphoric nature of our religious language, is scientifically committed to a realist point of view.

At this stage it should be clear that scientists and theologians construct theories in order to explain, as fully and successfully as possible, the hidden structures of the studied matter. At the same time the metaphoric origins[7] of our theological theories reveal the explicatory potential and dynamics of models handled in the context of a theology that has learned to see itself as a creative, conceptual construct. Despite frequent paradigmatic shifts and breaks in the development of theological knowledge, theology has shown steady and indisput-

---

7. For an analogous interpretation of metaphoric language, as we have analyzed in Black, Botha, TeSelle, and McFague, cf. also E. McMullin, 1984:30ff.

able growth (as will become apparent in the discussion of our third criterion). As in the other sciences, this type of critical realism in systematic theology has by its nature nothing in common with the accumulation of the so-called proved facts of the positivistic standard model for science.

All our theological models are theoretic constructs. And although the object of systematic theology (for example, God, Jesus Christ, the Trinity, Atonement, or Predestination) is in principle inaccessible to observation (as are related areas in, for example, microbiology, chemistry, geology, and nuclear physics),[8] our theories have enabled us—thanks to the metaphoric roots preserved in our religious language through the formulation of models and concepts—to define in our statements certain provisional conceptual boundaries for the object of our discussion. Once again—now from a realist commitment, and hence the reality depiction of our statements—it appears that the hypothetical statements of scientific realism, as defined in philosophy of science terms, may be translated in systematic theology into the eschatological nature and structure of our theological language. It now becomes clear—not only theologically, from the theologian's religious commitment, but also in philosophy of science terms—that our theological theories do indeed refer to a Reality beyond and greater than ours.

The creative conceptual construction of theological models, even models and theories that may become dominant in theological history and thus gain a certain linguistic permanence, does not imply that those models or theories provide, as rational constructs, a full description of the Reality to which they refer. On the contrary, our models serve, as Sallie McFague has shown, to make provisional and tentative statements. Yet such statements also reveal real structures and thus creatively discover and construct.[9]

Apart from what has been defined here in speaking of reality depiction as cognitivity, theology has a further reality to take into account in a creditable rationality model: the reality of the sociocultural context or contexts in which we make our statements about God. Those contexts are not only the living space of theology but also vital levels on which theology will ultimately discover and attempt to solve its essential problems.

Reality Depiction as Contextuality

The context in which a vital and dynamic systematic theology develops is at the same time the context(s) to which it is inseparably bound, from which it re-

8. For especially interesting examples from these sciences, see E. McMullin, 1984:12ff.

9. In the complex context of contemporary philosophy of science pursuits it is remarkable that Michael Polanyi (1962:64), as a chemist, could already in 1962 say the following about the development of knowledge: "Yet personal knowledge in science is not made but discovered, and as such it claims to establish contact with reality beyond the clues on which it relies. It commits us, passionately and far beyond our comprehension, to a vision of reality."

lationally draws its problems, and to which it attempts to give maximal mean-ing through topical and valid answers to actual problems.[10] Here we may dis-tinguish between three contexts,[11] each of which—although closely linked to the others—in its own fashion structures a framework in which the systematic theologian has to make relevant, contextual, and therefore realist statements about God. The three are the broad *context of religious experience,* the more specific *context of the church,* and the *context of theological reflection* as such. These three contexts are interdependent, although each has its own right of exis-tence in a particular dimension. The wider context of religious experience pro-vides a basis for the specific context of the church. Through a lengthy process of theorizing, the reality of these two contexts, as well as the problems crystal-lizing within them, eventually generates a context of theological reflection. Through critical analysis and the identification and solving of problems, that context of scientific reflection reaches out far beyond its origins, the contexts of religious experience and the church. Nevertheless, theological reflection al-ways comes back to those sources; for precisely there theologians must speak out—individually and confessionally—in a valid commitment to reality and contextuality, and may eventually even construct models for real religious ex-perience and a true church.

In my view, then, each of these three contexts—religious experience, the church, and theological reflection—may be seen as a valid way to the Re-ality referred to in the religious dimension of our own reality.

Religious Experience as a Context

By its nature, all religious experience is finally rooted in a quite specific re-ligious ultimate commitment. All religious language, in turn, is an expression and objectification of that which is perceived as true or meaningful in the re-ligious sense. Religious experience and language are thus always bound to a specific religion or religious tradition. In that sense, religions may also be seen as comprehensive interpretative frameworks based on myths or narration and, as such, often strongly ritualized. Thus religions always create space for the es-tablishment, use, and description of certain symbols, for the formulation of cer-tain convictions, and for definitive inner experiences, emotions, and sentiments within the religious dimension. Religions, of whatever nature, provide the broad

10. What issues could be truly problematic for systematic theology is discussed in detail under the next criterion for a creditable theological rationality model, namely, the critical and prob-lem-solving capacity of theological statements.

11. Despite significant links in content, these three contexts should not be confused with the three *publics* David Tracy identifies as target audiences or discursive partners for systematic theology. For Tracy, these publics or entities are the community, the academy, and the church, which ultimately correlate with a subdivision of theology into the three disciplines of practical theology, fundamental theology, and systematic theology. See D. Tracy, 1981:1-98.

paradigmatic context for cultural and religious frameworks that may ultimately govern not only individual religious experiences but life in its totality. How prescientific or everyday religious experience functions is stated succinctly by George Lindbeck (1984:35): "The primary knowledge is not about the religion, nor that the religion teaches such and such, but rather how to be religious in such and such ways."

All we have so far said about religion and religious experience applies equally to our Christian faith. In the context of pretheological, prereflective religious experience, too, phenomena such as ritual, prayer, meditation, and, on an ecclesiastical level, liturgy are often more important than any statement of what is believed. In the framework of Christianity, too, music, art, and certain rituals in the context of religious experience never function as a mere external facade of the essence of our faith; they have the integral function of cultural and hence also religious expressions of our perception of the essence of our faith. In fact, not only prayer, meditation, and liturgy but also music, art, and ritual serve to internalize, to shape, to express, and to communicate our commitment in the context of religious experience.

In our earlier examination of the origins of theological statements it became apparent, however, that our language in particular—and here our religious language—ultimately creates an arena for religious experience. For a theology that has learned to recognize the origins of its statements in the language of religious experience and that wishes to speak out contextually to the field of religious experience it is vital to realize that believers learn to feel, to act, and to think in accordance with a religious tradition which, in its internal structure, is much richer and subtler than any conscious articulation of it. Behind the metaphors of our religious language, and beneath the submerged models of our religious traditions, lies the inarticulable that we try tentatively to convey: religious experience as an encounter with God.

In the context of religious experience it is therefore of the utmost importance that whatever is experienced, expressed, and understood should be coherent with the broader, comprehensive interpretative framework of Christian faith.[12] If religious statements are not coherent with the total context of the Christian religious tradition, a statement that may normally be true or even central in that context may become untrue or a lie. We find a striking example of that in a reference by Lindbeck (1984:64) to the Crusaders' battle cry *Christus est Dominus* (Christ is the Lord), with which they attempted, out of context, to legitimize the killing of numerous nonbelievers in the course of the Crusades, thus negating through its noncoherent abuse the essential truth of Christianity.

For a theology that seeks, as a form of critical accounting of faith, to appeal not only to intellectual insight but also to religious experience, it is vital

---

12. "Thus for a Christian, 'God is Three and One,' or 'Christ is Lord' are true only as parts of a total pattern of speaking, thinking, feeling and acting" (Lindbeck, 1984:64).

especially on this plane that our examination of the origins of theological statements should lead us back to religious experience as such. If systematic theology would speak contextually within the arena of religious experience, it is
essential that it should realize that most of its theological questions and problems will ultimately be found and identified on a level preceding all theologizing: the context of religious experience, and, moreover, religious experience
as found and practiced in everyday life. In that sense we might say that the theologian is identifying and formulating problems that are already active in the
minds of believers (cf. Kuitert, 1975:98).

Systematic theology, then, is not concerned solely with its own theoretic
reflection or exclusively church-confessional problems; theology's task is also
to help a particular community solve its religious problems, thus opening up a
maximally meaningful religious dimension for life in our world. As a rule, the
community in which a theologian works is involved in certain ecclesiastical
groupings, but people grapple with religious experience also outside established
denominations, and therefore the theologian is functioning contextually also by
defining and attempting to solve valid problems outside existing churches. Thus
the task of a theology striving creatively and constructively to find lucid and
precise meanings of the ambiguous, ambivalent images of religious language
(cf. McFague, 1982:26) gains an even broader and more contextual dimension.

This has yet further implications if we realize that religious experience
is never a purely individual event. The truth or credibility of particular religious
statements is always truth or credibility for a specific group of people. Perceiv-
ing something as true in the context of religious experience without its being
true also for a particular community or group is hardly imaginable, given the
hazards of totally random subjectivism. Kuitert (1977:25) points out rightly that
the above is sociologically of the utmost importance if a religious truth is to
carry any power of conviction. A religious truth is convincing when it proves
itself to be plausible.

To the question, When is a religious truth plausible? Peter Berger
(1969:127-128) replied with his well-known analysis of the indissoluble relationship between plausibility and plausibility structures. By *plausibility structures* Berger meant that religions and philosophical convictions may gain or lose
plausibility through structural developments within social contexts. Thus the
social structures in which a certain community lives have a strong bearing on
the plausibility of accepted religious truths or statements of faith. Such structures (as established in the historical, cultural, traditional, and hence sociological context) are called plausibility structures because they act as supports or as
reinforcement for what people regard as true or plausible in their religious experience. If, for example, plausibility structures change through sociocultural
or sociopolitical factors to such an extent that they no longer bolster the plausibility of certain Christian truths, it is possible either that the Christian faith has
lost credibility because its essential message has lost contextual plausibility, or

that the social structures of a society have become so secularized that it has lost its essential religious dimension, so that the message of Christ can no longer be heard or understood.

Theologians inquiring critically into cognitivity, and thus into the claims to truth of their own faith, in the broader social context of religious experience, will therefore have to develop a critical sensitivity to the sociocultural context of religious experience and the special problems it may pose. This constitutes the essential relationship between religious experience and contextuality. In this area the theologian is also a believer among believers, someone whose contextual thought model is bolstered by its reality depiction, also on the cognitive level. In fact, it is on this plane of everyday religious experience, as a way to God's reality, that individual believers are already demonstrating the plausibility or implausibility of the claims to truth in their religious language.

Church as Context

Theological statements and models become concrete and referential not only in the context of religious experience but also most specifically within the church. In this sense one might refer to the context of the church for the realist reference of theological statements. The church may of course be seen both as a theological and as a sociological phenomenon. Sociologically, the church is one of the three contexts in which theological statements become contextually committed to reality. In the broadest sense of the word the church is by its nature an interpersonal religious community with a tradition of communal, basic convictions. Critical theologians who as a rule feel committed to a particular church group would wish to reflect on the dominant models of their own church tradition, not only to find greater theological clarity on their own confessional origins but also to gain full and responsible involvement in the life of the church.[13]

Therefore theologians who would critically account for their faith, in a contextual commitment to reality, will see their task as at least an attempt at plausible interpretation of the tradition of the church. And since systematic theologians would interpret that tradition from their own explicit self-concept within the contemporary problem-consciousness, they could never allow the context of the church to become the exclusive horizon of their theology, since both the context of religious experience and that of theological reflection have a bearing on the structuring of the church. For that reason alone any creditable interpretation of church tradition demands explicit historical, sociocognitive, hermeneutical, systematic-theological, and philosophy of science criteria. Pre-

---

13. David Tracy (1981:130) says rightly, "the theologian . . . is involved, consciously or unconsciously, in an ongoing process of reflection upon one's voluntary commitment and loyalty to the Christian church and, ordinarily, to some particular church tradition."

cisely because systematic theology must ultimately face the question of the truth of its statements, the plausibility structures of its conceptual models must be subjected to critical examination. Of theology's commitment to the context of the church, Tracy (1981:29) rightly said: "To the theologian, at least, there is in fact no real choice but explicitness." The systematic theologian who opts consciously, and on sound grounds, for a confessional theology in which the Christian church must function as a referential framework will have to realize that, over and above narrower or broader confessional and dogmatic problems, the question of the truth of theological statements always lies latent, ready to show up suddenly as an essential, concrete problem on the broader plane of fundamental theology.

Our earlier analysis of theorizing in systematic theology is particularly appropriate to ecclesiastical doctrine or dogma. As norms of a common faith, as rules of dialogue of a particular ecclesiastical community, doctrine is of course a focal point for systematic theology's exploration and identification of valid theological problems. The eventual solving of doctrinal or dogmatic problems is of the utmost importance, both intraconfessionally and ecumenically.

I therefore find it exceptionally problematic that George Lindbeck (1984:69), in an attempt to design a creditable model for ecumenical theology, should ask whether it might be possible to formulate ecclesiastical doctrines that would have a nonreferential structure but might nonetheless serve as permanent and normative rules for the Christian faith. Later Lindbeck (1984:80) did add, "To say that doctrines are rules is not to deny that they involve propositions," but he immediately pointed out that by propositions he meant not ontological but intrasystematic claims to truth. For him, therefore, the issue of the divergent confessional and doctrinal positions in the various churches was the quest for a kind of consensus truth. Lindbeck sees church dogma neither as propositions reaching out to an alleged reality nor as merely expressive symbols; they are, rather, grammatical rules controlling and regulating the language of a particular paradigm.

In any dogmatic consensus model, however, the question of the potential for truth in theological models must naturally arise, given the metaphoric, referential nature of our models—if not in the form of truth as literal correspondence, then as a critical-realist, tentative reference to truth. Thus is preserved not only the provisionality of our theological statements and the meaningful plurality of the church but also the essential insistence on a more and more precise description of the root metaphor or central truth of our Christian faith.

If we fail to integrate and reckon with the appeals to both insight (the cognitive, propositional aspect) and experience (the expressive aspect), our theologies remain one-sided, and our confessional and dogmatic models—as a blending of metaphor and theoretic concept—will not come into their own. We have in fact discovered that referential, relational element in metaphoric religious language by analyzing, from a critical-realist point of view, the process of theorizing in theology. By their nature, dogmas or doctrines, as rules of dialogue, have a regulatory function in the church. They become problematic only if there is a loss of cognitivity and expressivity.[14]

When Lindbeck (1984:134) further says of theology, "The ultimate test is performance. There is no other way of testing the merits and demerits of a theological method apart from its performance," his pragmatic statement is understandable, given the context of the wider ecumenical problem. But such a narrowing of the reality depiction and contextuality of theological statements into a functional contextuality is ultimately a narrowing of the question of theological contextuality. A theology, too—even if it could formulate functional doctrines or statements—would be a-contextual if it ended up seeking only criteria for performance and no longer also ones for a creditable rationality model for theology. Theological models may be functional or intersubjectively meaningful without necessarily offering a plausible anticipation of the truth that forms the ultimate object of theology.

In more theological terms: the church is by definition a community sustained by a specific memory and attuned to a future rich in promise. It is by definition a community living by a common hope, a particular trust, a promised future (cf. Smit, 1986:52ff.). That hope and expectation also fully engages a systematic theology that would plausibly—both in theological and in philosophy of science terms—explore the fundamental problems of theology. In that context, however, the systematic theologian can never adopt the role of a group ideologist. The role of theologians committed to reality is to serve the context of the church while nonetheless maintaining their independence as scientists through critical, constructive involvement in the academic context.

In its own historical context the church always has a specific confessional task and mission. Therefore the theoretic nature of a theology that critically examines theorizing in its own thought can never be prevented—given its commitment to the church as a context—from reaching out beyond theoretic reflection to contextual confessional problems. On the contrary, a rational model founded on committed reflection must always lead back to involvement in the confessional and sociocritical praxis of the church.

I therefore find it highly problematic that de Gruchy (1985:28ff.) should ask: "In other words, to what extent is Van Huyssteen's espousal of the model he uses affected by the desire to de-politicize theology and so prevent the Christian confession in our context from speaking directly to political issues?" A the-

---

14. That Lindbeck (1984:130), in his own conceptual model, relates strongly to Thomas S. Kuhn is evident from the following interesting and significant statement: "basic religious and theological positions, like Kuhn's scientific paradigms, are invulnerable to definitive refutation (as well as to confirmation) but can nevertheless be tested and argued about in various ways, and these tests and arguments in the long run make a difference."

ology that defines its contextuality inter alia also as confessional can by no
means separate confessional from theoretical language, nor can it depoliticize
the theological task and thereby prevent the center of the Christian confession
from speaking out directly on sociopolitical problems in our sociocultural context. The theologian also has the critical task of preventing the ideologizing of
models precisely in respect of church praxis, and thus of preventing both
depoliticizing and politicizing by remaining mindful of the origin of our religious language: the relativizing but constructive power of the metaphor.

Theological Reflection as Context

Our attempt to define the reality depiction of theological statements in terms of
contextuality has led us to the contexts of religious experience and of the
church. But theologians are not only believers among other believers, nor are
they always confessionally involved in some traditional context. They are first
and last theoreticians, fully involved—through analysis and critical interpretation in the academic scientific context—with the content to which their tradition also testifies. As such theologians also form part of the broader scientific
community.

The involvement of theologians in the reflective context of their own
field has implicitly and explicitly formed the theme of this work. Nevertheless,
I should like to sum up and elaborate briefly: In its broadest sense, theological
reflection may be seen as scientific engagement, from whatever point of view,
with the long-standing Christian tradition and the way the Bible—as the classic document of Christianity—has provided and still provides a basis for reflection on what that religious tradition holds to be its central truth, namely, that the
true God finally revealed Himself in Jesus of Nazareth.

Against that background, a theology that sees its own reflection as a
critical accounting for the content of the Christian religious tradition is by no
means threatening the religious certainty of believers with its critical approach;
on the contrary, it is helping—as we have seen in the case of religious experience as a context for theology—consciously to examine the questions and un-
certainties that may arise from a community's religious experience. In that sense
the final objective of theological reflection is again to be found on the existential religious plane. But to regain a perception of the religious events that we
call a religious experience, the theologian must constantly engage in a lengthy
and complex process of interpretative reflection in order to achieve the utmost
conceptual clarity,[15] precisely for the sake of his or her beliefs. Systematic theologians who, for the sake of the contextual reality depiction of their own reflection, cannot be contented with a type of privatistic ghetto existence, or even a

---

15. Cf. S. McFague, 1982:121: "The conceptual level provides this distance without which
we wander in a land of images that, while rich, is chaotic and unilluminated."

vaguely defined peripheral existence in the wider context of scientific reflection, are therefore compelled to articulate the claims to truth of their own religious tradition as validly and plausibly as possible.

An inevitable implication of the contextualizing of theological reflection is the specific question of the theologian's self-concept. By its nature that self-concept is directly determined by whether the theologian is operating in the context of a confessional seminary, at a university with a broader nonconfessional but nonetheless Christian commitment, as part of a program of biblical and religious instruction, or in a fully secularized academic context. The theologian's self-concept, and ultimately his or her conceptual model, is also naturally determined by the specific cultural-historical and sociopolitical framework of his or her own historical context. In that sense one might indeed say that the question, What is theology? ought to be preceded by another: Who is the theologian, and what is the nature of the theologian's self-concept? (cf. Tracy, 1981:5).

An analysis of the theologian's self-concept would also lead directly to analysis of the sociological frame of reference in which the theologian reflects, and thus to a description of the three contexts (religious experience, church, and theological reflection) in which and on which the theologian has to make statements. Whatever the answer to the question of the theologians' self-concept, and even if they deliberately chose to work in an exclusively confessional context, for example, they would always—given the nature of their own reflection and the implications of the claims to truth in their beliefs—be committed to intersubjectively demonstrable clarity. Although personally involved in their statements and theories, theologians can never again retreat esoterically into an irrational commitment to a particular theology, with the absolutism, exclusivity, and ideologizing that retreat would inevitably imply for their conceptual model.

Irrespective of the specific sociological context assigned to theological reflection, the first priority for any form of Christian theology is to be finally and radically theocentric. In that sense any theological model must preserve its incompleteness, provisionality, relationality, and openness if its statements and theories are to be plausible, both theologically and from a philosophy of science perspective. Thus theology may strive through critical realism to make its language more and more lucid in its attempts to illuminate the mystery of God's presence in the ambiguity of our everyday reality.

By its nature theology is sustained by a religious commitment to the truth of its particular religious tradition. The systematic theologian therefore focuses more often than not on reinterpretations and new creative applications of that tradition to our perception of reality. In that sense all systematic theology may be said to be basically interpretative or hermeneutical, but then hermeneutical in a sense that concerns not only meaning but also the question of truth. This is so because the language of the Christian tradition, as also the language of its source document, has in itself metaphoric potential for exploring creatively, albeit provisionally, the Reality with which our religious commitment and theology are concerned. And this, once again, commits systematic theologians to the fundamental-theological question of a valid rationality model for their own reflection: a critical question which, as we have seen, also provides theological reflection with an essential and valid scientific contextuality.

Seen in this light, the multiplicity of systematic-theological perspectives can no longer pose a threat; they become a meaningful and complementing diversity which in any event is characteristic of the relational nature of theological language. From the critical-realist perspective, plurality, which in the Kuhnian modal would probably make systematic theology a preparadigmatic or immature science by philosophy of science standards, can thus become valid by those standards without necessarily raising fundamental communicative problems through the irreconcilability of conceptual models. Furthermore, theological plurality may be the mark of maturity and democratic openness in the social framework in which that reflective plurality is functioning. The context of theological reflection thus becomes a fundamental part of the realist commitment of theologians, both in the cognitive and in the contextual sense, and also provides the context in which they are creditably theologians. From that context they might eventually also examine the intratheological nature and encyclopedic relationship of the various subdisciplines in theological science.

From the context of theological reflection it becomes clear that a creditable contextual theology must find its reality depiction in all three of the contexts mentioned above (religious experience, church, and theological reflection). If a theologian's situation becomes so exclusive that his or her theological conceptual model is determined solely by religious experience or the church or theological reflection itself, such a model must inevitably become positivistic, since it would elevate a particular perspective into the only acceptable—and therefore an ideological—conceptual model. And any form of ideologizing, despite its striving for a particular form of contextuality, impoverishes theology into an a-contextual pursuit, theoretically invalid and practically even hazardous.

The Critical and Problem-Solving Ability
of Theological Statements

From the reality depiction of theological statements, as a first and basic criterion for a creditable rationality model for systematic theology, we can now proceed to a next criterion: theological statements must be able critically to identify and analyze real problems and to formulate theories that might provide valid and adequate solutions to those problems.

In contemporary philosophy of science, science and scientific thought can be defined in various and divergent ways. It is essential to all scientific thought, however, that it must be able to provide analytic and theoretical-abstract definitions of problems (cf. Strauss, 1971:6), and that it must be directed fundamentally at problem solving (cf. Laudan, 1977:12). This presents a stimulating challenge for a theology that claims to be a critical accounting of faith. From a fundamental-theological point of view, this book has consistently defined the problems of theology as the question of reclaiming and revitalizing the concept of rationality for theology, the quest for a valid model of rationality for theology, and critical analysis of the process of theorizing in theology.

From the perspective of systematic theology a number of further problems can now be identified, confronting theology with difficult questions such as the following:

1. What would qualify as a problem in systematic theology?
2. What types of problems confront systematic theology?
3. What is it that sometimes makes one problem more important than another?
4. What is the relationship between scientific and nonscientific problems in theology?
5. What criteria would be valid for problem solving in the theological context? In other words, what guidelines could be used to ascertain whether our answers to real problems are in fact adequate?

In contemporary philosophy of science, Larry Laudan (1977), in particular, has offered a model for scientific problem solving, progress, and rationality—the last of which could be critically broadened, as we shall see—that may provide very interesting links with theological reflection. Like Kuhn, Laudan sought to demonstrate that important nonempirical, even nonscientific, factors play a key role in rational development. He (Laudan, 1977:7ff.) argued that the rationality and ultimate progressiveness of a theory are closely related, not in terms of justification or falsification but in its capacity for effective problem solving in a given context. Laudan also points out that scientific progress is not so much a matter of individual theories as the potential for scientific progress and growth, especially in global theories, which he called research traditions (or paradigms).

Laudan makes it clear that scientific and other problems are not all that different, and that the differences are often largely a matter of degree. In fact, he shows that his perspective on scientific problems could, with a few qualifications, be applied to all forms of intellectual problems (Laudan, 1977:13). For him the analysis of problems is the true focus of all forms of scientific thought, with the end result of that reflection to be found in our scientific theories. Therefore theories are important only insofar as they offer adequate solutions to real problems.[16] The basic dialectics of science—and ultimately also of systematic-theological thought—is shaped by problems formulated as questions, and by theories in response to the challenge of those problems.

For theologians this spells out what has already become apparent: as theologians, they must learn to identify the real problems that arise on the plane of religious experience, and they must try to find valid solutions to them. This implies what Kuhn has already shown us: by reclaiming a broader concept of rationality theologians are now finally freed from a typical positivistically re-duced conceptual model; instead of having to ask whether a given theory is provable, correct, or true, they can now first ask whether that theory offers ade-quate solutions to meaningful problems.

Laudan (1977:190) points out that scientific theories have to cope with two kinds of problems, and he states explicitly that this model might also be ap-plied to theology. The two types we can now distinguish are empirical and con-ceptual problems.

Regarding the first type, Laudan (1977:15) wrote: "generally, anything about the natural world which strikes us as odd, or otherwise in need of explana-tion, constitutes an empirical problem." In this context Laudan (1977:11-70) has shown that the concept *empirical problem* can be stripped of its positivistic con-notations and fruitfully explored for theology. Our earlier examination of the origins of our theological statements and conceptual models clearly led to the conclusion that problems—whatever their nature—always arise in a specific context of inquiry and are to some extent even defined by that context.

Issues that are valid and of high priority in one context are not neces-sarily problematic in a different theological model. This is true also of a criti-cal-realist theology: whether something is seen as problematic depends largely on the models and theories of the conceptual framework we bring to bear on the world around us. What theologians see as problematic is influenced not only by their religious commitment but especially also by their theoretic commitment to a particular theological model or models. All theological problems—both empirical and conceptual—are therefore determined largely by context: whether the context of religious experience, that of the church, or that of the complex field of theological reflection in itself.

Scientific progress in solving empirical problems may be seen as the transformation of unsolved problems into ones that have been solved as effectu-ally as possible. Laudan's (1977:120) model for problem solving, however, be-comes problematic when he writes: "Determinations of truth and falsity are ir-relevant to the acceptability or the pursuitability of theories or research traditions." This perspective McMullin (1984:25) rightly sees, from a philoso-phy of science point of view, as a broad anti-realist approach that negates the

---

16. "If problems constitute the questions of science, it is theories which constitute the an-swers" (Laudan, 1977:13).

ontological status of theoretic entities in science in general. Yet Laudan (1977:126) suggests that his model for progressive problem solving does not in principle exclude the possibility that scientific theories might be true, or might even be advancing toward the truth; what he wishes to avoid is the striving for some utopian nearer-to-the-truth ideal which is in any event not scientifically ascertainable. He would therefore prefer to deal with the concrete capacity of theories for finding meaningful solutions to intracontextual problems.

With reference to the third criterion for a creditable rationality model for theology—the constructive and progressive quality of theological statements—closer examination of Laudan's criterion for progress will show that rationality, in his conceptual model, can be defined as exercising the most progressive choices. In a criterion for progress, too, we shall have to leave space for a hypothetical reference to the ontological status of that with regard to which problems are solved progressively (cf. Peacocke, 1984:46).

For systematic theology, an empirical problem might be anything that strikes us as unusual, and hence as calling for explanation, in the Christian religious paradigm. Thus the following might be identified as empirical problems for theology: the reality of evil or sin; the meaning of suffering and death in the light of faith in a good, loving God; the experiential basis of faith and the problems it poses; sociopolitical issues; ethical questions; etc.

In all intellectual development—in the strict sciences as well as the broader human sciences, and therefore also in philosophy and theology—a second type of problem is, however, as important as empirical ones to the advancement of scientific thought. This type has already been identified by Kuhn, but Laudan (1977:45-46) further examines and defines them as conceptual problems, with the specific aim of providing a broader and richer theory of problem solving than the merely empirical.

In his identification of conceptual problems Laudan draws attention to a quite specific aspect of problems: insight into problems arising not on the empirical but on the conceptual level as a result of intellectual interaction between protagonists of divergent (even conflicting) theories that seem to be supported in equal measure by the same data. Laudan refines this definition by drawing a further distinction between, on the one hand, internal conceptual problems, which arise from apparent inconsistencies or ambiguities in a particular theory, and, on the other hand, external conceptual problems, which may arise from broad philosophical conflicts between two theories: problems, therefore, that might have scientific, methodological, or even religious causes.

Systematic theology would find its conceptual problems—both internal and external—in all three contexts in which it also finds its reality depiction, namely, in religious experience, in the church, and in theological reflection as such. To mention some examples: typical conceptual problems might be ones arising from classical theological theories such as the Trinity doctrine, predestination, redemption, and the Christological problem of Christ's divinity and humanity. Typical external conceptual problems for systematic theology might be methodological ones arising from the handling and choice of certain hermeneutical theories; confessional problems arising from ecumenical theological questions about baptism or communion; the question of truth or error in Christian faith, and therefore the problem of heresy; and of course also the fundamental-theological question that has consistently engaged us, namely, the problem of a valid rationality model for theology. With regard to the last-mentioned: scientific conceptions of theology, no matter how veiled, subtle, or nuanced, present theology with some of its most severe conceptual problems through their impact on systematic theology. For theology, Laudan's useful distinction between internal and external conceptual problems would in my view need further refinement, in the sense that what might normally be identified as an empirical problem in theology often conceals a more profound conceptual one; and what may appear to be internal conceptual problems often refer to more profound external conceptual ones.

As for our earlier reference to what McMullin calls Laudan's general anti-realism, Laudan's definition of conceptual problems has in itself a strong bearing on the question of possible claims to truth in science, and hence also in theology. Conceptual problems would not arise in the first place if divergent theories did not already contain conflicting claims to truth or plausibility. A theology seeking to construct creative conceptual theories from a critical-realist perspective is thus immediately confronted with the question: by what criteria or guidelines can we determine whether the solutions we offer to real theological problems (empirical or conceptual) are in fact adequate, to such an extent that we might be able to judge why one solution is better or more plausible than another?

In our eventual discussion of the third and last criterion for a creditable rationality model, namely, the constructive and progressive quality of theological statements, it will be seen that the solving—no matter how provisionally—of either empirical or conceptual theological problems may well be the crux of a model of progress for systematic theology. Meanwhile, however, we may say that if a theory offers a satisfactory solution to a problem, the aim of scientific thought in general and of theology in particular is to give that solution the maximum scope or impact by applying it as widely as possible. Thus a scriptural theory might be developed as a solution to the problem of scriptural authority and the valid application of Scripture. If theologians succeeded in showing that their theory about scriptural authority and the use of Scripture could reduce or minimize real problems in a given theological community, and could do so validly and according to definitive hermeneutical criteria, such a theory might be seen as successful and valid, until such time as it in turn raised empirical or conceptual problems, in which case it might be replaced by an even more plausible and intellectually sophisticated theory. We might also put it as follows: in theology, too, a theory gains if it can offer provisional solutions to empirical problems; it loses if it raises conceptual problems.

For systematic theologians who are critically aware of the process of theorizing in their own reflective pursuit of theories that might solve real theological problems, we might isolate from the broader Christian religious paradigm three guidelines or basic criteria to serve as preconditions but also as beacons for plausible and critical problem solving. That model with its basic criteria can function plausibly only if both it and its three basic criteria are structured on the three much more comprehensive criteria for a creditable model of rationality for theology.

This structuring can be summed up briefly as follows: The basic criteria or guidelines for a problem-solving model in systematic theology are the Bible, as the classic source of Christianity; the tradition of Christian reflection; and contemporary scientific thought. For systematic theology these three basic criteria construct a model for creative problem solving, but each of the three also lays down quite specific conditions for credibility in theology.

If it is assumed from a critical-realist viewpoint that our theological models do in fact refer to a specific reality, it means that in that reference the object of our Christian belief is constantly redescribed by our theological theories. The Bible, the tradition of theological reflection, and the context of contemporary thought then function as criteria by which to evaluate as plausible, less plausible, or unsound the theoretic solutions purportedly given by our interpretative redescription and contextualizing of the content of our beliefs.

Theology and Holy Scripture

The Bible takes a central place not only in the contexts of religious experience and the church but also in theological reflection; and there, too, it has for nearly two thousand years provided a yardstick for adherence to the basic metaphor of the Christian religion: the credo that God has wrought salvation for this world through Jesus of Nazareth.

As the classic source document[17] of Christianity the inherited and oft-translated text of the Bible has been and remains our only access to the Jesus of Nazareth in whom God finally reveals Himself to the Christian. In that sense the Bible is essentially a book of faith, with a radical religious dimension. That the Bible is a book of faith means, quite concretely, that its wide-ranging and complex text provides written evidence of the relational manner in which believing people conveyed, in metaphoric religious language, their perception

---

17. It will soon become clear that this definition of the Bible should not be confused with what both David Tracy and Sallie McFague mean when they speak of the Bible as *classic*. McFague (1982:121) states clearly: "We shall argue that the authority of Scripture is the authority of a classic poetic text." In a similar context Tracy (1977:390) states: "For a classic possesses both the concreteness of its own historical context and, by its self-transcending fidelity to that concrete historicity, a certain universality of significance." Cf. also Tracy, 1981:99-154.

of God from a total religious commitment. In a certain historical sense, faith in Jesus of Nazareth was, of course, a living reality even before the Bible existed (in the recording of the New Testament, but also in the final canonization of the Old and New Testaments). As long as it has existed, however, the Bible has been a living collection of documents about and for believers (cf. van Huyssteen, 1983a:7), and as such it still lives as the Word of God among believers.

Our earlier analysis of religious language as metaphoric language showed that referring to the Bible as the Word of God is a fascinating example of a religious metaphor that has developed into a dominant model in the context of the Christian religious paradigm. In a specific sense the description *Word of God* may also be seen as the primary metaphor for God's relationship with mankind.[18] As a metaphor, the Bible is God's Word brought to us in human language, and metaphorically that Word opens up a reality that systematic theology may describe as God's revelation—yet another metaphor.

In most theological traditions, such as the Reformed theological paradigm, it is, however, the metaphor of inspiration that has through the years developed into the dominant model (and divergent theories as well as conceptual problems) to convey the relationship between God and biblical authors. I think this original biblical metaphor still has enough metaphoric potential to be reclaimed through hermeneutical restoration as the basic definition of the inherent religious dimension of the Bible, which—as a book of faith—can never be dismissed, whether by literary, historical, linguistic, or any other argument (cf. van Huyssteen, 1985a:7).

Therefore any scriptural theory will have to reckon with the fact that the Bible's authority in the Christian context cannot be made dependent on particular theories of inspiration or conceptions of authority. The Bible's authority—also as a basic criterion for a systematic-theological model of problem solving—is fundamentally religious and thus ultimately rooted in an encounter with Jesus Christ. That encounter is primarily through the Bible, since our only access to the Jesus of Nazareth who lived, died, and was resurrected 2000 years ago is to be found in the writings of the many well-known but also anonymous believers, and finally in those of a number of early Christians. In that sense the Bible's authority may be summed up as redemptive authority.[19] God's Word

18. Sallie McFague (1982:54), by describing the Bible as a classic retaining the metaphoric character of the Word of God and then nonetheless stating that "as metaphor it cannot be absolute, divinely inspired, or final," loses her own original definition of the referential, revelatory, or exploratory character of metaphors, which would have enabled her to regain creatively the metaphor "divinely inspired." Since she fails to do so, it is logical that the Bible should be described as a mere poetic *classic,* a conclusion that in my view does not follow logically from the original object of defining religious metaphors. In fact, describing the Bible finally as a *classic,* a poetic/religious text, means absolutizing a model of which the original metaphoric potential—also and especially in the religious sense—has been sacrificed.

19. Cf. here also B. J. du Toit (1984:75ff.), who in his own way proceeds from a relational epistemology to a redefinition of the Bible as Christological authority.

may itself be seen as revelation, since the authority of the essentially religious text derives from the basic metaphor of salvation in Jesus Christ, and since the metaphors *word, inspiration,* and *revelation* also anticipate the Reality that is here, through faith, revealed metaphorically and tentatively.

To be able to use the Bible as a criterion or guideline for the solution of meaningful theological problems is not only a complex hermeneutical and exegetical conceptual problem but also demands of all theologians a thorough critical analysis of their own scriptural conception. A scriptural conception is a model and, as a theory, a structured way of looking at the Bible. As such it fully determines the theologian's manner of problem solving and may function either as a considered, critically responsible model or uncritically as a submerged model serving as an invisible filter in the theologian's provisional and hence limited perspective on the Bible. As believing Christians, theologians relate directly and quite specifically to the Bible. Their respect for the Bible, their acceptance of it as God's Word, and its directive impact on their daily life are at all times governed by how they see the Bible—in other words, by their biblical or scriptural conception.

A scriptural conception is not something some theologians have and others lack: a specific conception of Scripture is undeniably part of everyone's way of thinking and acting. As such, it is a human, provisional, and fallible perspective on the Bible. Thus a scriptural conception forms the essential filter through which the professing theologian reads the Bible, and as a human construct it must always be partly determined by sociocultural, divergent circumstances. This simple but crucial fact implies that a certain (perhaps trusted) conception of Scripture is not necessarily true, the best, or the most biblical simply because it has come down to us from an authoritative tradition. Ultimately it may, of course, prove to be the most valid and plausible conception of Scripture, but then it would have to be constantly tested and, if need be, adjusted or corrected by the nature, structure, and message of the Bible itself.

When theologians accept through the redemptive authority of the Bible that this book is the Word of God, a basic conviction is already at work in that religious acceptance. The problem, then, is not that religious commitment brings theologians to accept and perceive the Bible as God's Word, but rather what theologians mean when they speak of the authority of the Bible. Yet again: a conception of Scripture is the theologian's only access to the Bible, but that conception—as a model—is vulnerable (and corrigible) precisely because faith and religious experience are always rooted in the wider framework of definitive contextual views and opinions, which are always sociohistorically determined.

The worst conceptual problems, however, arise when scriptural conceptions, as models, are absolutized in a fundamentalist manner.[20] A fundamentalistic conceptual model is positivistic; in its passion for firm and final certitudes it trades the security of a relationship of faith with Jesus Christ for a supposedly

---

20. On fundamentalism, see Wentzel van Huyssteen, 1985a:5.

greater certainty, which can often be equated with historical certitude, reliability, and lack of error. Such a conception of Scripture is not only the death of the most essential biblical metaphors[21] but in fact disqualifies the Bible from offering any kind of direction as a hermeneutical criterion for problem solving. Such a fundamentalism usually also functions as a naïve biblicism in which—often with a view to a so-called ultimate scriptural proof—isolated biblical texts are invoked unquestioningly, uncritically, and uncontextually (to support and thus affirm what has become even more important than Scripture to fundamentalists: their own conception of Scripture).

Since fundamentalist biblicism in any form leads to a random use of Scripture, in which biblical citations usurp the role of valid argument, it must be totally unacceptable to any theologian who is seriously concerned with the Bible as God's Word. Ironically, that approach puts excessive stress on the human, subjective factor (one particular conception of Scripture), which all fundamentalists would surely wish to eliminate in their quest for enduring, immutable, and objective truths. I do not mean, of course, that it is necessarily fundamentalistic to accept the Bible, as God's Word, as the absolute authority in church doctrine or in the life of the believer; what is fundamentalistic is to tie the authority of the Bible to extrabiblical theories, for instance, of historical infallibility or timeless ethical norms.

The danger of fundamentalism is not only that it would make the Bible's authority dependent on an extrabiblical notion of general perfection or infallibility; but also, and far worse, is that the belief in the authority of the Bible is (through one absolutized scriptural conception) made into an immunization technique to ensure that the Bible will henceforth speak only in terms of that conception or model. What is speaking is no longer the Bible but merely those abusing their conception of Scripture to make the Bible speak for them and their standpoint. The very soul of the Reformational heritage has rejected this from the outset.

Systematic theological statements must attempt to convey the essence of the biblical message in terms of an explicit theory. They can do so only if all fundamentalistic methods of scriptural proof are abandoned in favor of a broader, hermeneutically responsible form of scriptural appeal in which the deepest intention of the text, with all its hermeneutical complexity, can still direct our religious experience.

Theology and Tradition

Apart from appealing to Scripture in terms of valid hermeneutical and well-considered exegetical criteria, systematic theologians must also be familiar

---

21. David Tracy (1978:126) makes the following striking point about the problem of any naïvely biblicistic, directly biblical use of language: "Literalize that language and that super-everyday world of supernaturalism called fundamentalism emerges."

with the long history of reflection in the Christian religious tradition. In fact, in a certain sense any theological model derives its plausibility from a direct or indirect appeal to a quite specific Christian tradition. Thus all theologians are inevitably and directly involved in some form of tradition (cf. Tracy, 1981:59). Reflection above all on the constant elements or so-called enduring achievements of their tradition—in the formulation of dogmas and confessions—once again confronts systematic theologians with a crucial hermeneutical problem. But the implications are unavoidable: theological statements and theories will gain an ability for criticism and problem solving once the solutions to real empirical or conceptual problems in theology are pursued in direct relation to the tradition of theological reflection on what may be seen as the central truths of the Christian religious paradigm. In fact, as basic metaphors some of the core elements of the global Christian tradition are so central that they finally typify and constantly structure that tradition. But the traditional context thus created in its turn directs the interpretation of the core elements of such a tradition, so that the interpretation of theological tradition becomes a truly complex hermeneutical, historical, doctrinal, and sociology of knowledge problem.

In that sense, reflection on the enduring achievements or rules of dialogue of Christian tradition is an appeal for constant, continuous interpretation. Interpretation of the content of dogma and the authority and nature of confessions will, in fact, ultimately determine the role doctrines and confessions should play as possible guidelines or even as criteria for theorizing in contemporary theology. As theological models and theories, dogmas and confessions are constructs produced in a creative process of historicotheological theorizing, within quite specific sociocultural frameworks and with a view to quite specific empirical or conceptual problems. After all, every Christian doctrine and every confession has its own history and has been created in the context of a specific historical problem-consciousness.

For that reason alone dogmas and confessions cannot be seen as timeless truths and infallible criteria for further theological reflection but must—as theological models—be constantly reclaimed as guidelines for contemporary theological reflection,[22] through a kind of restorative hermeneutics. Therefore dogmas and specific credos or confessional theses cannot become exclusive criteria for theological reflection. In fact, as rules of dialogue in a tradition, dogmas or doctrines in the confessional sense are ultimately the precipitation of certain metaphors that have grown into models through their dominance. Both dogmas and confessions can, however, be absolutized into ideologies. Otherwise their metaphoric roots and the success of their permanence give them great potential for creatively restoring, from the relational, metaphoric nature of re-

---

22. This applies even to the theory-laden "biblical truths" or basic metaphors of our Christian faith: which—conceptually—add immensely to the problem of truth and error (or heresy) in contemporary theological debates.

ligious language, what TeSelle (1975:93) has strikingly called "revelatory participation" in theology.

In attempting a closer definition of the relationship between the languages of our religious experience, of confessions, and of theological reflection, the theologian will not only have to ask what happens when our figurative and metaphoric religious language is theologically transformed into theoretic reflection, but also where the language of confession and dogma fits into that process.

Here we should not lose sight of the distinction between religious and confessional statements on the one hand and theological statements on the other. Religious and confessional statements purport to be answers, and as such reveal a certain decisiveness. Theological statements are argumentative, provisional, and critically directed at the cognitive quality of religious and confessional statements. Therefore theological statements cannot be justified naïvely with a direct or literal appeal to religious or confessional statements. If we did that, we might be dangerously close to a type of ecclesiastical or confessional theology that would ultimately have to function as an isolated ghetto theology because it had severed itself, through an essentially unproblematic confessionalist vindication, from the problem-consciousness of our time.

We have already (cf. Chapter 8 above) distinguished between the metaphoric nature of religious language and the more theoretic nature of theological language. A further refinement to the definition of the relationship between confessional language and the language of theological reflection is the use of the term *model,* a term that is very apt for confessional language, which lies between the metaphoric nature of religious language and the theoretic nature of theological language, thus showing features of both language modes.

By now the task of systematic theology can by no means be seen either as a mere explication or definition of the metaphoric sources of its own linguistic roots, or as the mere definition of the meaning of metaphors and models, as if they are simply illustrations for certain theological concepts. Its task in this area is rather to deal with the critical hermeneutical question of the way figurative religious language and the theoretic language of theological reflection have blended in confessional formulation, to offer valid interpretations of the biblical message for specific problems or crisis situations.

In this respect, what is true of the text of the Bible is also true of any confession. A confession speaks from a certain complex context to someone in a different, equally complex context. In that sense, confessional language precipitates a specific blending of religious language and theological interpretation and should be heard and interpreted as such in any new situation. The context of confessional language is therefore always interpretative, and the complex hermeneutical triangle of author, text, and reader offers a multitude of possibilities for understanding, misunderstanding, dissent, divergent interpretation, and the inevitable revision of earlier interpretations.

No confessional thesis or dogmatic creed can ever exist in isolation; it is always relational to the persons who created it interpretatively, and to those hearing it through further interpretation. In this sense confessions and their systematized doctrines, as systematized interpretations of the biblical message and thus as a blending of figurative religious language and theoretic theological language in certain concrete situations, develop into theological conceptual models: into explicatory guidelines and basic criteria for future theological reflection. Given the model character of confessions, however, one cannot see confession or dogma as an absolute interpretation or as a full perspective on God's will.[23]

Both confessions and specific dogmas can therefore be seen as systematic, relatively permanent theological models, and as such form a critical link between the language of religious experience and the theoretic plane of theological reflection.[24] Thus the tradition of theological reflection offers stimulating interpretative access to the events and Person that provide the grounds for our religious commitment. In that sense tradition offers us valuable guidelines, for through the metaphoric roots of its biblical religious language its dominant models enable us to account critically for all kinds of problems that might arise from interpretation of both the essence and the implications of our Christian faith. Only through the responsible interpretative use of tradition as a directive, basic criterion for concrete, realistically committed theological reflection can theology also enable the church to speak out contextually through its confession and witness on the empirical or conceptual problems of its own cultural-historical or sociopolitical situation.

The critical implications this argument has for confessional formulation may be summed up as follows (cf. van Huyssteen, du Toit, Swanepoel, Rousseau, 1983d:6-7):

1. There is no such thing as a timeless, objective, ahistorical, or omnivalent truth in the meaning of the term confession *or* confessional *authority.*

Churches in the Reformed tradition, in particular, have always regarded themselves as confessional. This implies, however, that we should also critically examine the origins of confessional concepts, and especially of our conceptions of the authority of confessions. If we want to apply ourselves in the context of the modern theological situation to a Reformed examination of the origins of our confessions—and of our conception of confessional texts—we must begin to examine the factors that have affected confessional formulation, the reasons

23. For a detailed discussion of the process of confessionalizing, as well as the nature and authority of confessions as such, cf. van Huyssteen, 1985:7ff.

24. What Sallie McFague (1982:103) says of theological models in general is particularly true of confessions: "Models, like metaphors, retain the tension at the heart of all religious language and, like concepts, order the images of a tradition so that they may become an intelligible pattern for life."

for the formulation of confessions, the validity of the claim that confessions carry authority because they follow the Bible, and, of course, the nature and function of that authority.

A crucial problem that arises immediately is the question of the relationship between the Bible and confessions, the question of the relationship between conceptions of Scripture and of confession, and the indisputable fact that the definition of confessional authority frequently determines how biblical authority is seen (and not the other way around, as we often and too readily assume). Only when I have defined as precisely as possible what the authority of the Bible means to me can I venture a formulation of the authority of a confession. As conceptual models and expressions of ecclesiastical faith, our credos purport to interpret the Bible and thus synoptically and systematically affirm what we regard as biblical truth. Since confessions claim to follow the Bible interpretatively—and not to become a timeless Bible in themselves—every credo reflects the theological and nontheological intellectual climate of its time and is as such already a theological model, regardless of the authority it has in the course of time acquired in that tradition.

It is of cardinal importance that since even the earliest days of the Reformation there has been no timelessly valid conception of what confessional authority means. In the earliest days of the Reformation in Switzerland, theologians such as Bucer and Zwingli, with their typical Reformed passion for *sola scriptura,* saw the multitude of confessions that had sprung up everywhere as provisional, concise commentaries on the Bible, with an educational, catechetic, contextual function (in other words, as dealing with specific problems), which as a point of departure (never as an end in themselves) always referred only to the Bible. Only some 100 years later—especially in 1618, with the synod at Dordt—did confessions in the Reformed paradigm develop from brief occasional pieces into comprehensive theological documents corresponding in all things with God's Word (cf. Augustijn, 1969)—a naïve-realist stand that has since become highly problematic, both epistemologically and methodologically.

2. Any viewpoint on the authority of confessions is sociohistorically determined, either through an acquired mode of reflection or through a mode of reflection that people have come to find convincing, for whatever reason.

In the Reformed tradition, and specifically for Calvin, credos have had an ecumenical function. Through its confession the church offers communion and seeks communion with other churches. For Calvin this was always a matter of unity of doctrine and faith, a unity of direction, and never merely a unity of confession: a kind of exclusivism that developed early in the history of Lutheranism around the Augsburg Confession. In the early days of the Reformation confessions were exchanged among churches and congregations as a token of communion. Augustijn (1969) has shown convincingly that Calvin concurred with what may be seen as the original and classical view of the nature and authority of a confession. It was therefore accepted that confessions had an ecumenical function, but that the Three Formulas of Unity, for example, had to be accepted by all churches and believers as inviolable is refuted by the factual situation of various churches, each with its own confession.

It is clear, then, that in the Reformed tradition there has been a definite development not only in the history of confessions but also in conceptions of their authority. And the logical conclusion is that if we cannot read the Bible biblicistically, we also cannot read the confessions confessionalistically. If the Bible, as Word of God, now confronts us with radical hermeneutical problems, then all the more so the confessions, which, as children of their time, would have to lead us back to the Word of God. The basis of our faith is not the confessions but the Bible itself, which is still to be read, heard, and understood as the Word of God.

3. As an interpretation of the Bible within the bounds of a particular historical situation, each confession is a sociocultural reflection of both the theological and the nontheological thought of its time, as the scriptural truths that must be valid for all times and must therefore be constantly reinterpreted.

How confessions interpret and formulate the biblical message is governed by the insight, religious language, and hermeneutical apparatus of that particular era or situation. If we failed to recognize that and tried to canonize confession confessionally by naïve-realist or literal interpretation, we would immediately rule out any claim to creditable theological reflection. Confessions, no matter how much historical or spiritual authority they have may have gained over the years, must still be seen as theological constructs or conceptual models. And if they are to be read and appreciated from a new and contemporary point of view, they can no longer be understood literally or confessionally.

Confessions are not conclusive documents that can be interpreted literalistically and venerated as timeless, spiritual icons. As a blending of metaphorical religious language and theoretic theological language, they are models that, as guidelines for the convictions of the church, interpretatively anticipate what is regarded on biblical grounds as the will of God for our time. In that sense credos can never be seen as the conclusion of theological reflection but must always form a point of departure for new theological reflection.

The more convinced the church is of its own confession, the more confidently will it allow critical testing of that confession by theology (Heyns and Jonker, 1974:204). Even more importantly, from the Reformed point of view, for example, confessions are not intended as norms to be set up beside the Bible and binding on biblical exegesis. They can therefore never assume an independent significance, outside the control of scriptural interpretation. Confessions, too, must be interpreted hermeneutically for our time and have spiritual authority because they derive from the Bible itself.

4. Our confessions reflect our continuity with the church of Christ through all ages.

As such they define boundaries for us from our past and underline our still living heritage. In the history of the church God has been present through His Holy Spirit, leading the faithful back to the Bible itself according to the demands of contemporary circumstances.

As a Luther or a Calvin never claimed obedience to themselves but demanded it for the Word of God, the church can never claim obedience to confessionally interpreted confessions as ends in themselves. Our confessions are not ends but points of departure: pointers to the Bible, which, as source document, is our only real access to Jesus Christ. A confession is a document in which the church professes faith in Jesus Christ. It is not a systematizing of the opinions, convictions, or ideals of a particular group of people, or a canonized program for dogmatic or ethical thought; nor, however, is it a political, ethical, or even religious platform, to be abused by one or another pressure group for the sake of whatever ideals it may cherish.

Our interpretation of our confessions must therefore always focus solely on the Bible and on Jesus Christ. Despite their historicity and contemporaneity, our confessions contain strong allusions to Holy Scripture and also have the challenge to profess Jesus Christ contextually in our time and our circumstances. The authority of confessions is, therefore, subservient to the Bible's. That authority is not legalistic but spiritual, founded on the fact that Jesus Christ is still professed essentially in order that we might experience His salvation in concrete, living situations. In that sense the theological thinking reflected in tradition is a valid way to the reality in which we believe. And it is also the only valid authority of a confession.

5. A theology that wishes to account for the authority of God's revelation must bear in mind that this authority does not come to us unproblematically through Scripture or confessions.

As we have seen, the reason for this lies in the theorizing implied in our conceptions of Scripture and confessions. Therefore authority cannot be identified uncritically and dogmatistically with particular conceptual models; theologically, it must be approached as a problem.

Theology and Contemporary Scientific Thought

Systematic theologians who critically examine the process of theorizing underlying their own thought cannot but discover that they are in a sense balancing on the line of tension between, on the one hand, the crucial truths of Christian tradition, which derive from the central biblical message, and, on the other hand, the complex but ineluctable challenge of contemporary thought and problem-consciousness. A theologian who fails to sense that tension can only be hiding behind the barricades of some or other form of theological ghetto-thought (cf. also de Gruchy, 1985).

The specific task of theologians is to grapple with the empirical and conceptual problems now being discovered in the contexts of religious experience, the church, and theological reflection itself. In that sense theologians have to try to articulate and contextualize the essence of the biblical message and Christian traditions in a contemporary situation that confronts them not only with very specific philosophical and ideological challenges but also with incisive sociocultural questions.

To be able to meet that challenge creditably, theologians must be able to speak with confidence, having considered as thoroughly as possible the conceptual problems surrounding the nature and structure of their own reflection. Thus the context of theological reflection brings its own empirical and conceptual problems. Furthermore, some of theology's most difficult conceptual problems are in fact raised by the question, What is theology?

That exceptionally complex question might, of course, be answered differently from different perspectives. In this work the approach has been to examine the problems of systematic theology from a fundamental-theological point of view; therefore our inquiry has had to crystallize constantly into specific questions such as the following: Can the concept of rationality be reclaimed meaningfully and validly for theology as an intellectual activity? Can a valid rationality model be constructed for systematic theology through a critical analysis of the theorizing underlying all its statements, models, and theories—a model that would be reality depicting, both cognitively and contextually, that could lead to the valid analysis and solution of problems, and that could thus stimulate progress in theological thought?

To be able to ask questions such as these from a fundamental-theological angle we had to enter into a dialogue with the philosophy of science inquiries of our time, from logical positivism to critical rationalism, Kuhn, Laudan, and scientific realism. The reason for that engagement was self-evident, but it was nonetheless reiterated time and again. Fundamental epistemological issues such as the nature of scientific thought, the nature of rationality and objectivity, the origins of conceptual models and theories in the process of theorizing, are in fact treated as specific problems in philosophy of science terms. That kind of inquiry is vital to any form of science. Not only does a philosophy of science examination of theological reflection engage the theologian in interscientific dialogue, but a type of scientific problem-consciousness is created that theology dare not lack in its attempt to find a valid problem-solving model.

Even more important is that, in the context of modern scientific thought, it is in fact philosophy of science that can help systematic theology to fulfil its commitment to rationality[25] in the formulation of criteria for a valid rationality model. For that reason a second criterion, the critical and problem-solving capacity of theological statements, has been identified in addition to the first, the criterion of reality depiction in theological statements.

Apart from the basic guidelines found in the Bible as the classic document of Christianity and the tradition of dogma and credal formulation, a theology engaging in the critical analysis and solving of problems will therefore—for the sake of the scientific conceptualizing of its reflection—have to turn to contemporary scientific thought for specific philosophy of science guidelines if its own reasoning is to be epistemologically and methodologically plausible. In systematic theology, too, a broad range of historical, philosophical, hermeneutical, sociological, and sociology of knowledge criteria could and should eventually come up for discussion, depending on the specific angle of approach and type of problem statement.

Systematic theologians have a commitment to the church as a religious community and to society as a whole. Nevertheless, theologians offer their services from within a university. The consequent commitment to scientific credibility makes very high demands of professing theologians but ultimately also implies testifying to the Truth to which they have totally committed themselves in faith.

The specific philosophy of science problematization of systematic theology is not only an aid to regaining a creditable rationality model but also presents systematic theology with challenging conceptual problems. Some of these have already been raised, especially in our discussion of the theological models of Wolfhart Pannenberg and Gerhard Sauter, as in the new type of problem-consciousness philosophers of science such as Thomas S. Kuhn, Larry Laudan, and Ernan McMullin have brought home to systematic theology. I should now like to outline some other problems as critical implications of a philosophy of science analysis of theology:

1. In analyzing the nature and limits of theologians' rationality model, the problem is not so much their personal faith or basic convictions as the way their theory-laden religious commitment—already conceptualized and theorized—helps to shape their theological viewpoints.

2. Theologians have to be especially wary of using their pretheoretic commitment to God and His revelation as a rational pretext for irrationally developing their theological models on unexamined premises. Systematic theologians must beware of taking refuge in a supposedly unique and esoteric epistemology as an ideological immunization against criticism. Once the premises of such a theology have been critically ex-

25. For a discussion of what is meant by this commitment to rationality, cf. also A. König, 1978:399-411.

posed, its conceptions of God and revelation often show up as subjective and random conceptual constructs.[26]

3. Claiming that God's Word or His revelation is the direct starting point of theology offers no cure for theological subjectivism. Methodologically, a positive religious encounter with revelation provides no alternative to subjectivism in theology. After all, theologians who appeal directly to God's Word—whether in Scripture, ecclesiastical pronouncements, or a personal encounter with Jesus Christ—are still fully bound to their own subjective, theory-laden, and hence pretheorized premises, despite that appeal to the Word of God.

4. A theology that would account for the authority of God's revelation must bear in mind that we do not receive that authority unproblematically from Scripture or doctrine. It is made problematic by the theorizing inherent in our conceptions of Scripture and doctrine; therefore that authority cannot be identified uncritically and dogmatistically with certain conceptual models but should be approached as a theological problem. If we failed to do so, theological language would be perverted into a purely expressive language; in other words, into statements of certain theologians' subjective convictions and decisions. And if that happened theology would lose any claim to cognitivity and be reduced to just another form of social ideology.

5. In the paradigmatic context of a religious tradition in which the Bible is recognized as the authoritative Word of God, theologians have to be wary of an epistemological naïveté in which theological statements are founded solely on references to certain scriptural proofs. Even the Reformed *sola scriptura* principle, for example, might lapse into a type of exegetical positivism. A method of exegesis in which the Bible, as the Word of God, is hermeneutically and historically explored to account for faith could, however, express the ultimate intent of the Reformed *sola scriptura*.

6. In seeking to answer the question of its identity, systematic theology need not prefer theoretic thought to religious experience in order to salvage its claim to rationality. Christian faith itself, and the very way it is experienced and conceptualized, offers realist grounds for critical reflection, and thus for rational reflection. Our faith in Jesus Christ is in fact articulated in statements about that faith—statements committed, in

26. For the way the concept of God must be shaped through a process of imaginative construction in the process of theological theorizing in terms of concrete constructs, cf. Gordon Kaufman, 1975; 1979; 1981. Kaufman's reconstruction of the concept of God as a regulatory symbol—consciously also apart from biblical metaphors and with a consequent loss of cognitivity—is so complex and problematic that it is not dealt with here. Essentially, he is attempting to construct a valid rationality model for systematic theology while totally ignoring contemporary debates and the divergent redefinitions of the concepts of rationality and objectivity in contemporary philosophy of science.

turn, to a network of argumentative constructs. Such a creative conceptualizing is, as a critical justification of faith, the very essence of systematic theology.

Our philosophy of science examination of the concept of rationality has shown how that concept has evolved since logical positivism, critical rationalism, Kuhn's historicist turn, Laudan's anti-realism, and McMullin's scientific realism. I am convinced that no rationality model in modern philosophy of science can finally and conclusively define the term *rationality.* Therefore all rationality models must be provisional and inconclusive. If we have found, in what is here called a critical-realist rationality model, a provisional answer to the most basic fundamental-theological conceptual problems, then that model, too—and the criteria structuring it—must remain fully provisional and susceptible to richer, subtler, and more refined forms of rationality.

Meanwhile such a model may structure and offer guidelines for a plausible systematic-theological process of creative, conceptual construction in the context of contemporary scientific thought—a process which, through the creative formulation of theological theories, may further systematic reflection on God in this world.

The Constructive and Progressive Nature of Theological Statements

Our examination of the nature of theorizing in theology has shown that systematic theology, by transforming metaphoric religious language into the clearest possible theoretic conceptual language, constructs theories in response to concrete empirical or conceptual problems. Such problems are found in the contexts of religious experience, the church, and theological reflection itself. The theories or answers we produce to solve those problems are creatively and constructively founded on a theological problem-solving model which serves as a directive, interpretative framework and incorporates, as basic criteria, the Bible, the Christian confessional tradition, and the modern scientific problem-consciousness.

These insights emerged even more specifically from our discussion of the second criterion for a creditable rationality model for systematic theology, namely, the critical and problem-solving capacity of theological statements. The rationality of a theological statement, theory, or conceptual model is no longer seen as dependent on its supposed ability to state the truth unproblematically, in a fundamentalist manner; it depends, rather, on whether such statements, theories, or models can show some form of progress by reducing or solving problems, whether empirical or conceptual.

By this means we have learned that the rationality of a given theory must be defined in terms of its progressiveness, and not the other way round, as is normally assumed. Larry Laudan rightly suggests that we can learn something about rationality by looking at progress, simply because our model for scientific progress is normally far clearer than ones for the elusive and problematic concept of rationality. Thus Laudan (1977:6) could conclude that rationality consists in making the most progressive theory choices, and that progress is not a matter of accepting the most rational theories.

Working rationally and progressively in systematic theology is therefore bound up with the creative construction of theological theories in an attempt to solve clearly identified problems as effectively as possible. I should like to put it even more strongly: even the development of a sophisticated problem-consciousness, and from that the identification—albeit approximately, tentatively, and provisionally—of a specific theological problem, can be seen as definite progress. Above all, however, the interpretative handling of our problem-solving model in an attempt to solve problems as effectively as possible and thus find maximal meaning in a particular problem context may be seen as the essence of progress in systematic theology.

From the above it follows that if a certain theory in systematic theology (for instance, on scriptural authority, on redemption, on predestination, or on the theodicy problem) is somehow modified or finally even replaced by another, such a change is progressive only if the modified or new theory is a better or more effective problem-solver than its predecessor. We might also find interesting examples in Christological theories and in recent debates on the heresy problem. In the early church, for instance, theories about Christ's dual nature related directly to the issue of heresy. At the famous councils of Nicea (A.D. 325) and Chalcedon (A.D. 451), any theories that might detract from the true divinity and true humanity of Jesus Christ, or from His unity of person, were rejected as heretical.

Since then the Christological problem has developed into divergent Christological theories in attempts to solve the problem of Chalcedon in terms of the Bible, with due regard for tradition and in accordance with our contemporary problem-consciousness. Heresy, however, is no longer central to the development of such Christological theories; in fact, the heresy issue—as a typical external conceptual problem—has since developed into a quite specific contemporary issue. In the present South African context heresy is no longer an issue governed by a theory about the unity of Christ. The far more contextual question is the visible unity of the church, and specifically the question whether apartheid, as a political system, is essentially heretical because it discredits and negates salvation through Jesus Christ and thus directly jeopardizes the truth of Christianity. This type of conceptualizing of theological problems—irrespective of how they might be answered or resolved—can already be seen as valid progress in systematic theology.

We see a further example of this kind of progress when conceptual problems caused in the Reformed reflective tradition by an obsolete scriptural theory led to a new theory. The ultimate interpretation of the metaphor of inspiration will naturally be a central problem in that context. In the Reformed theological model the concept of inspiration, more than any other (cf. van Huyssteen and du Toit, 1982:31ff.), has over the years been used and abused to express the special relationship between God and the biblical authors. Systematic theologians have used it to suggest that God had in a special sense employed people to convey the message of His revelation by experiencing and finally recording their religious encounters. In orthodox Reformed circles (cf. Deist, 1974:2ff.), however, a comprehensive mechanistic inspirational theory was eventually developed in fundamentalist fashion: a conceptual model in which the truth of the Bible was made directly dependent on its purported literal, historical infallibility or inerrancy.

If a biblical text such as the story of creation (Gen. 1–3) is read in a naïve-realist way as literal history, as may be done through a positivistically structured fundamentalist model, its ancient Near Eastern literary form is ignored and numerous insurmountable problems are raised. These problems, as specific conceptual theological problems, are caused directly by the consequent conflicting claims of (supposedly) biblical and scientific stands on the origins of our world. In such a situation theology and science are inevitably plunged into direct and irreconcilable confrontation, ruling out any creative reinterpretation of the story of creation in the light of the most recent scientific knowledge and archeological and paleontological discoveries.

In designing a new scriptural theory to incorporate our problem-solving model, we again have to look for a theory of the Bible in terms of its own nature, the tradition of reflection on it, and contemporary hermeneutical criteria. As an ancient Near Eastern book composed of many books with divergent literary forms (the Bible's own nature), and as a book that has to be interpreted according to its own nature (in the Reformed tradition the *sola scriptura sui ipsius interpres*—the Bible is its own interpreter), the Bible now stands before us as a book of faith with a nonnegotiable religious dimension. If that book is to be understood according to its own character, no contemporary hermeneutics can dismiss its religious dimension.

With such a scriptural theory, commitment to the Bible's redemptive authority becomes possible, as does the insight that its authority cannot be confused with historical accuracy. Insight into the nature of biblical literary genres—in itself a form of theological progress—now also enables us to grasp that the biblical accounts of Genesis are not concerned with historiography in the Western sense but with archetypal history conveyed to us by biblical authors in a confessional, narrative, and pretheoretical form.

In contrast to a traditional mechanistic or even organic scriptural theory we now have here a theory in which the historical question (whether the world was actually created in six days; whether Adam and Eve were in fact the first people) is made relative to the deeper religious intent of the text. Such a theory of Scripture ensures progress in theology, not only because the text as a literary form is given its due more than in the earlier theory, but also because it eliminates some conceptual problems in the sense that theological statements need no longer form (conflicting) alternatives to theories of natural science about the origins of our world.

That the Bible's historical authority is not equal to its redemptive authority does not, of course, imply that the question whether certain biblical events did in fact occur is always of secondary importance. In the light of the context and particular literary form we should also ask the important question of the specific gravity of the historicity of certain events—a question that would clearly demand different answers for different parts of the Bible.

Theologians might well disagree strongly on whether the metaphor of inspiration should be retained in any new or alternative scriptural theory. Despite its traditional connotations I should prefer to reclaim and retain it, at least for a Reformed theory of Scripture. The concept of inspiration is an original biblical metaphor that might be revitalized with a new openness to convey the special religious dimension of the biblical text. The concept of inspiration also signifies that the Word of God did not drop into our world in some supernatural fashion, as an objective revelatory truth and without human intervention. By choosing the metaphor of inspiration we also profess God's care and preordination throughout the biblical account of creation. That account comprises events and stories from a distant past, the words of patriarchs and prophets, traditions, various sources, the work of scribes, of editors, and of individual authors.

In professing that the secret of biblical authority lies most profoundly in the workings of the Holy Spirit, we mean that in the divergent texts of the Bible believers testified in writing to the revelation of God as they had experienced it in faith. This inherent religious dimension of the Bible cannot be dismissed by any argument, whether literary-historical, linguistic, or otherwise. In that sense the Bible is a book by believers for believers, and its authority lives and works only in relation to the religious bond between God and professing Christians.

In the light of the care and creative presence of God's Spirit in the biblical account of creation, the Bible's ultimate authority is not founded on its mechanical immutability, as if one can interpret it without any scriptural conception. On the contrary, the Bible is above all a gateway to the reality in which we believe. Its authority is therefore deeply rooted in the religious level, and thus in the encounter with Jesus Christ. That encounter is mediated primarily by the Bible, since the writings of many known and anonymous believers, and finally also of some of the first Christians, provide our only access to the reality of the Jesus of Nazareth who lived, died, and was resurrected nearly 2000 years ago.

In that sense the authority of the Bible can ultimately be defined as redemptive and experienced in faith as God's revelation. The Bible also gives us the intellectual and experiential framework in which Jesus Christ expressed His message in His time—a still living message, but one that can be heard and interpreted clearly and lucidly only through a scriptural theory that has been corrected and refined as accurately as possible.

It is now also clear why the basic criteria of our problem-solving model (the Bible, Christian tradition, and the modern scientific problem-consciousness) first had to be developed as a directive, interpretative context. The relationship between the theologian (within the contemporary problem-consciousness), through the long process of reflection on central Christian truths (tradition), to the source document of our Christian faith and theological reflection (the Bible) remains the historical and hermeneutical context in which the critical theologian constantly refers back and attempts to reflectively penetrate to the original religious intent of the Word of God for all times, but in particular for the present and its contemporary problems. More simply: theological progress means renewed but also better understanding of the biblical message in each new context or problem situation.

In a philosophy of science sense, the role played by theoretic constructs and hence by conceptualizing in the process of theorizing is now clearer than ever. That in itself is of course a form of intellectual progress in theological reflection. But progress in systematic theology is far more than intellectual insight into the process of creative, conceptual construction with which theology seeks to solve problems by designing theories. As theoretic conceptual constructs against the background of the metaphoric structure of our theological knowledge, those solutions in themselves also creatively reveal—true to their metaphoric roots—something of the reality that such theories anticipate provisionally. In a new and better scriptural theory, something of the nature and structure of the Bible itself has been grasped and described more validly than before.

This line of thought in the structure of systematic-theological knowledge is not only the essence of the theological rationality model we have described as critical realism but ultimately also the basis of any progress in theology. In a theology that sees itself as a form of critical justification of faith, the theologian constructs theories that provisionally postulate the still hidden structures and nature of what is being studied. At the same time, the metaphoric origins and hypothetical structure of our systematic-theological theories provide a key to their explicatory potential. Such theories can be evaluated as sound or unsound, as plausible or implausible, as biblical or unbiblical,[27] in terms of our contemporary insights in handling our problem-solving model, but also comparatively, in terms of alternative and earlier theories.

---

27. These so-called zero terms, like *scriptural* and *nonscriptural, Christian* and *unchristian*, etc., can still be used only with full cognizance of the complex tridimensionality (Bible, tradition, modern scientific problem-consciousness) of our problem-solving model, as well as the hermeneutical and other criteria that become fully functional through that model.

As in all other sciences, our theological models and theories may also be seen as theoretic constructs. And although that of which we speak in theology (including, for example, God, Jesus Christ, the Holy Spirit, salvation) is in principle inaccessible, our theories have enabled us to draw certain tentative, provisional conceptual lines toward the object of our statements. As we have seen, this opens the door to a critical realism that may be translated into systematic-theological terms as the anticipatory, eschatological structure of our theological language.

In that sense we could earlier claim ontological status or also a cognitive core for our theological statements. That we can, in the context of our problem-solving model, eventually compare and prefer some theories to others because the solutions they offer to concrete problems provide, by current insights, maximal meaning, is enough reason for us to assume that sound theological theories do not only refer to a Reality beyond and greater than ours but can in fact speak more and more accurately—through hermeneutical, historical, and exegetical refinement—about the Object of theological reflection. Thus such new theories show real progress without losing their tentative and provisional character.

As metaphors work by tentative suggestion in our religious language and in science (cf. McMullin, 1984:31), so our theological models and theories contain something of this inherent metaphoric dynamics.[28] In the context of our problem-solving model it may also become apparent that original metaphors or dominant models gradually grow more and more extensive, testifying to the constructive and progressive nature of our theological statements by broadening meaning in the most concrete sense of the word.

Theological theories therefore never aspire to literal reflection of the mystery of God, which is always directly or indirectly the object of their statements. Like religious language, as the origin of our theological statements, theological statements always function relationally within the relationship between God and mankind. In that relational context systematic theology has to strive for the broadening of well-known metaphors, and even for new and creative ones,[29] in order to achieve a redescription of the hidden Reality it seeks to convey. In such a gaining of a more plausible understanding of theology's object lies the essence of its progress.

To some extent, then, acceptance of a successful model or theory in theology must always be provisional. No model should be ideologized, as if it were absolutely and eternally true. In terms of loyalty to the essence of the biblical message and its reflection in history, a theory may be the best available, but then

---

28. Cf. S. McFague, 1982:91: "Models, the products of imagination, are neither literal pictures of reality nor mere useful fictions, but partial, though inadequate, ways of dealing with what really is."

29. Cf. also S. McFague, 1982:177ff., who from a reformist-feminist perspective examines the value of metaphors such as *friend* and *lover* in respect of a modern conception of God.

the best because it offers a better grasp and a better solution of a particular problem in a particular, concrete situation.

A good theory is therefore always the basis for further research and reflection (McMullin, 1984:35), thus contributing substantially to theological progress in the scientific sense. Hence the language of theological theories is—in terms of a critical-realist model—always tentative, provisional, and capable of further development. For precisely that reason systematic theology must be tolerant of a multiplicity of theories, even if the structuring and handling of its own problem-solving model give it a preference for certain theories or models. Like their original metaphors, good theories offer us, through their metaphoric structures, filters and perspectives by which to gain a more plausible insight into the Reality we speak of in our theological statements. Apart from the framework of our problem-solving model and the effect of the Bible as a directive basic criterion in that model, it is in the history of our theological reflection, too, that the success of certain theories over a long period not only guarantees continuity with the basic biblical metaphors but also provides adequate grounds to believe that certain models or theories do indeed refer to something, and that something of the Reality theologians speak of is constructively and progressively revealed in that reference. Good examples may be found in the dominance of models such as *Father* (in respect of God) and *Word of God* (for the Bible).

Of cardinal importance to systematic theologians is not only that their own thought derives consciously or unconsciously, ideologically or critically, from a quite specific theological research tradition; by imaginatively but responsibly evaluating theological theories, theologians can ultimately also help to develop and broaden that tradition or conceptual paradigm as a whole. Analyzing theological thought and its progress in terms of such global theories, theological and confessional traditions will, of course, reveal a highly complex meshing of conceptual, theoretic, religious, and confessional commitments. But that multiplicity could also be meaningful and need not in any way contradict a critical-realist approach to theological research traditions, inasmuch as it demonstrably and validly reflects, in the interpretation of the basic biblical metaphor, a definite congruity in interpretations of the essence of Christian faith. Comprehensive theological traditions are therefore by no means outside the problem-solving and hence progressive process of theological cognitive development. In fact, such traditions even partly determine the empirical or conceptual problems of a particular tradition.

Significant changes—not necessarily with the revolutionary implications of the Kuhnian paradigm shift—can also occur in a particular theological tradition through the modification or revision of a certain central theory or theories. Thus, for example, a hermeneutical and exegetical broadening of scriptural theory might enhance the biblical theory of a particular Reformed tradition while at the same time incisively revising and refining the problem-solving capacities of other theories that appeal to that scriptural theory within a particular theological paradigm.

Laudan (1977:98) points out rightly that significant internal shifts in a particular tradition—and therefore also in a specific theological tradition—might lead to the natural evolution of a conceptual paradigm. In theology, too, we find—over and above paradigmatic conceptual transformations—a kind of natural development of specific reflective or confessional traditions which, at the same time, provides insight into the continuity of a creatively developing tradition. In both cases—paradigmatic shifts as well as natural development and broadening—we see the essence of systematic-theological progress.

The essence of the constructive and progressive nature of theological statements is perhaps best summed up by David Tracy (1981:14): "If any human being, if any religious thinker or theologian, produces some classical expression of the human spirit on a particular journey in a particular tradition, that person discloses permanent possibilities for human existence both personal and communal." Theologians who critically and responsibly examine the essence of their own theological reflective mode realize that God is greater than all our theological constructs. Our knowledge of God grows not through the sudden gift of infallible theological propositions but through His guiding us to new situations and new experiences that must, in terms of our problem-solving model, constantly demand a new and creative mode of theological reflection.

In that process the Bible, as our exclusive access to Jesus of Nazareth, as well as the creative, constructive capacity of our theological reflection, presents us with an enduring challenge, namely, to make critical-realist and tentative but plausible statements on the reality of the Object on Whom we reflect in anticipation, and in Whom we believe. In the typical metaphoric religious language of the Bible we might conclude: "For now we see through a glass darkly, but then face to face" (1 Cor. 13:12).

The tentative knowledge revealed for us in these simple images, as well as the hidden mysteries they preserve, is an essential part of the structure and tension of our religious language. The special task of systematic theology is to preserve that tension in creatively designing concepts, models, and finally theological theories, while nonetheless progressing through a problem-solving and thus maximally meaningful appeal to both our insight and our experience.

Bibliography

Albert, Hans. 1982. *Die Wissenschaft und die Fehlbarkeit der Vernunft.* Tübingen: J. C. B. Mohr (Paul Siebeck).

————. 1968. *Traktat über kritische Vernunft.* Tübingen: J. C. B. Mohr (Paul Siebeck).

Augustijn, C. 1969. *Kerk en Belydenis.* Kampen: J. H. Kok.

Barbour, Ian G. 1976. *Myths, Models and Paradigms. A Comparative Study in Science and Religion.* New York: Harper & Row.

————. 1985. "A review of A. Peacocke's *Intimations of Reality. Critical Realism in Science and Religion.*" In: *Religion and Intellectual Life,* II/4:111ff.

Barth, Karl. 1928. "Die dogmatische Prinzipienlehre bei Wilhelm Herrmann." In: *Die Theologie und die Kirche.* Munich: EVZ-Verlag.

————. 1932. *Kirchliche Dogmatik,* I/1. Munich: EVZ-Verlag.

Bartley, William W. 1964. *The Retreat to Commitment.* London: Chatto and Windus.

Berger, Peter L. 1969. *The Sacred Canopy: Elements of a Sociological Theory of Religion.* New York: Doubleday.

Biser, E. 1970. *Theologische Sprachtheorie und Hermeneutik.* Munich: Kosel.

Black, Max. 1969. *Models and Metaphors. Studies in Language and Philosophy.* Ithaca: Cornell University Press.

Bosman, H. L. 1987. "Modelle van Skrifuitleg." In *Scriptura: Tydskrif vir Bybelkunde.*

Botha, M. Elaine. 1984. *Metaforiese perspektief en fokus in die wetenskap. Die rol van geloof, mite en taal in wetenskaplike teorievorming.* Potchefstroom: PU vir CHO Central Publications Dpt.

Botha, R. P. 1977. *Generatiewe taalondersoek. 'n Sistematiese inleiding.* Cape Town: HAUM.

Boyd, R. N. 1984. "The Current Status of Scientific Realism." In: *Scientific Realism*. Ed. J. Leplin. Los Angeles: University of California Press. Pp. 41-82.

Burnham, F. B. 1985. "Response to Arthur Peacocke." In: *Religion and Intellectual Life*, II:27-31.

Chryssides, G. D. 1985. "Meaning, Metaphor and Meta-theology." *Scottish Journal of Theology*, 38/2.

Daecke, S. M., Janowski, H. N., Pannenberg, W., and Sauter, G. 1974a. "Theologie als Wissenschaft. Ein Gespräch." In: *Grundlagen der Theologie. Ein Diskurs*. Stuttgart: Kohlhammer. Pp. 58-120.

Daecke, S. M. 1974b. "Soll die Theologie an der Universität Bleiben?" In: *Grundlagen der Theologie. Ein Diskurs*. Stuttgart: Kohlhammer. Pp. 7-28.

De Gruchy, John W. 1985. "Wentzel van Huyssteen's Belydenis as denkmodel. A Critical Response." In: *Teologie-Belydenis-Politiek/Theology-Confession-Politics*. Bellville: U.W.K. Publishers. Pp. 28-32.

Deist, F. E. 1974. *Die Woord in beweging. Bybeluitleg vir die moderne tyd*. Cape Town: Tafelberg.

De Ruiter, A. 1979. "A contrecoeur contra Kuhn." In: *Algemeen Nederlandsch Tydschrift voor Wysbegeerte*, 71/4.

De Vries, G. 1984. *De ontwikkeling van wetenschap. Een inleiding in de Wetenschapsfilosofie*. Groningen: Wolters-Noordhoff.

Doppelt, G. 1978. "Kuhn's Epistemological Relativism: An Interpretation and Defense." In: *Inquiry*, 21.

Du Toit, B. J. 1984. "Die aard van skrifgesag en waarheid." Unpublished M.A. Thesis. University of Port Elizabeth.

————. 1984. "Die metaforiese spreke oor God." D.D. Thesis, University of Pretoria.

Hare, R. M. 1957. "Religion and Morals." In: *Faith and Logic*. Ed. B. Mitchell. London: Allen & Unwin.

Hart, Hendrik. 1983. "The Articulation of Belief. A Link between Rationality and Commitment. In: *Rationality in the Calvinian Tradition*. Ed. H. Hart, J. Vander Hoeven, and N. Wolterstorff. Lanham: University Press of America. Pp. 209-248.

Hefner, P. 1985. "Just How Much Can We Intimate about Reality? A Response to Arthur Peacocke." In: *Religion and Intellectual Life*, II/4:32-37.

Hempelmann, Heinzpeter. 1980. *Kritischer Rationalismus und Theologie als Wissenschaft*. Wuppertal: Brockhaus.

Hesse, Hermann. 1973. *Siddhartha*. London: PAN Books Limited.

Hesse, M. 1984. "The Cognitive Claims of Metaphor." In: *Metaphor and Religion*. Ed. J. P. Von Noppen. Brussels: Theolinguistics. Pp. 27-45.

Heyns, J. A., Jonker, W. D. 1974. *Op weg met die teologie*. Pretoria: D. R. Church Publishers.

Hodges, H. A. 1979. *God beyond Knowlege.* London: Macmillan Press.

Jüngel, Eberhard. 1967. *Die Freiheit der Theologie.* Theologische Studien, 88. Zürich: EVZ-Verlag.

Kaufman, Gordon D. 1975. *An Essay on Theological Method.* Missoula, Montana: Scholars Press.

————. 1979. *God the Problem.* Cambridge: Harvard University Press.

————. 1981. *The Theological Imagination. Constructing the Concept of God.* Philadelphia: Westminster Press.

Klooster, Fred H. 1977. *Quests for the Historical Jesus.* Grand Rapids: Baker Book House.

König, Adrio. 1978. "In gesprek met prof. Van Huyssteen." In: *Koers,* 43/4.

Koningsveld, H. 1977. *Het verschijnsel wetenschap.* Meppel: Boom.

Kuhn, H. 1978. "Die Theologie vor dem Tribunal der Wissenschaftstheorie." In: *Philosophische Rundschau,* 25/3-4.

Kuhn, Thomas S. 1970a. *The Structure of Scientific Revolutions.* 2nd ed. Chicago: University of Chicago Press.

————. 1970b. "Logic of Discovery or Psychology of Research." In: *Criticism and the Growth of Knowlege.* Ed. I. Lakatos and A. Musgrave. Cambridge: Cambridge University Press.

————. 1970c. "Reflections on My Critics." In: *Criticism and the Growth of Knowlege.* Cambridge: Cambridge University Press.

Kuitert, H. M. 1974. *Zonder geloof vaart niemand wel. Een plaatsbepaling van Christendom en kerk.* Baarn: Ten Have.

————. 1977. *Wat heet geloven? Struktuur en herkomst van de christelijke geloofsuitspraken.* Baarn: Ten Have.

Laudan, L. *Progress and Its Problems: Towards a Theory of Scientific Growth.* London: Routledge and Kegan Paul.

Leplin, Jarrett, ed. 1984. *Essays on Scientific Realism.* Los Angeles: University of California Press.

Lindbeck, G. A. 1984. *The Nature of Doctrine. Religion and Theology in a Post-liberal Age.* Philadelphia: Westminster Press.

McCormack, B. L. 1985. "Divine Revelation and Human Imagination: Must We Choose between the Two?" In: *Scottish Journal of Theology,* 37.

McFague, Sallie. 1983. *Metaphorical Theology. Models of God in Religious Language.* London: SCM Press.

McMullin, Ernan. 1984. "A Case for Scientific Realism." In: *Essays on Scientific Realism.* Ed. J. Leplin. Los Angeles: University of California Press. Pp. 8-40.

————. 1982. "The Motive for Metaphor." In: *Infinity,* 55.

————. 1984. "A Case for Scientific Realism." In: *Essays on Scientific Realism.* Ed. J. Leplin. Los Angeles: University of California Press.

————. 1985. "Realism in Theology and Science. A Response to Peacocke." In: *Religion and Intellectual Life.* II/4.

Mouton, Johann, and Marais, H. C. 1985. *Metodologie van die geesteswetenskappe: Basiese begripe. RGN-Studies in Navorsingsmetodologie.* Pretoria: HSRC.

O'Hear, A. 1984. *Experience, Explanation and Faith.* London: Routledge & Kegan Paul.

Pannenberg, Wolfhart. 1967. "Die Krise des Schriftprinzips." In: *Grundfragen Systematischer Theologie. Gesammelte Aufsätze.* Göttingen: Vandenhoeck & Ruprecht.

————. 1973a. "Ein Leben mit Stil." In: *Gegenwart Gottes: Predigten.* Munich: Claudius.

————. 1973b. *Wissenschaftstheorie und Theologie.* Frankfurt am Main: Suhrkamp.

————. 1974. "Wie wahr ist das Reden von Gott?" In: *Grundlagen der Theologie.* Ed. S. Daecke and N. Janowski. Stuttgart: Kohlhammer. Pp. 29-41.

————. 1980. "Antwort auf G. Sauters Überlegungen." In: *Evangelische Theologie,* 40/2.

Peacocke, Arthur. 1984. *Intimations of Reality. Critical Realism in Science and Religion.* Notre Dame: University of Notre Dame Press.

Polanyi, Michael. 1962. *Personal Knowledge: Towards a Postcritical Philosophy.* Chicago: University of Chicago Press.

Popper, Karl. 1963. *Conjectures and Refutations.* London: Routledge and Kegan Paul.

————. 1968. *The Logic of Scientific Discovery.* London: Hutchinson.

————. 1970. "Normal Science and Its Dangers." In: *Criticism and the Growth of Knowlege.* Ed. I. Lakatos and A. Musgrave. Cambridge: Cambridge University Press.

————. 1973. *Objective Knowledge.* Oxford: Clarendon Press.

————. 1980. *Unended Quest: An Intellectual Autobiography.* 5th ed. Glasgow: Fontana.

Putnam, H. 1984. "What Is Realism?" In: *Essays on Scientific Realism.* Ed. J. Leplin. Los Angeles: University of California Press.

Russell, R. J. 1985. "A Critical Appraisal of Peacocke's Thought on Religion and Science." In: *Religion and Intellectual Life,* II/4.

Sauter, Gerhard. 1970a. *Von einem neuen Methodenstreit in der Theologie?* Munich: Kaiser.

————. 1970b. "Die Aufgabe der Theorie in der Theologie." In: *Evangelische Theologie,* 30/9.

————. 1971a. "Theologie als Wissenschaft. Historisch-Systematische Einleitung." In: *Theologie als Wissenschaft.* Ed. G. Sauter. Theologische Bucherei 43. Munich: Kaiser. Pp. 9-72.

————. 1971b. "Die begründung theologischer Aussagen Wissenschaftstheoretisch gesehen." In: *Zeitschrift für Evangelische Ethik,* 15.

————. 1971c. "Möglichkeiten der Theoriebildung in der Theologie." In: *Die Theologie in der Interdiziplinären Forschung*. Düsseldorf.

————. 1973. *Wissenschaftstheoretische Kritik der Theologie. Die Theologie und die neuere wissenschaftstheoretische Diskussion*. Munich: Kaiser.

————. 1975a. "Wissenschaftstheoretische Kritik der Theologie." In: *Der Wissenschaftsbegriff in der Natur- und die Geisteswissenschaften*. Studia Leibnitiana (Sonderheft). Wiesbaden: Franz Steiner Verlag.

————. 1975b. Der Wissenschaftsbegriff der Theologie." In: *Der Wissenschaftsbegriff in der Natur- und die Geisteswissenschaften*. Studia Leibnitiana (Sonderheft). Wiesbaden: Franz Steiner Verlag.

————. 1975c. "Grundzüge einer Wissenschaftstheorie der Theologie." In: *Wissenschaftstheoretische Kritik der Theologie*. Munich: Kaiser.

————. 1980. "Überlegungen zu einem weiteren Gesprächsgang über *Theologie und Wissenschaftstheorie*." In: *Evangelische Theologie*, 40/2 (March/April).

Schillebeeckx, Edward. 1973. "The Crisis in the Language of Faith as Hermeneutical Problem." In: *Concilium*, 5/9.

Scholz, Heinrich. 1971a. "Wie ist eine Theologie als Wissenschaft möglich?" In: *Zwischen den Zeiten* (1931). Repr. in: *Theologie als Wissenschaft*. Ed. G. Sauter. Munich: Kaiser. Pp. 265-278.

————. 1971b. "Was ist unter einer theologischen Aussage zu verstehen?" In: *Theologische Aufsätze Karl Barth zum 50. Geburtstag*. Munich: Kaiser, 1936. Repr. in: *Theologie als Wissenschaft*. Ed. G. Sauter. Munich: Kaiser. Pp. 221-265.

Smit, D. 1985. Die droom van bybelse geregtigheid. *Scriptura, Tydskrif vir Bybelkunde*, 15.

Soskice, J. M. 1985. *Metaphor and Religious Language*. Oxford: Clarendon Press.

Strauss, D. F. M. 1971. *Wetenskap en werklikheid. Oriëntering in die algemene wetenskapsleer*. Bloemfontein: SACUM.

Strauss, D. F. M., and Visagie, P. J. 1983. *Die verhouding tussen nie-teologiese wetenskappe en die teologie*. Interim.

TeSelle, Sallie (McFague). 1975. *Speaking in Parables. A Study in Metaphor and Theology*. London: SCM Press.

Tracy, David. 1977. "Modes of Theological Argument." In: *Theology Today*, 33/4.

————. 1978. *Blessed Rage for Order. The New Pluralism in Theology*. New York: Seabury Press.

————. 1981. *The Analogical Imagination: Christian Theology and the Culture of Pluralism*. New York: Crossroad.

Trigg, Roger. 1977. *Reason and Commitment*. Cambridge: Cambridge University Press.

Van Buren, Paul M. 1963. *The Secular Meaning of the Gospel*. London: SCM.

Van Huyssteen, Wentzel. 1970. *Teologie van die rede. Die funksie van die rasionele in die denke van Wolfhart Pannenberg.* Kampen: J. H. Kok.

————. 1978a. "Teologie en metode." In: *Koers,* 43/4.

————. 1978b. "Antwoord aan prof. König." In: *Koers,* 43/4.

————. 1981. "Die Sistematiese teoloog en persoonlike geloofsbetrokkenheid." In: *Nederduitse Gereformeerde Teologiese Tydskrif.* 22/4:291-302.

————. 1983a. "Die bybel is tog 'n geloofsboek en ook woord van God." *Die Kerkbode,* 13 July 1983.

————. 1983b. "Rasionaliteit en kreatiwiteit. Ontwerp vir 'n kritiese, konstruktiewe teologie." In: *Koers, Bulletin vir Christelike Wetenskap,* 48/3.

————. 1983c. "Thomas S. Kuhn en die vraag na die herkoms van ons teologiese denkmodelle." In: *Nederduitse Gereformeerde Teologiese Tydskrif,* 24/3.

————. 1985a. "Die bybel en die gelowige: 'n probleemverhouding." In: *Die Kerkbode,* 27 Feb. 1985.

————. 1985b. "Belydenis as denkmodel. 'n Teologie tussen insig en ervaring." In: *Teologie-Belydenis-Politiek/Theology-Confession-Politics.* Ed. D. Smit. Bellville: U.W.K. Publishers. Pp. 7-27.

Van Huyssteen, W., and du Toit, B. J. 1982. *Geloof en Skrifgesag.* Pretoria: N. G. Kerkboekhandel.

Van Huyssteen, W., du Toit, B., Swanepoel, F., and Rousseau, J. 1983d. "Die ware gesag van 'n geloofsbelydenis." In: *Die Kerkbode,* 28 Sept. 1983.

Van Niekerk, A. 1982. "Rasionaliteit, wetenskap en geloof." In: *Nederduitse Gereformeerde Teologiese Tydskrif,* 23/2.

Van Niekerk, A. A. 1984. "Analogie en teologie: Humphrey Palmer en die moontlikheid van 'n kognitiewe spreke oor God." In: *S. A. Tydskrif vir Wysbegeerte,* 3(2).

Van Niekerk, Erasmus. 1984. "Methodological Aspects in Karl Barth's *Church Dogmatics.*" D.D. Thesis. Pretoria (UNISA).

Index

Albert, H., 35ff., 78ff., 84ff., 99-100
Apologetic theology, 74ff.
Argumentative theology, 101ff.
Axiomatic theology, 40, 63ff., 112ff.
Ayer, A., 3, 6

Barth, K., 11ff.
Bartley, W. W., 33ff., 47ff., 78, 90-91, 100, 143ff.
Basic convictions, 49ff., 71ff., 93ff.
Basic metaphor, root metaphor, 140ff., 177ff.
Biblicism, 178ff.
Bonhoeffer, D., 4

Calvin, J., 64, 184ff.
Carnap, R., 3
Cognitive, cognitivity, 3, 110-111, 147ff.
Coherence, coherence postulate, 18, 83, 120ff.
Concept of God, 78ff., 86-87, 98-99
Conceptual problem, 174ff.
Conceptual transformation, 53ff.
Confessions, 183ff.
Confessional language, 171
Confessional theology, 91-92, 168ff., 171ff.
Context of discovery, 7ff., 49-50, 80ff.
Context of justification, 7ff., 49-50, 80ff., 105ff.

Contextuality of theological statements, 163ff.
Conventions, 27ff., 80-81
Critical rationalism, 24ff.
Critical realism, 142ff.

Degree of corroboration, 30-31
Demand of irrefutability, 17
Demand of testability, 18, 87, 118
Demarcation criteria, 12-13, 30ff., 62ff.
Dialectical theology, 23ff.
Disciplinary matrix, 49ff.
Doctrine of creation, 88
Doctrine of faith, 16ff.
Dogmatic exclusivism, 67
Dogmatistic, dogmatism, 39ff., 49, 66-67, 144-145

Ebeling, G., 35, 114ff.
Ecclesiastic theology, 72
Empirical problem, 174ff.
Empiricism, 4
Empiricist criterion for meaning, 114ff.

Falsifiability principle, 29ff., 52
Fideism, 39ff., 78
Fundamental theology, xiff., 92ff., 125

Gadamer, H. G., 96, 100
Gestalt switch, 53, 66ff.

Ghetto theology, 72ff.

Hempelmann, H., 35, 73, 118
Hermeneutics, 16, 19, 96, 106ff.
Heyns, J. A., 19ff.
Hypothesis, 81ff., 113ff., 131ff.

Immunization tactics, 21ff., 35ff.
Incommensurability, 57ff., 177ff.
Irrationalism, 37ff., 60ff.

Kaufman, G., 73, 131, 189 n.26
Koningsveld, H., 9,
Kuhn, T. S., 47ff., 80-81, 98-99, 128ff.,
    148ff., 188ff.
Kuitert, H., 131, 166

Laudan, L., 173ff., 187ff.
Lindbeck, G., 165, 168ff.
Logical positivism, 3ff.
Luther, M., 64

McFague (TeSelle), S., 73, 131, 135,
    138, 140-141, 163, 178n.18
McMullin, E., 148ff., 188, 195ff.
Metaphor, 132ff., 151-52, 153ff.
Metaphysical statements, 6ff., 30ff., 80-
    81
Model, xv, 137ff.

Normal science, 51ff.

Objectivity, 7ff., 25-26, 47ff., 126ff.,
    147ff.

Pancritical rationalism, 40ff.
Pannenberg, W., 70ff., 101-102, 113-114
Paradigm, xv, 49ff.
Peacocke, A., 156ff.
Popper, K., 24ff., 55ff., 77, 118
Preparadigmatic sciences, 50ff.
Problem-solving, problem-solving
    model, 49ff., 108-109, 172ff.
Protocol statements, 7
Psychological subjectivism, 14-15

Rationality, xv, 8-9, 24ff., 47ff., 72-73,

    104ff., 125-126, 145ff., 187ff.
Rationality model, xvff., 131-132
Rationality of religious language, 126ff.
Reality depiction, 147ff., 163ff.
Referential theory, 147ff.
Relativism, 58ff.
Religious commitment, 36ff., 44ff.,
    78ff., 159ff.
Religious experience, 86-87, 89ff., 97-
    98, 126ff.
Revelatory positivism, 4, 81ff.
Revelatory theology, xvi, 11ff., 44

Sauter, G., 101ff., 127
Schlick, M., 3-4
Scholz, H., 15, 17ff., 83ff., 87ff., 96,
    105, 118ff.
Scientific realism, 148ff.
Scientific revolutions, 53ff.
Scriptural authority, 177ff.
Sensory perception, 5ff.
Sociology of knowledge, 16, 50
Sola scriptura principle, 110, 116,
    177ff., 189
Standard conception of science, 7
Subjectivism, 19, 22-23, 36ff.

TeSelle, S. (McFague), 134, 137
Theological progress, 190ff.
Theological statements, 125ff.
Theology of religions, 92ff.
Theory-ladenness, 27ff., 81ff., 109ff.
Tracy, D., 73, 126, 129, 197
Tradition (theological), 180ff.
Transcendence, 136
Truth, 60ff., 144ff.
Tu quoque argument, 38ff.

Ultimate commitment, 36ff., 131ff.,
    144ff.

Verifiability criterion, 7ff., 25ff.
Verisimilitude, 31ff.
Vienna Circle, 3ff.

Wittgenstein, L., 4, 6